Maya Cultural Heritage

ARCHAEOLOGY IN SOCIETY SERIES

Series Editors
Ian Hodder, Stanford University, ihodder@stanford.edu
Robert W. Preucel, Brown University, Robert_Preucel@brown.edu
Rowman & Littlefield Senior Editor: Leanne Silverman, lsilverman@rowman.com

In recent decades, archaeology has expanded beyond a narrow focus on economics and environmental adaptation to address issues of ideology, power, and meaning. These trends, sometimes termed "postprocessual," deal with both the interpretation of the past and the complex and politically charged interrelationships of past and present. Today, archaeology is responding to and incorporating aspects of the debates on identity, meaning, and politics currently being explored in varying fields: social anthropology, sociology, geography, history, linguistics, and psychology. There is a growing realization that ancient studies and material culture can be aligned within the contemporary construction of identities under the rubrics of nationalism, ethnoscapes, and globalization. This international series will help connect the contemporary practice of archaeology with these trends in research and, in the process, demonstrate the relevance of archaeology to related fields and society in general.

Books in this series:

Maya Cultural Heritage: How Archaeologists and Indigenous Communities Engage the Past, by Patricia A. McAnany (2016)

An Archaeology of Resistance: Materiality and Time in an African Borderland, by Alfredo González-Ruibal (2014)

Archaeology beyond Postmodernity: A Science of the Social, by Andrew M. Martin (2013)

UNESCO, Cultural Heritage, and Outstanding Universal Value: Value-based Analyses of the World Heritage and Intangible Cultural Heritage Conventions, by Sophia Labadi (2013)

The Dark Abyss of Time: Archaeology and Memory, by Laurent Oliver (2011)

In Defense of Things: Archaeology and the Ontology of Objects, by Bjørnar Olsen (2010)

Dwelling, Identity, and the Maya: Relational Archaeology at Chunchucmil, by Scott Hutson (2009)

The Social Construction of Communities: Agency, Structure, and Identity in the Prehispanic Southwest, edited by Mark D. Varien and James M. Potter (2008)

Archaeology and the Postcolonial Critique, edited by Matthew Liebmann and Uzma Z. Rizvi (2008)

Collaboration in Archaeological Practice: Engaging Descendant Communities, edited by Chip Colwell-Chanthaphonh and T. J. Ferguson (2007)

Appropriated Pasts: Indigenous Peoples and the Colonial Culture of Archaeology, by Ian J. McNiven and Lynette Russell (2005)

Archaeology of Performance: Theatre, Power, and Community, edited by Takeshi Inomata and Lawrence S. Coben (2005)

Maya Cultural Heritage

How Archaeologists and Indigenous Communities Engage the Past

Patricia A. McAnany

ROWMAN & LITTLEFIELD
Lanham • Boulder • New York • London

Published by Rowman & Littlefield
A wholly owned subsidiary of The Rowman & Littlefield Publishing Group, Inc.
4501 Forbes Boulevard, Suite 200, Lanham, Maryland 20706
www.rowman.com

Unit A, Whitacre Mews, 26-34 Stannary Street, London SE11 4AB, United Kingdom

British Library Cataloguing in Publication Information Available

Library of Congress Cataloging-in-Publication Data
Names: McAnany, Patricia Ann, author.
Title: Maya cultural heritage : how archaeologists and indigenous communities
  engage the past / Patricia A. McAnany.
Description: Lanham : Rowman & Littlefield, [2016] | Series: Archaeology in
  society series | Includes bibliographical references and index.
Identifiers: LCCN 2016019402 (print) | LCCN 2016031038 (ebook) |
  ISBN 9781442241275 (cloth : alkaline paper) | ISBN 9781442241282 (electronic)
Subjects: LCSH: Mayas—Antiquities. | Mayas—Antiquities—Collection and
  preservation. | Mayas—Social conditions. | Community life—Mexico. |
  Community life—Central America. | Archaeology—Social aspects—Mexico. |
  Archaeology—Social aspects—Central America. | Cultural
  property—Protection—Mexico. | Cultural property—Protection—Central
  America.
Classification: LCC F1435 .M485 2016 (print) | LCC F1435 (ebook) |
  DDC 972/.6—dc23
LC record available at https://lccn.loc.gov/2016019402

♾™ The paper used in this publication meets the minimum requirements of American
National Standard for Information Sciences—Permanence of Paper for Printed Library
Materials, ANSI/NISO Z39.48-1992.

Printed in the United States of America

For Peter

Contents

Figures and Tables

FIGURES

TABLES

Foreword

On a hot July day with the desert sun beating down, promising rain clouds building to the west, a Zuni religious leader and I walked across a bladed archaeological site called Amity Pueblo in northeastern Arizona. It had been cleared of vegetation and top soil, the result of activities related to construction of a public fishing pond. The site had been extensively damaged due to a federal agency's negligent compliance, destroying numerous archaeological features including fourteen human burials. Scores of human bone fragments and artifacts littered the bladed surface of the site. The Zuni religious leader and I surveyed the damage, and I witnessed his emotional pain as he viewed the broken and scattered remains of his ancestors.

As an archaeologist, naturally I was troubled by the needless destruction of this archaeological site, the desecration of human burials, and the unfortunate loss of scientific and historical information. I was more profoundly moved, however, by the emotional turmoil in my companion. Not only was this religious leader emotionally traumatized to see the physical remains of his ancestors scattered across the site, he also wrestled with how to resolve the effects of this desecration on the spirits of his ancestors, for whom he is, in a way, responsible as a steward of familial relationships between ancestors and descendants. The spiritual imbalance caused by unearthing and destroying the graves—the eternal homes—of the ancestors was enormous for him.

The deep visceral response of a Zuni religious leader to the destruction of Amity Pueblo parallels the strong impulse towards conservation among descendant Maya communities that is revealed in Patricia McAnany's book. And although it comes from a very different place than does the campaign for conservation of archaeological sites, nonetheless, I agree with McAnany that it represents common ground that holds potential for deeply significant future collaborations.

The incident in the Arizona desert occurred more than five years ago. The period between then and now can only be characterized as frustrating and futile. Numerous meetings with federal agencies, state agencies, tribal nations, and professional archaeological organizations punctuated this period with little constructive progress toward reaching a consensus on how to "fix" the damage. As I write this foreword, archaeological crews are just beginning to collect all the scattered human remains for reburial. It took five years for the Federal agency to initiate necessary actions to mitigate the adverse effect and address Zuni concerns. One of the less controversial but still contentious issues that delayed immediate action was the degree to which archaeological data recovery would be required to mitigate the physical damage. Throughout the process, Zuni representatives repeatedly stressed that their primary concern was to begin spiritually healing the site through the respectful treatment of their ancestors' remains in the form of immediate collection and reburial. The Zuni position was not only borne out of a real sense of personal responsibility to their ancestors, but also fueled by a view that additional archaeological excavation would only contribute to the existing damage.

Two state agencies and one national archaeological organization maintained the position that some form of scientific data recovery was necessary. In fact, one state agency terminated consultation over this issue, stating that the proposed level of scientific analysis was unacceptable. That state agency was silent on their views of the Zuni position, which stressed conservation over additional excavation.

In part, this example demonstrates the customary privileging of a scientific materialist view of history (and prehistory) and how historical "truth"—which in this view can only be achieved through objective, scientific archeological research—underpins the National Historic Preservation Program. It also underscores the disparity that exists between Native American attitudes toward their heritage resources and how those heritage resources are treated through the standard federal historic preservation compliance process. More importantly, but often overlooked, this example highlights the underlying, deeply entrenched, and subtly enduring colonialist attitudes toward Indigenous people that continue to shape the manner in which the dominant settler society routinely rejects Native American rights of primacy to the landscape by subjecting Native Americans to Western ideologies of prehistory, history, and historical presentation. Only within the last few decades have archaeologists—working globally—come to scrutinize their role in distancing Indigenous peoples from stewardship of their ancestral landscapes. As a result, there has been significant, if halting, changes in the practice of archaeological research. This book represents one such effort to examine how archaeologists and Indigenous Mayan peoples engage the past and each other.

Organizations like the American Anthropological Association, the Society for American Archaeology, and the Register of Professional Archaeologists all have stated research ethics and codes of conduct that recognize an anthropologist's or archaeologist's responsibility to the Native (Indigenous) people they study or to "groups whose culture histories are the subjects of archaeological investigation" (http://rpanet.org/?page=CodesandStandards#tothepublic). Commonplace archaeological narratives about the past, however, continue to be generated in a traditional third person voice which fails to acknowledge the personal ongoing relationships that Native Americans have with their heritage sites. There remains a vast disparity between actualizing these research ethics and the resultant historical narratives generated by archaeologists. I believe that by acknowledging the connections and contributions of contemporary Native Americans to the past, we might move beyond the problem of incommensurability that is discussed in the pages to come. Additionally, I believe that this failure to acknowledge has the unintended consequence of contributing to the enduring deleterious effects of colonialism through ignoring and thereby disenfranchising contemporary Native Americans from their deep past which intensifies feelings of depression, despair, and existential nihilism.

South of the border, the story for Native people has not been much different. Here, as McAnany demonstrates, Indigenous Maya peoples have experienced similar effects of colonialism, which are intensified and lengthened by highly constrained legal recourse and far fewer treaty commitments. In *Maya Cultural Heritage: How Archaeologists and Indigenous Communities Engage the Past,* McAnany directly addresses this disparity and demonstrates how archaeologists can build mutually beneficial bridges that engage local communities and Indigenous peoples in the development of heritage narratives and the conservation of heritage locales. By meaningfully engaging Indigenous people (and other stakeholder communities) directly in archaeological research, McAnany shows us how this can create a context for equitable research and sustainable heritage conservation. The lessons we learn from Indigenous responses to this experimental and pioneering plunge into cultural heritage programs can be taken to other parts of the world and particularly to the United States, where more collaborative programs like the ones McAnany describes need to be implemented.

Kurt E. Dongoske
Pueblo of Zuni, New Mexico
29 June 2016

Acknowledgments

In a book about collaborative approaches to the past, an attempt to call out all who contributed to the efforts discussed in the pages to follow would be equivalent to the precise expression of π—an infinite series of nonrepeating entities. Regardless of the immensity of the task, acknowledgments are probably the most important words that appear in the pages of this book, and I welcome the opportunity to feature those who played a role in funding, designing, conducting, and participating in the heritage programs discussed in the pages to follow.

In accordance with the adage *follow the money*, I begin with the foundations and fellowship programs that funded projects and academic leaves. First, I want to acknowledge with deepest gratitude the family foundation, and particularly the foundation director, who in 2005 brought to me the idea of expanding the scope of my fieldwork beyond survey and excavation and then supported our efforts to establish a deeper dialogue with communities living proximate to archaeological sites in the Maya region. Other generous private donors also contributed to the effort. Pearl Gottstein at Lush Cosmetics supported our proposal to provide funding for community mapping in the Guatemala highlands and the Archaeological Institute of America generously funded our community heritage conservation efforts at Tahcabo, Yucatán, México. The National Science Foundation OISE, Program for Catalyzing New International Collaboration (#1134331), provided key support toward initiating archaeological research and heritage programs in eastern Yucatán. Funds from the Kenan Foundation of the University of North Carolina at Chapel Hill contributed annually toward heritage work.

Fellowships from the Institute for the Arts and Humanities at the University of North Carolina at Chapel Hill, the John Simon Guggenheim Memorial Foundation, and the John Carter Brown Library ensured time not only to write this book but also to interact with scholars who provided critical feedback that substantially improved the writing effort. The Department of Archaeology at Boston University, the Department of Anthropology at UNC–Chapel Hill, and the Research Labs of Archaeology at Chapel Hill administered grant funding and exhibited great tolerance for countless requests to wire money internationally to our program collaborators in foreign places. The Institutional Review Boards (IRB) at Boston University and at UNC–Chapel Hill vetted the program questionnaires and, by requesting further clarification, played an important role in strengthening survey design. The Board of the Alliance for Heritage Conservation kept the fledgling nonprofit on course. For this, my thanks go to Barbara Arroyo, Emilio Escalante del Valle, Florence Peacock, Stephan Wittkowsky, and Alicia McGill.

As detailed in chapter 5, the Maya Area Cultural Heritage Initiative (MA-CHI) was hatched in a lab at Boston University with two graduate students: Shoshaunna Parks and Satoru Murata. While Shoshaunna took the lead in program design, Satoru designed and managed the initial website. Throughout her time as program director of MACHI and the later launch of InHerit: Indigenous Heritage Passed to Present, Shoshaunna displayed an amazing ability to conceptualize programs, develop them into operational entities, and conduct critical evaluative surveys at the end of each cycle of programming. She was a driving force in the success of MACHI, and no words are sufficient to acknowledge her dedication to Maya cultural heritage.

Several more former graduate students played critical roles in the incubation and maturation of MACHI programs: Reiko Ishihara-Brito and Claire Novotny were instrumental in shaping the classroom heritage modules in Toledo, Belize. Crista Cesario wrote storyboards for the puppet-mentary and accompanied Shoshaunna across the breadth and length of Yucatán to deliver the puppet-mentary DVD and accompanying teaching materials to schools and to retrieve valuable survey data.

Each of the partnering organizations in the Maya region brought different issues and concerns to the table and helped to translate the heritage programs into local idiom. I endeavor to mention by name those who helped to launch, maintain, and evaluate the MACHI, InHerit, and Alliance programs. Throughout the run of all the programs, our partnership with Arte Acción Copán Ruinas, directed by Carin Steen, proved instrumental to the look and feel of MACHI programs. An artist who loves to create books, Steen designed the classroom workbooks for fourth-, fifth-, and sixth-grade schoolchildren in Honduras, created four different multilingual coloring books, and provided annual reports that were both beautiful and informative. She attracted to Proyecto Maya, as she called it, young and energetic facilitators who taught weekly cultural heritage modules in the *aldeas* around Copán Ruinas. Bringing the material to life and infusing the workshops with fun and caring, the facilitators included Londin Velásquez, Moisés Mancia, Elsa Morales, and Marlen Vásquez. Support and advice from Copán archaeologist Allan Maca helped to ground the project and after

Carin closed the doors of Arte Acción, the local nonprofit Asociación Copán managed the program under the directorship of archaeologist Ricardo Agurcia. To the students and teachers in the small community schools around Copán, many heartfelt thanks for your participation.

Christina Coc, director of the Julian Cho Society in Punta Gorda, Belize, supported the school workshops and worked with us to make them more effective. Marvin Coc, the facilitator and teacher, steadfastly traveled from school to school—with a generator and PowerPoint projector—to teach about Maya cultural heritage. Faustina Coc, accountant for the Julian Cho Society, provided encouragement and constancy. The alternative Maya school of Tumul K'in provided a radio venue for the Q'eqchi'-language radio *novelas*, and the staff was a source of support and inspiration—first from Pablo Mis and later from Esther N. Sanchez Sho and Aurelio Sho. To the Toledo students, teachers, and community members who participated in the classroom workshops and questionnaires, I extend my deepest gratitude.

Throughout the Departments of El Petén and Alta Verapaz in Guatemala, a hearty thank-you goes to all of the radio listeners who tuned into the radio *novela* called *Entre Dos Caminos* (*Between Two Roads*) to hear about the latest heritage-related drama in the fictitious town of San Jerónimo. The *novelas* were crafted by a skilled storyteller, Yadira Vargas, who works at ProPetén. A nonprofit located in Flores, Petén, Guatemala, Fundación ProPetén was directed by the energetic Rosa Chan, who always knew how to get the job done. The listening audience was augmented by the publicity efforts of multitalented Edy Romero, who advertised the shows via a bullhorn mounted on top of a car, served as radio announcer, and conducted focus groups and individual interviews after the shows aired. Spanish and Q'eqchi' radio performers brought the stories alive, particularly with the addition of sound effects that contributed a convincing rural Petén ambience to the shows. To the students and teachers in schools throughout the Petén where the new experimental curriculum based on the radio *novelas* has launched, few words can express the joy and relief of seeing expensive radio productions integrated into a sustainable school curriculum.

Tomás Gallareta Negrón guided the creation and production of the puppet-mentary (filmed on location in Yucatán) to completion and pulled together a dedicated production staff. The collaborating nonprofit—Kaxil Kiuic—helmed by George Bey—provided administrative support for the endeavor and a home for the marionettes. James Callahan—director of the Kaxil Kiuic Biocultural Reserve—assisted with film production. During the filming process, Director Sergio Garcia-Agundis displayed his brilliant ability to convincingly film puppets in contexts built to human rather than marionette scale. The puppeteers were devoted to the production and traveled from shoot to shoot. Storyboards were composed by Miguel Gallareta Negrón, Christa Cesario, and Shoshaunna Parks with translation into Yucatec by Patricia Huchim. Thanks to the local Yucatec performers who provided voice-over for the marionettes and, of course, to the puppet-maker, Victor Carbajal. Finally, to the students and teachers across the State of Yucatán who agreed to preview the heritage film and provide feedback, many thanks. We sincerely hope that children continue to enjoy the film for years to come.

In addition to the Yucatán collaboration with Kaxil Kiuic, we initiated two other heritage programs in the northern lowlands. First, with Amadeé Collí of Mayaón—an organization located in Felipe Carrillo Puerto, Quintana Roo, that is dedicated to Maya cultural issues. Amadeé wowed her radio listeners with Yucatec-language presentations about Maya cultural heritage. Second, a collaboration with Adolfo Ivan Batun-Alpuche of the Universidad de Oriente (UNO, in Valladolid) led to the formation of Proyecto Arqueológico Colaborativo del Oriente de Yucatán (PACOY), which ultimately focused on Tahcabo, Yucatán.

An ongoing research and heritage effort, the PACOY project has included graduate students from UNC–Chapel Hill (Maia Dedrick and Mary Margaret Morgan-Smith), former undergraduates of UNO (Lourdes Chan Caamal, Miguel Kanxoc, Alejandro Tuz Bacab, Ricardo Pootchuc, Ricardo Cabañashaas, Itzel Batun Meza), as well as the university in Mérida (UADY, represented by Miriam Batun and Ivan Batun Cante). Alfred Berry, Guy Duke, Nicolas Smilovsky, and Danielle Williamson Smilovsky provided additional fieldwork expertise, and Norma Cante Poot provided daily sustenance and ensured that we always had a place to live in Valladolid. To these talented students and colleagues, as well as the townspeople of Tahcabo, Che Balam, and Tixhualactun, who tolerated our constant questions about the old colonial structures, I extend heartfelt gratitude.

In the highlands of Guatemala, our collaboration with the Riecken Foundation began under the directorship of Paul Guggenheim and continued through subsequent leadership. Riecken staff and local community representatives—in particular Israel Quic Cholotio, Evelyn Caniz Menchú, and Jose Mendoza Quic—were committed to the community mapping program and worked tirelessly to launch mapping forays, present and discuss maps at community meetings, and ensure that participating communities controlled the process and the product. To members of the five communities involved in the mapping project—Cabricán, Chiché, Huitán, San Juan la Laguna, and Xolsacmaljá—as well as the librarians of the Riecken community libraries, I thank you for your participation and willingness to perform collaborative mapping with the goal of increasing community autonomy.

Several of the heritage efforts discussed in this book were funded as a result of competitions sponsored by MACHI or InHerit. The two competitions— Community Heritage Conservation Grants and Bidirectional Knowledge Exchange Grants—targeted different constituencies. The former were awarded to Indigenous community organizations that proposed a program of heritage conservation, while the latter focused on archaeologists who proposed to expand traditional programs of field research to encompass an exchange of knowledge between communities and archaeological projects. I am indebted to the following persons and programs that worked with us to effect change in business as usual.

For working toward community heritage conservation, I acknowledge the director and staff of the following organizations: Parque A'ak, a heritage park north of Mérida; ADIPES, a Motul-based nonprofit that emphasizes heritage education for children; Manejo Cultural in Quintana Roo, focusing on environmental conservation via TV documentaries; the Aguacate (Toledo, Belize) Conservation Committee, which proposed to transform an archaeological site into a heritage park; Kaxil Kiuic and descendants of Rancho Kiuic with a proposal to refurbish the historic cemetery at Kiuic; Asociación CDRO in association with ArtCorps (Totonicapán, Guatemala) with a proposal to strengthen cultural and environmental heritage; and the Seine Bight (Belize) Village Council with a proposal to create a community heritage center.

For working toward a bidirectional knowledge exchange between archaeologists and communities, I acknowledge and thank the following: in Yucatán, the team of Scott Hutson and Can Herrera and in a separate project, Jessica Wheeler; in Guatemala, Brent Woodfill and Seleste Sanchez; in Honduras, Kristin Landau and Fredy Rodriguez; in Toledo, Belize, Rebecca Zarger and Kristina Baines; and in Cayo, Belize, Terry Powis and Jessie Burnette.

Sarah M. Rowe succeeded Shoshaunna Parks as program director of InHerit and was instrumental in launching the nonprofit Alliance for Heritage Conservation. She brought to the effort new perspectives and ideas about how InHerit could be expanded into the Andean region. Her successor, Claire Novotny, continues the same tradition of enthusiasm, dedication, and the ability to operationalize great ideas about collaborative heritage work.

In the wider world of archaeology, I thank Richard Leventhal, director of the Penn Cultural Heritage Center, for co-organizing with MACHI the 2008 conference called Indigenous Perspectives on Cultural Heritage and for extending a collegial hand to me years ago when I was an assistant professor at Boston University. For encouraging me to write this book and to submit the manuscript to the Archaeology in Society series at Rowman & Littlefield, I thank Ian Hodder and Robert Preucel. The acquisitions team at Rowman & Littlefield, Leanne Silverman and Andrea O. Kendrick, provided critical feedback and encouragement as they managed me through the production of a completed manuscript and the review process. Mary Margaret Morgan-Smith, Ashley Peles, and Tomás Gallareta Cervera contributed technical and translation expertise to this effort. Four external reviewers who generated fourteen pages (single-spaced) of comments on the manuscript challenged me to reach higher and drill deeper into the topic. Through it all, my partner Peter Joyce remained supportive and tolerant of the many hours I spent word crafting this book in an attempt to communicate the significance of collaborative approaches to Maya cultural heritage. As an educated layperson, Peter gave me the courage to write a book without the parenthetical in-text references that distance nonarchaeologists from our prose form.

I am fortunate to have supportive colleagues in the discipline and through the years at my home institutions. These colleagues carried me through a time of human frailty. I especially would like to thank Deborah Nichols for organizing the support network that got me through the worst of times. This experience helped me to realize that resilience isn't possible without a network of community support, and it galvanized my desire to work toward a more resilient and sustainable kind of Maya archaeology.

PART I

Background and the Big Ideas

This book is divided into three sections: each sequentially drills into topics of heritage and Indigenous voices more specifically. In part I, background themes and the big ideas that frame a consideration of Maya cultural heritage are considered. Chapter 1 begins with a haunting question from a young Yucatec Maya girl. This query leads to a "road map" of the many constituencies—particularly Indigenous peoples and archaeologists—who hold a compelling interest in Maya cultural heritage. Although potential incommensurability between constituencies looms large, the art of bridging divides—both ontological and epistemological—is argued to provide an effective means of moving forward and beyond the irony of the present moment.

Chapter 2 contains historical background that is focused on the relationship between Native peoples of the Maya region and the exclusionary processes of nation building and the equally exclusionary definition of archaeological space that has been a corollary of nationhood in this part of the world. How this space was "disciplined" and came to be managed and interpreted within the frame of archaeology provides the subject of chapter 3.

Concerns of the present are the topic of chapter 4: specifically, the impact of subaltern voices on the conduct of both anthropology and archaeology. A consideration of postcolonialism, particularly as practiced south of the U.S. border, brings us ever closer to the Maya region. The uniformity suggested by terms such as the *Maya* and the *ancient Maya* is critically evaluated in chapter 5, followed by an exploration of the diversity of Maya voices and ways of relating to things and places of the past.

With background and big ideas digested, part II considers the art of bridge building between archaeologists and communities around issues of cultural heritage (chapter 6). In chapter 7, the specifics of collaborative heritage programs initiated first by the Maya Cultural Heritage Initiative (MACHI) and then by InHerit: Indigenous Heritage Passed to Present are presented. Part III, titled "In Their Own Words," details the response to heritage programs that were designed to level the playing field, acquaint members of local communities with archaeological ways of knowing, and provide a space for other ways of knowing about and caring for a much-valorized past (chapters 8 and 9). The final chapter, chapter 10, returns to the question of incommensurability and the challenges of working toward collaborative research with Indigenous and local communities. I leave readers with the final thought that we need to engage with the reality of today's challenges while simultaneously nurturing a utopian vision for the future.

1

⌒

Haunting Questions

"Why did all the Maya have to die?" The question came from a young girl with shoulder-length jet-black hair who looked at me with a sad, quizzical face. She was part of a school group from the nearby Yucatec Maya town of San José and had come to see the archaeological site of K'axob (*k'aah-shobe*) in northern Belize, where, in 1995, I was directing a field school through Boston University. Although early morning, field school students were already troweling and sifting sediments from a four-by-four-meter excavation at the locale of a possible pottery kiln. I looked at the young girl of Yucatec ancestry and tried to explain that although the ninth century had been a time of political turmoil, not all Maya people, and probably not even the majority, had met with an untimely death. Many had migrated elsewhere in search of new opportunities. Finally, I declared that her ancestors could have lived right here at K'axob. But she didn't seem convinced, and I was unable to bring a smile to her face.

A few years later, I was investigating ancient cacao (cocoa) production in the Sibun Valley of central Belize when an equally unsettling event took place. While leaving a restaurant, an expatriate cross-examined me in a somewhat hostile tone of voice. "Did the short, brown-skinned Maya people really build the pyramids or were they built by another people altogether?" "If they did build them," my interrogator insisted, "then why are the skeletons from classic Maya tombs so much taller than Maya people are today?" I tried to explain the negative effect of five hundred years of malnutrition on height and the overwhelming biological, linguistic, and cultural evidence that linked contemporary Maya people with remains of the past, but my answer was met with skepticism.

The more that I thought about these questions, the more I was forced to conclude that something was terribly wrong—few people were connecting the dots between the past and present and archaeologists were not challenging the disconnect. In

2005, when I was given an opportunity to work on this problem, I accepted the challenge and began to invest time and energy on what proved to be a complex issue with deep colonial roots and tentacles reaching all the way to the banana-boat piers of Boston, Massachusetts. As I formed a team and we began to formulate heritage programs that we hoped would respond to these unsettling questions, Boston University ran a story in their alumni magazine on my newly founded organization, the Maya Area Cultural Heritage Initiative (MACHI). I received many responses from alumni—mostly positive—but yet another disturbing question.

The alumna placed a direct call to me and voiced effusive appreciation for the work we were doing, but then she asked if any Maya people still existed. She thought they had "all died off" at the end of the classic period. Our conversation was cut short because I needed to get to class, but as I hurried down a long corridor, I kept thinking about what the woman had said. Among archaeologists, she is called an "interested layperson," someone who is fascinated by the techniques and interpretations of archaeologists, probably subscribes to *National Geographic* and maybe *Archaeology* magazine. How could she overlook five million–plus Maya people who live in southern México and the northern part of Central America and who increasingly were coming to the United States in search of employment?

These three questions—one from a young Yucatec schoolgirl, another from a North American expatriate living in Belize, and a final quizzical statement from an educated U.S. citizen with an interest in the Maya region—share a sadness that continues to haunt me. Strong forces—colonization, nation building, orientalism, neoliberalism, and the expediencies of heritage tourism—created and have maintained the inequities and politics of exclusion that lurk beneath the surface of such seemingly innocent questions.[1]

This book reports on community heritage programs that seek to unsettle these forces of inequality. But how does one begin to unpack what took five hundred years to coalesce into some of the most enduring myths of the Western imaginary? Case in point: the notion that the ninth-century end of the Classic Maya divine rulers—and their departure from the great southern cities—spelled the end of Maya peoples surely ranks as unlikely as the yarn that a continent called Atlantis sunk without a trace somewhere in the Atlantic Ocean. Likewise, valorization of the remains of Classic Maya peoples (some call them a celebrity archaeological culture) stands in great contrast to the stigmatized existence of most Indigenous Maya people today. Together they feed the myth that ancestors of descendant populations could not possibly have built the extraordinary buildings of the Classic period. Redolent of a colonial strategy of land disenfranchisement and usurpation, this myth takes its place alongside a similar myth about pre-Colonial mound constructions in the midcontinent of the United States and equally outlandish tales about the builders of the impressive political capital of Zimbabwe in east Africa.[2] *The point of this book is not to debunk such myths but rather to ask how they came to be and how the structural inequities that form the struts of such storytelling might be effectively challenged.* To go down this path as an archaeologist is to move from secluded trails through tropical forests in search of archaeological sites to bustling and bristling pathways that converge on a congested intersection called heritage—where there are few agreed upon traffic rules.

This book relates a journey and an attempt to understand the role of archaeologists in relation to the people who are affected by our research activities and our narratives about the past.[3] Throughout the chapters to come, the reader will note a shift in voice from "I" to "we" as I move from more traditional egocentric research to collaborative arrangements with heritage teams that bridge the academic and the local in selected parts of what is called the Maya region (more on this term soon). In an attempt to make this text more accessible to students and nonacademics, I forgo in-text parenthetical referencing in favor of endnotes. The latter, in addition to the references section at the end of the book, provide a resource for those who want to follow up on issues raised in the pages to come.

CONFRONTING THE HAUNTING

Archaeologists are trained to design research, conduct fieldwork, analyze collected information, and publish their findings, ideally while engaging with current theoretical constructs throughout this process. Archaeology is a heady profession because we literally create the past—or narratives about the past—based on our capacity to recognize important pieces of evidence in materials that we examine. We are closely entangled with the materiality of human existence, but what about our entanglements with each other? To practice professionally means to follow standards of survey, excavation, laboratory analysis, and conservation upon which most archaeologists can agree even if the reality of practice doesn't always match professional standards. More contentious and slower to codify are standards and expectations for how we deal with each other as professionals, with interested laypersons, descendant populations, and communities that are proximate to places of archaeological interest. There is growing concern among archaeologists that neglect of this social realm is resulting in harm to local populations and, in the long run, compromising the sustainability of the discipline.

The realm of archaeological ethics,[4] principles of best practices, or, as some of my colleagues see it, the politics of archaeology often are not part of the graduate curriculum. Leo Groarke and Gary Warrick criticize the "Principles of Archaeological Ethics" adopted by the Society for American Archaeology for employing the trope of stewardship to describe the responsibility of archaeologists to things of the past. They point out that stewards report to other humans (usually supervisors) and not to things.[5] The increasingly social turn in archaeological ethics unsettles the intimate and dyadic relationship between archaeologists and things of the past. Instead, we find ourselves in a triadic relationship, and the third member of the triad unquestionably possesses agency and can object to our professional practices and interpretive narratives.

In confronting the haunting, we enter the shifting terrain of academic IRB (Institutional Review Board) approval and the AAA (American Anthropological Association) "Code of Ethics"[6]—both of which emphasize that the research process should provide benefit to impacted communities and do no harm. As archaeologists, we have been able to give passing deference to these guidelines by breezily stating that we work with things of the past and not with people of the present; we are comfortably and professionally marginalized as asocial.

But wait a minute . . . what about those haunting questions that came from a young girl of Yucatec descent, a Maya enthusiast, and an educated layperson? Weren't they impacted greatly by archaeological research? Shall we simply characterize them as poorly informed and go about the business of investigating the past with a bit more attention paid to public outreach and education? To look deeper, to work to unsettle the status quo and dismantle the struts of inequality requires consciously rewiring archaeological practice to make it more inclusive in scope and participation.[7] This seems major. . . . Retreating to labs and jungle trails is an understandable response but not a realistic alternative.

In this book, I argue that there is much to gain by confronting *the haunting* and that the outcome will be a strengthening of archaeology as a discipline. On the other hand, to ignore the need for transformation of the traditional role and activities of archaeologists is to endanger the discipline and flirt with societal and academic irrelevance.[8] To a large degree, this book is about process rather than product. Specifically, the focus resides on how we can engage with local communities and move toward a more collaborative model—in the conjoined realms of heritage conservation and archaeological research. In response to the reviewer who asked what new knowledge has been gained by the heritage programs and the local voices with whom the programs were in dialogue (presented in chapters 7 to 9), I respond that the reader will learn many new things about community perspectives on archaeology, archaeologists, and local concerns with heritage conservation.

In the chapters to follow, I outline why we are obliged to leave the quiet jungle path and engage with an archaeological practice that is more uncertain but more inclusive. If the young girl who asked me why all the Maya had to die were to grow up and become an archaeologist, would that alter narratives about the ninth-century time of political troubles? You bet it would. And would the expatriate think differently about classic and colonial times if tour guides and archaeologists who lead tours of sites spoke from an Indigenous perspective about the past and present? Definitely. And finally, how can we kill definitively the myth of extinction that pervades any popular discussion of the original inhabitants of the Americas? Listening and providing space for Indigenous voices to be heard is a place to start and a path that is followed in this book.

Although this path may be less traveled in the Maya region, the trail has been blazed by archaeologists working in other parts of the world, particularly in Canada, the United States, Australia, and New Zealand, where post-sixteenth-century colonizing populations reside uneasily alongside original populations. Heritage activities and transformation in the conduct of archaeology in these parts of the world are discussed in chapters 3, 4, and 6. The heritage programs presented here build upon these innovative approaches to the problems of colonialism that continue to haunt archaeology today.

NAVIGATING BUSY INTERSECTIONS

While a graduate student at the University of New Mexico, one of my professors, Lewis R. Binford, advised us to actively engage with issues that were critical to the well-being of archaeology. In his charismatic southern style of speech, he would advise us: *Don't stand in the middle of the road; you might get run over.* But deciding which side of the road to follow is relatively easy compared to navigating intersections with other avenues that carry people who travel from very different places. The crossroads of cultural heritage include heritage tourists, artifact thieves, state bureaucrats, local communities, and descendant populations. Some intersections contain feeder roads from an even larger number of constituencies or stakeholders, but for the purposes of the Maya region, the above listing will suffice.[9]

Archaeologists have a multifaceted relationship with the past that primarily focuses on investigating and interpreting archaeological materials, but others relate to the past in terms of identity, emotion, politics (national or otherwise), curiosity, or economics. Cultural heritage is just that—a relationship to a past that is expressed through tangible and intangible media.[10] Generally forged within a self-identified community, heritage relationships are social—a community of persons who speak a mutually intelligible language, perform social practices together, or think of themselves as rooted in a landscape that contains material traces of deeply historicized inhabitation. The term *heritage management*, which has become so fashionable in the Anglo world, is increasingly the study and practice of managing the diverse relations that exist between people and their material imprint, often with an eye to conservation.[11] Such interested clusters of people are referenced as stakeholders, communities, or constituencies, and their participation in research and conservation activities is highly variable. In chapters 4 and 6, I return to the subject of stakeholders and critically examine historical shifts in their perceived role vis-à-vis anthropology and particularly archaeology.

This complex entanglement between people and things with a historical dimension is the place where archaeologists confront the commodification of the past in terms of illegal looting and a softer kind of commodification that results in heritage tourism or the apocryphal hope of such tourism, which is often expressed by local communities in the Maya region. At this locale, archaeologists often align with government regulatory ministries and effect exchanges (generally financial and informational) in order to conduct field research. Finally, at this crossroads archaeologists find themselves face-to-face with local landowners, residents of spatially proximate communities, and people who are culturally, ethnically, economically, or politically linked with the landscapes we seek to study.

I suggest that this freighted intersection holds the key to disciplinary transformation or conversely to stasis, depending on our navigational skills.[12]

In the pages of this book, I relate one path of navigation—there are many—through this intersection. It is a routing that includes bridge building with local and Indigenous peoples, many of Maya cultural affinity. For archaeologists, this work is a kind of activist research in the sense that we acknowledge the importance of listening to and affirming the value of those who are impacted by our studies, and we also acknowledge that there are multiple ways of relating to the landscapes and features we term archaeological. Finally, we attempt to engage that multiplicity in a positive fashion. In fact, archaeological engagement contains an additional layer of complexity over sociocultural anthropology because of its triadic structure, which includes archaeologists, lay participants, and materials of interest.

For sociocultural anthropologist Charles Hale, activist research is "a method through which we affirm a political alignment with an organized group of people in struggle and allow dialogue with them to shape each phase of the [research] process, from conception of the research topic to data collection to verification and dissemination of results."[13] This descriptor emphasizes social justice as a motivator of activist research and also details the ways in which activist researchers share authority in the research process. These two characteristics deviate decisively from archaeological business as usual and are examined further in chapters 4 and 6. Battle-hardened by the trenches of anthropological fieldwork in Central America, Hale describes the place of activism as "compromised spaces" that are difficult to occupy "without losing sight of the utopian horizons that keep such efforts on track."[14] Within this book, such compromised spaces and shaky bridges are related in detail and from multiple voices. The final chapter focuses on what are admittedly—to borrow the words of Charles Hale—utopian horizons.

Finally, Hale observes that many conceptually innovative ideas that form the stock-in-trade of anthropology have come not from cultural critique within anthropology but from activist research. Popular examples include the work of Antonio Gramsci on hegemony, Frantz Fanon on decolonization, or Audre Lorde on intersectionality.[15] Also chaotic and compromised, the intersection of archaeology with cultural heritage is a place from which new kinds of knowledge can emerge. Knowledge produced through participatory heritage programs forms one of the utopian horizons that we glimpse throughout this book. In large measure, this study seeks to move beyond the perceived irony of postmodernity in which contradictions are observed from a detached perspective. Here a different way of grappling with the challenges of a twenty-first-century world is explored through the forging of new epistemic communities of archaeological practice that might provide a context for equitable research and sustainable heritage conservation.[16]

In the chapters to come, we take a close look at intersecting interests in a part of the world generally called the Maya region (southern Mexico, Guatemala, Belize, western Honduras and El Salvador; see figure 1.1). While acknowledging the multiple agents that buzz around this intersection, the focus here is trained on the juncture of archaeologists with local, rural communities, which in the Maya

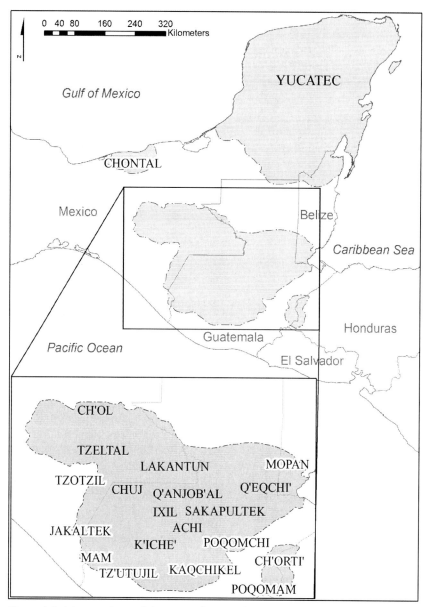

Figure 1.1. Maya region with location of Maya ethnolinguistic groups referenced in text (map by Ashley Peles).

region often self-identify as Native or Indigenous peoples. In the pages to come, there is much discussion of the term *Indigenous* and acknowledgment that not all peoples whose ancestors lived (since before the time of Columbus) in what is now called the Maya region choose to identify as Indigenous[17] or to claim ancestry within one of the many ethnolinguistic groupings that have been bundled together by linguists and labeled Maya. Regardless of whether one invokes the durable "viscerality" of Indigenous identity, an enduring connection to place, or the historical circumstances of colonization, the term *Indigenous* carries heavy freight and is not embraced lightly in this book.[18] As Maori scholar Linda Tuhiwai Smith notes, "The term 'indigenous' is problematic in that it appears to collectivize many distinct populations whose experiences under imperialism have been vastly different."[19] Even within an area that today is homogenized as the Maya region, there were vast differences in the impositions of colonialism, not to mention the diversity of languages, cultural expressions, and cultural hybridities that formed in response to colonialism. In a book that aims to reckon with the past in order to create a more inclusive archaeology of the future, the term *Indigenous*—carrying the freight of colonial exclusion—is used because it helps to stabilize and focus the work at hand.

ENGAGING MAYA CULTURAL HERITAGE

What is Maya cultural heritage? The term provides the title for this book, but what does it mean? Previously, *heritage* was defined as a relationship with tangible matter and, of course, heritage includes intangible, embodied practices such as language and cultural performance. The many languages (over two dozen) spoken by Maya peoples today constitute a form of cultural heritage, as does *traje* or traditional dress, which is so distinctive and yet so regionally and temporally dynamic. Regionally diverse ritual practices that range from rain-bringing Ch'a' Chaak ceremonies in Yucatán to ceremonies focused on appeasing the earth spirit Tzuultaq'a prior to planting in highland Guatemala constitute other forms of heritage.

And then there are distant times—such as the Classic period—when divine rulers who were carried in palanquins across an intricately built landscape oversaw the construction of massive shrines and palaces. That deeper heritage—yes, we can call it history—coincided with the Carolingian Empire of Charlemagne in Europe and is over a thousand years distant. Just as the Carolingian Empire is perceived as a very distant time and not particularly relevant to the identity of current residents of Aachen—once Charlemagne's capital—so residents of Pisté, Yucatán, deeply appreciate nearby Chichén Itzá, but their contemporary identity is not necessarily shaped in reference to this place that once was a powerful Itzá capital. In both situations, there are strong economic entanglements between the old places and contemporary residents by way of heritage tourism. And in the case of Pisté, what has been called a patrimonialist discourse is increasingly deployed to counter government efforts to curtail access to Chichén Itzá for mercantile transactions.[20] Such complexities of Maya cultural heritage are examined in further detail in the chapters to come.

The uniformity of terms that work to classify tends to dissolve upon closer scrutiny. Such is the case for *Maya cultural heritage*, the *Maya*, and even the *Maya region*. As Monica Smith has noted, most boundaries or delimiters prove inadequate when examined in depth.[21] In actuality, the Maya region is composed of a network of ethnolinguistic groups (figure 1.1) that speak (or spoke) a language classified as a member of the large Mayan language family. The outer limits of this grouping have been mapped on to places of deep history (some as old as one thousand years BCE); this mapping has conflated heritage and history to a large degree. At these old places, cultural practices, governance, and their material expression are more internally related to each other than to old places farther to the west and to the south. Never consolidated in the past into a single political entity, this region (and people speaking Mayan languages) likewise were subjected to distinctive colonialities that—mostly in the nineteenth century—resulted in the following nation-states: México (southern states of Tabasco, Chiapas, Campeche, Yucatán, and Quintana Roo), all of Belize and Guatemala, and the western parts of Honduras and El Salvador.

Just as few Europeans relate in any direct way to the Carolingian Empire of Charlemagne, few people who inhabit the Maya region today identify with the distant reality of Classic-period kings and queens. When popular depictions characterize the end of the Classic period as a bloody free-for-all, the distancing can become even greater.[22] But there are powerful forces of exclusion that also distance Indigenous and local peoples from their past and from participation in the heritage tourism industry built upon the ancient cities.[23] While the popularity of La Ruta Maya may be waning at the moment, there is no denying that classic Maya archaeology carries a cachet that is unrivaled in the Americas. Indeed, the busy intersection described earlier becomes even more congested if filmmakers, avocational enthusiasts, New Age prophets, and doomsday seers are included.

Contributing factors to the allure of Maya archaeology include complex hieroglyphic writing, intricate calendrical reckoning, an aesthetic that included idealized portraiture in permanent media, and an architectural prowess emulated by Frank Lloyd Wright. At the start of the nineteenth century, the Western eye was enchanted by Aztec heritage as presented by the nascent state of México,[24] but as urbanization and industrialization overran the contemporary capital of México (which is superimposed upon the old Aztec capital), fascination shifted to the ruined buildings in the jungles of the lowlands. Beatriz González-Stephan characterizes this enchantment as the Orientalizing of Latin America.[25]

This imaginary created places without history—only a prehistory in ruins. Correspondingly, inhabitants became the eponymous *people without history*.[26] Not surprisingly, portrayal of an abandoned landscape available for foreign investment served the needs of emergent Latin American nation-states badly in need of capital. As explored in further detail in chapter 2, this need coincided with the desire of the global north for tropical foods such as coffee, bananas, and sugar, as well as botanical and antiquarian specimens that could be collected and transported to the global north.[27] Yucatán stepped forward to supply the world with rope and twine tediously and painfully processed from thorny henequen plants by an indentured Yucatec Maya labor force. In the past and also today, disused stone structures covered by tropical forest accentuated the exoticism of the Maya lowlands.

From the ironic perspective of postmodernism, there is much to appreciate here. As descendants became more distanced from their precolonial past (and withdrew or were ejected from the busy intersection discussed above), other groups (archaeologists included) drew closer to and were ever more enamored by what they found in the forest. In chapter 3, we examine the historical trajectory by which Indigenous peoples were increasingly alienated from the deep history of the Maya region. With a nod to Annette Weiner, we might characterize the Maya region as composed of people of value and things of renown[28]—the living heritage of people who experience their culture today and the powerfully evocative things that have survived the ravages of time in a tropical climate. For the last century or two, these two arcs of Maya cultural heritage have been on a divergent trajectory, but the trend is shifting toward one of convergence. This convergence supercharges the complexity of the busy intersection that is cultural heritage but also infuses well-tread terrain with fresh perspectives. This book details an effort to nurture this convergence through collaborative programs designed to jump-start a dialogue within local schools and communities about the deep past and what it means to twenty-first-century children, adolescents, and adults living in the Maya region.

BUILDING BRIDGES

Like the shaky banana-truck bridge that spans the Río Sixaola separating Costa Rica from Panama, collaboration and alliance building are fragile endeavors. Archaeologists are obliged to move from their comfortable perch as scientists of the past and seek common ground with community organizations that may be distrustful of foreign researchers or interested in the past primarily for political or economic advantage. Within the Maya region, local partnering organizations inevitably operate on a shoestring budget. Of tenuous construction and liable to collapse if not maintained, such bridges nonetheless provide a pathway toward a new kind of endeavor that can hybridize archaeology with cultural heritage. This new kind of engagement goes by many different names, which are dependent on disciplinary boundaries (varieties are discussed in chapters 4 and 6), but all approaches share an impulse toward greater inclusivity by restructuring how knowledge is created.

Bridges are built to serve a purpose; here the purpose is to spark dialogue about heritage and encourage participation in its study and conservation. Cultural heritage programs are a means to this end. Deciding from the onset to build out in several directions, the Maya Cultural Heritage Initiative (introduced formally in chapter 7) became an endeavor of bridge building and content production. A bridge to Arte Acción—an art nonprofit in Copán Ruinas—led to cultural heritage workshops in the small *aldeas* (villages) around the world-renowned site of Copán.[29] Another bridge to the Julian Cho Society (an organization dedicated to land claims settlement in southern Belize) led to cultural enrichment programs for grade-school children. Radio *novelas* that tell the story of heritage and archaeology in the Guatemalan lowlands resulted from an alliance with ProPetén—a grassroots environmental nongovernmental organization (NGO) based in Flores, Petén. Elsewhere, marionettes were created and pressed into service to tell a story of Yucatec Maya cultural heritage via an alliance with an international NGO called Kaxil Kiuic A.C., based in the Puuc region. Collaboration with the Riecken Foundation of highland Guatemala and Honduras, an organization that has built small libraries in more than sixty communities, resulted in a community-mapping program that proved to be particularly useful to local communities.[30]

In chapters 8 and 9, those who participated in these programs speak out. Responses to questionnaires provided by hundreds of participants in these transcultural projects are at times surprising, sometimes predictable, and also can be unsettling. We learn, for instance, of a deep interest in the tools and narratives of archaeology and a desire to be more involved in research and conservation. Answers hint at the power of a deeper engagement with the past to tackle seemingly intractable problems such as racism, low self-esteem, and a desire for greater self-determination. Taken together, opinions voiced by participants point toward a conclusion that is significant for Maya archaeology: the entanglement of Western praxis with non-Western local knowledge holds transformational potential for archaeology and potentially can strengthen both local communities and heritage conservation. This book is particularly concerned with how the busy intersection that forms the nexus of cultural heritage is navigated through (a) partnerships, (b) activities engendered by collaboration, and (c) the possibility of lasting impact in terms of both heritage conservation and the democratization of knowledge. These issues are critically evaluated in the final chapter.

BETWEEN THE COVERS OF THIS BOOK

Without a time line, an archaeological approach to a topic takes on the feel of Salvador Dalí's melting timepieces. I begin this book with nineteenth-century nation building in Latin America. This birth of nations focused on the *lettered cities*[31] and, by and large, encouraged foreign investment that produced wealth for a small urban sector at the expense of a rural, Indigenous, and largely illiterate sector. Chapter 2 tells the story of emerging nations—often *unimaginable* communities of horrific violence for Native peoples. As these new nations claimed and then leased or sold national resources (including Indigenous traditional-use lands), *cultural patrimony* increasingly became another resource to be commodified and removed from Indigenous jurisdiction.

Chapter 3 is an examination of how Maya archaeology emerged amid the economic turbulence and political violence of nineteenth-century Latin America, and it did not escape unscathed. The neocolonialism that permeated rural-urban and north-south relations through the nineteenth and twentieth centuries imprinted itself on archaeological practice in a profound fashion. As archaeologists explored rural areas, local men became guides and excavators for archaeological projects, while women and daughters cooked, cleaned, and laundered the clothes of archaeologists. The intimacy to these relationships was deeply contextualized in place. Local guides led archaeologists to the "lost cities," the "discovery" of which often was announced in the pages of *National Geographic*.[32] Knowledge of landscape and how to survive in a tropical environment was profound and immediate for the explorers from the north, but the contribution of this kind of intelligence to knowing the past often went unremarked as archaeologists forged ahead with publicity, publications, and funding for more discoveries.

Maya archaeology is not unique in this regard. During the last quarter of the twentieth century, a clarion call for the examination of practice sounded throughout sociocultural anthropology and then through the discipline of archaeology since the 1990s. This general critique and its relevance to Maya archaeology is the concern of chapter 4. In the latter part of this chapter, we leave behind the postcolonial critique and examine a newer approach that can be called *transmodern*. This approach is typified by theory and methods that aim to confront and creatively deconstruct the structural inequalities exposed by the postcolonial critique. Collaborative approaches are one kind of transmodern approach considered in chapters 4 and 6.

Chapter 5 returns to the Maya region to consider the impact of nation building, neocolonialism, and neoliberalism on ethnolinguistic Maya communities. We learn how communities define themselves in very local terms—in great contrast to the monolithic term the *Maya*. This localness translates into tremendous variation in the experience and expression of cultural heritage within the Maya region and in the way in which people draw upon the trope of the *ancient Maya* to shape modern identities for different purposes.

Building bridges—transmodern style—is central to chapter 6, where the general value of community-participatory research and other collaborative approaches is considered. The very real challenge of building partnerships with communities in four of the nation-states within the Maya region is detailed in chapter 7. Shaky at first, each partnership was shaded by the national experience of local communities. Thus, each alliance is unique, as are the cultural heritage programs that were codesigned within each partnership.

The Maya cultural heritage programs discussed in this book tend to be either educational (sited within schools with field trips to local archaeological sites) or performative in the sense of radio or puppet shows. Community responses to these programs occupy chapters 8 and 9, which is coauthored with Sarah Rowe, who directed programs (until 2015) for an initiative called InHerit, which followed the Maya Area Cultural Heritage Initiative. While community mapping is not performative in the same way as radio shows, the practice of mapping can be considered a performance of cultural heritage and for this reason is discussed in chapter 9. Both chapters 8 and 9 provide the reader with access to the thoughts and opinions of rural inhabitants of the Maya region as they internalized and made sense of the cultural heritage initiatives.

Lessons learned from responses to heritage programs are taken back to archaeology where, in chapter 10, the notion of heritage without irony is engaged—what that might look like and what we might be able to accomplish if we can get there. The broader issue of heritage conservation is tackled within this context. I apply the knowledge gained from programs and responses to suggest that a United Nations top-down style of conservation will never be successful if not matched by grassroots programs and dialogue with local communities.

The pages to follow tackle the haunting questions that opened this chapter. Like the ominous sound of a creaky door hinge, those questions are harbingers of more issues that will continue to shape Maya archaeology as practitioners face the colonial history of the discipline, current practices of inquiry that need to be more inclusive, and a future that is inextricably linked with heritage conservation. The odyssey continues, but now it is time to consider the nineteenth-century world and the creation of a Maya region.

NOTES

1. For more on colonialism and the manner in which it haunts contemporary scholarship, see Stoler (2006).

2. For discussion of the myth of the mound builders in North America, see Silverberg (1968) and Willey and Sabloff (1993:21–28). For Zimbabwe, see the classic work by Caton-Thompson (1931) and the recent scholarship of Pikirayi (2001).

3. The conjoined personal and professional nature of this journey is presaged in similar accounts by Nicholas and Andrews (1997a) and also by Little and Shackel (2014).

4. For an edited book on archaeological ethics, see Vitelli and Colwell-Chanthaphonh (2006).

5. Groarke and Warrick (2006:164–67).

6. For an IRB guidebook, see www.hhs.gov/ohrp/archive/irb/irb_introduction.htm; for the AAA "Code of Ethics," see www.aaanet.org/issues/policy-advocacy/upload/AAA -Ethics-Code-2009.pdf

7. For several approaches to rewiring archaeological practice, see Atalay et al. (2014), McGuire (2008), and Pyburn (2003, 2011).

8. See McAnany (2014:163–64) and McAnany and Rowe (2015) for discussions of relevance in archaeology. This perspective places greater emphasis on the social relevance that emerges from the way in which archaeology is practiced vis-à-vis those who are impacted by archaeological activities and relies less on attempting to teach societal lessons based on tenuous archaeological findings.

9. See McGuire (2008:190–94) for a discussion of archaeological communities and praxis.

10. Smith and Waterton (2009:44) define *heritage* as "a cultural process or performance of meaning-making."

11. This burgeoning literature—particularly in the United Kingdom—is challenging to summarize succinctly; influential texts include the following: Dearborn and Stallmeyer (2010); Di Giovine (2009); Fairclough (2008); Labadi and Long (2010); Lowenthal (1985); Meskell (2012); Rowan and Baram (2004); Seneviratne (2008); Silverman (2002); Silverman and Ruggles (2007); and Smith (2008).

12. For a pertinent discussion of this freighted intersection of interest groups, see Bartu Candan (2007:93) on the myriad stakeholders of Çatalhöyük.

13. Hale (2006:97).

14. Hale (2011:205).

15. Hale (2006:101, 108).

16. Much has been written about the formation of new communities of archaeological practice, particularly in the United States. For instance, see Atalay (2012), Colwell-Chanthaphonh and Ferguson (2008), and Silliman (2008). Also Parks and McAnany (2011) discuss how heritage conservation cannot be sustained without the grassroots participation of local communities who need a compelling *raison d'être*.

17. See Castañeda (2004).

18. See the critical analysis of the term *Indigenous* in Colwell-Chanthaphonh (2012:269); Corntassel and Witmer (2008); Daes (1996); Haber (2007); Hinton (2002); Levy (2006); Martínez Cobo (1986); Merlan (2009); Niezen (2003); Ross et al. (2011:21); Sanjinés (2004); and Smith (2012).

19. Smith (2012:6).

20. Armstrong-Fumero (2013:178).

21. Smith (2005).

22. Using Mel Gibson's *Apocalypto* as a case in point, it's instructive to consider the divergent responses to the release of this violent chase film. Ricardo Cajas of Guatemala, presidential commissioner on racism, condemned the film (www.theguardian.com/film/2007/jan/10/news.melgibson). Yucatec primary school students and residents of Cobá, Quintana Roo, disassociated themselves from the violent past depicted in the film while simultaneously expressing pride that the movie was filmed in their native language (Callahan, 2007). A panel convened at the American Anthropological Association in 2007 and organized by Traci Ardren revealed a wide range of responses by scholars and Mayan intellectuals that included everything from condemnation to appreciation that the film contained dialogue in Yucatec Mayan.

23. McAnany and Parks (2012).

24. González-Stephan (2009:108) notes that the Mexican Palacio Azteca at the 1889 Paris World's fair was a pharonic imitation.

25. González-Stephan (2009:108).

26. A phrase coined by Eric Wolf (1982) to describe the manner in which Europeans dealt with cultural difference during European colonial expansion.

27. González-Stephan (2009:108–9).

28. Weiner (1987).

29. See McAnany and Parks (2012) for an in-depth analysis of this program.

30. See McAnany et al. (2015) for presentation of the Guatemala mapping project.

31. Angel Rama (1996:1–15) discusses the focus of Latin America colonialists and then nationalists on literacy and urban places as emblematic of social order and receptacles for transplanted European culture.

32. For more on the role of *National Geographic* in exoticizing the Maya region, see Lutz and Collins (1993) as well as Gero and Root (1990).

2

◡◠

Forging Nationalism
and Indenturing Labor

And here shall appear their faces, one by one, of each of the Quiché Lords . . .
Jaguar Quitze, origin of the Cauecs. . . .
Seven Thought and Cauatepech . . . eleventh in the sequence of lords.
Three Deer and Nine Dog, in the twelfth generation of lords.
And they were ruling when Tonatiuh [Pedro de Alvarado] arrived.
They were tortured by the Castilian people.
Black Butterfly and Tepepul were tributary to the Castilian people. . . .

—*Popol Vuh*, translation by Dennis Tedlock[1]

In the short but factual lines of the *Popol Vuh*, a creation narrative and royal genealogy of the Quiché (K'iche') Mayan people, we learn of the arrival of Spaniards in 1524. Twelfth-generation aristocratic rulers were tortured by invading Pedro de Alvarado, an infamous conquistador dubbed Tonatiuh or "he who goes along getting hot."[2] The following generation—that of Black Butterfly and Tepepul—became tributaries of the Castilians. Political and economic autonomy died with Three Deer and Nine Dog, and the Native aristocracies began a slow death. Military conquest (by Castilian rules) had occurred, and colonization would follow. During the nineteenth century, nation-states sputtered into existence throughout the Maya region along with a new kind of slavery (indentured labor) that signaled the participation of Latin America in neocolonial arrangements of early globalism. From the sixteenth through the eighteenth centuries, massive population loss among Indigenous peoples living within the region occurred as people coped with new and deadly diseases and the daily reality of forced labor. These are the historical realities that stand behind the haunting referenced both in chapter 1 and in the phrase used by Ann Stoler as the title of her edited volume, *Haunted by Empire*.[3]

18

During three hundred years of colonialism and brutality, such as that of Pedro de Alvarado, conquest and control of Native peoples was a recursive theme as clergy and crown fought for the body and soul of Indigenous Maya peoples.[4] Controlling Christianized souls was an influential point of entry for controlling the body—and more explicitly the labor—of Native peoples. Aristocracies—such as that of Three Deer and Nine Dog—were useful to colonialists because they could facilitate Spanish desires to amass large fortunes on the backs of Native laborers via taxes and forced labor.[5] Coerced relocation around mission churches (and burning Indigenous communities to the ground if they refused to relocate[6]) altered the way in which local landscape was experienced; it was a critical point of inflexion. Landscapes are imbued with meaning, which often are deeply religious and overtly historical. Colonialists worked actively to subvert Indigenous codes of meaning.

How did sixteenth-century colonialists perceive what had existed before their incursions? Did they comprehend the rich and deep heritage of those they sought to conquer and enslave? The answer to this question is complex and requires a longer treatment than is possible here. Certainly, Spaniards recognized the monumentality of classic-period Yucatec sites and recorded some amazingly accurate descriptions of places such as Uxmal and Chichén Itzá during the seventeenth century.[7] On the other hand, what is now called the Department of Petén remained *terra incognito* well into the nineteenth century. But colonial concerns with extirpation of Indigenous religious practices and with corralling a labor force took precedence over all else. Later, when eighteenth- and nineteenth-century explorers considered the tangible heritage of precolonial times and how it related to impoverished and disenfranchised Native inhabitants, thoughts turned increasingly to off-course sailing Phoenicians or Carthaginians, who were given credit for building the ancient cities.[8]

The nation-states that now occupy portions of the Maya region formed primarily during the early part of the nineteenth century. The birth of nations in this part of the world is significant for this study because nation-states codified laws and conditions of existence that greatly impacted Indigenous peoples and constrained the ways in which they could relate to the past.[9] These same governmental entities laid claim to the tangible cultural heritage of old places and the things that are found within them—ostensibly to protect cultural resources from the depredations of looting and development and later to encourage heritage tourism. Nation-states also codified laws and created permit procedures to control the activities of archaeologists and stem the outflow of artifacts. We return to the means and methods by which Maya archaeology was "disciplined" later in chapter 3.

As many have noted, the nineteenth-century liberation of Spanish-American colonies from Spain did not translate into more liberties for Native peoples. In fact, an intensification of coerced labor occurred in many parts of the Maya region. The violent encounters of the sixteenth century were replayed, and there ensued a new cycle of physical as well as structural violence. During the early colonial period, Native aristocrats negotiated with Spaniards for continuation of their rights and privileges, and they also mediated the blunt demands of colonizers. But when nineteenth-century nation building was underway, the Indigenous aristocracies of precolonial times had been all but leveled into an impoverished underclass. Politicians of the new republics could characterize this underclass as resistant to change and a white man's burden. Historian Terry Rugeley cites a speech given by prominent Yucatecan "Castilian" Néstor Rubio Alpuche in 1899 to students of Salesian College in Mexico City: "The proletariat class, full of vices, and the Indian, indifferent to progress, form a heavy burden for the state and cause it to march but slowly."[10] "Indifferent to progress" seems an odd way to describe people whose ancestors had independently invented the concept of zero, developed the most complex hieroglyphic writing system in the Americas, and engineered towering structures that are still standing today. The relentless violence of colonialism left Indigenous peoples with few weapons other than withdrawal.[11]

The focus of this chapter is primarily the nineteenth century for a number of reasons. Politically, this century bore witness to the transition from colony to nation in four of the five countries within the Maya region (see table 2.1). The outlier is Belize, formerly British Honduras, which did not become an independent nation until 1981. As former colonies crafted national identities, flags, and currencies, they engaged in the process of creating what Benedict Anderson calls *imagined communities*,[12] in which commonalities are emphasized and differences masked or erased, particularly when such differences were intricately woven into the maintenance of power relations and wealth accumulation. In Latin America, imagined communities as artificial constructs held together through persuasion, coercion, and identity crafting ultimately followed a process that Beatriz González-Stephan calls *café con leche* or whitening the nation.[13] This process greatly diminished opportunities for and representation of Native peoples within emergent nations.

Table 2.1. Characteristics of nation-states that comprise the Maya region.

Nation	Year of Independence	Former Colony of	Indigenous Symbols or People	
			On Flag	On Currency
Mexico	1822	Spain	yes	yes
Belize	1981	England	no	yes
Guatemala	1821 . . . 1838–1840[a]	Spain	yes	yes
Honduras	1821 . . . 1838–1840[a]	Spain	no	yes
El Salvador	1821 . . . 1841[a]	Spain	no	yes

[a]After independence from Spain in 1821, Guatemala, Honduras, and El Salvador became part of Provincias Unidas del Centro de América (United Provinces of Central America). The United Provinces were dissolved in 1838, and each province declared independence as a nation-state.

Although overt political imperialism began to fade in the nineteenth century, economic imperialism or neocolonialism rose to the fore as mercantile capitalism transformed into modern capitalist relations of production. The world became a smaller place and one in which thousands of miles might routinely separate places of production from those of consumption. People living in the increasingly powerful global north exhibited a growing appetite for food, drink, hardwoods, and other materials that could only be grown in the tropics or could be cultivated and harvested more cheaply in tropical locales because laborers were captives, indentured, or paid a pittance. In *Sweetness and Power*, Sidney Mintz documents how laborers captured in Africa and transported to Caribbean sugar plantations provided English tea-drinkers with their daily dollop of sugar.[14] Within the Maya region, vast amounts of land were needed for plantation agriculture to grow henequen (for rope and twine), coffee, bananas, and sugar. Tropical hardwood trees in mature forests were felled to feed the demand for mahogany furniture. In colonies like British Honduras where deep rivers provided navigable corridors to the sea, these conduits were choked with floating logs that had been painstakingly cut by enslaved (or recently emancipated) Africans.[15] Throughout the region, Indigenous farmers with small holdings were extremely vulnerable to land expropriation because they did not possess title to what had always been usufruct or inherited lands. Additionally, new forms of taxes were continually levied against them despite the fact that rural farmers had limited access to currency. Because of its direct bearing on how people relate to landscape and the past that is encoded within it, we examine the impact of burgeoning global capitalism on nineteenth-century Native peoples of the Maya region.

Archaeology as a scientific approach to the past also came of age during the nineteenth century, primarily in Europe. In England and on the Continent, archaeological pursuits often entailed a search for evidence of a primordial past that was useful to bolster ethnic identity and nationalism—the imagined communities of Benedict Anderson.[16] But in the Americas, archaeologists generally were of European descent and identified first as adventurers and then as scientists. Both monikers applied primarily to men who studied an exotic past with an uncertain (in the minds of those conducting the studies) relation to Native inhabitants. The methods of archaeology can be used in any time or place, but the political and economic context of pursuing the past in the Americas aligned archaeologists with the aspirations of emerging nations and with expansionistic U.S.-based enterprises.

How did the extraordinary past of the Maya region fit into nation building? Answering this question requires grappling with the complexities of studying the past of peoples who were perceived to be without history and whose place in the imagined communities of burgeoning nations was painfully ambivalent. Yet the allure and exoticism of that past to those of European extraction cannot be underestimated. Scores of scientific travel writers[17] as well as archaeologists were increasingly drawn to the region. Because of the manner in which this history shaped the contemporary practice of Maya archaeology, nineteenth-century archaeological discourse in reference to Indigenous inhabitants of the Maya region is examined here.

The purpose of this chapter is not to sketch a political or economic history of nation-states within the Maya region—these have already been written and far better than I can do—but rather to examine the interactions between nascent states and Indigenous peoples who lived within their newly demarcated boundaries. In the process, we hope to glimpse the strategies by which these imagined communities coalesced and attempted (or not) to make space for *café sin leche*.[18] Likewise, by examining neocolonial entanglements with the global north, we may come to a better understanding of the processes by which Indigenous peoples were disenfranchised from lands upon which their livelihood was based and also from ancestral landscapes that contained the old places that—during postcolonial times—became the property of a nation and the object of archaeological investigation.

LIMITS TO IMAGINATION

Benedict Anderson used the term *imagined communities* to describe the nineteenth-century turn toward nationalism on a global scale.[19] For Latin America, Anderson thought that the print medium and the circuits of colonial bureaucrats were important factors in promoting ideas of independence and the subsequent contours of emerging states.[20] But historians such as John Chasteen and others have shown that the power of letters in relation to nationalism followed rather than preceded the nineteenth-century wars of independence and that colonial bureaucratic circuits had little to do with the shape of nascent states in Latin America.[21]

Although Anderson may have been wrong in terms of the specific factors that led to state formation throughout Latin America, his thesis that imagined communalities play an indispensable role in cultivating a sentiment of nationalism is bolstered by empirical evidence. The challenge of cultivating a national sentiment proved formidable, however, in ethnically diverse postcolonial contexts in which perhaps 25 percent of the population were "American-born whites," another quarter were of mixed ancestry (some combination of white and Indigenous or African or all three), and the remaining 50 percent were Indigenous (except for plantation-intensive locales such as Brazil in which there were larger numbers of laborers with African ancestry).[22] This diversity coupled with Eurocentric illusions of superiority limited the ability of emerging nations to imagine a pluralistic state. The putative ethnic nationalisms of Europe simply could not be superimposed on Latin America without erasing over 50 percent of inhabitants—that is, Native peoples with a very deep and long-term relationship to the landscape.

Four of the five emerging nations under consideration—México, Guatemala, Honduras, and El Salvador—had been managed under colonial occupation for three hundred years when independence came. A precisely calculated social caste system was well established,[23] and rural as well as urban areas were integrated politically into colonial rule of law. The Indigenous population was large and internally diverse. In southern México, Guatemala, Belize, and the western parts of Honduras and El Salvador, Native peoples spoke languages that are classified by linguists as members of the Mayan language family. Distinct languages—not just dialects of one language—exist within this family. When ethnic identity is coupled with this linguistic diversity, there are approximately thirty-one distinct ethnolinguistic groups within the Maya region. This count does not include groups that did not survive the violence of colonization. Such diversity poses an additional challenge to an imagined uniformity of nationhood and "to the cultivation of a subject's willingness or desire to form part of a nation."[24]

POLITICS OF EXCLUSION IN THE LETTERED CITY

Terry Rugeley describes nineteenth-century Yucatán as a synthesis of "liberal positivist sensibilities pasted over unreformed colonial practices."[25] Although the wars of liberation were supposed to promote freedom and equality for all, in reality the American-born whites benefitted most from a break with the Spanish crown. In the words of John Chasteen, the native-born white minority sought "not to remake colonial society, but to assume control of it themselves."[26] While the participation of Indigenous peoples in the wars of liberation was much heralded, their position postindependence became more precarious. Under the old colonial República de Indios established by the Spanish crown, Indigenous peoples lived in "a parallel society organized in administratively designated 'Indian towns' where Iberian colonizers were not to intrude."[27] Independence nullified this arrangement and in many cases led to predatory seizing of lands that had been classified as Native holdings under the Spanish crown, even after the Bourbon Reforms of the eighteenth century. The mid-nineteenth-century eruption of the Caste War (pitting Yucatec Maya against Creoles) was inflamed by many factors, and among the causes were increasing incursions following Mexican independence onto *milpa* lands used for long-cycle swidden agriculture.[28]

Even though the printed word may not have fanned the flames of independence in Latin America, once independent "printed words and images . . . gave legitimacy to new states and the ideology of republicanism."[29] Angel Rama proposes that nineteenth-century urban places provided an indispensable context for the promulgation of nationalism within Latin America.[30] In the cities, rates of literacy were high due to the availability of education, and the written word was encouraged and reproduced via printing presses. Presses became widespread in Latin America during the nineteenth century and were actively deployed to craft nationalism and identity politics through the circulation of newspapers, novels, and pamphlets.[31] These publications were produced primarily for urban, literate audiences residing in the regional capitals of México (including Mérida in Yucatán), Guatemala City in Guatemala, and urban enclaves in Honduras and El Salvador. Indigenous peoples, many of whom continued to reside in rural areas and lacked access to education, were excluded from this enterprise of nation building by low rates of Spanish literacy as well as physical remoteness from the lettered cities.

The urban-rural dichotomy crystallized as a racialized romantic exoticism in the eyes of nineteenth-century explorers from northern latitudes. As Frederick Catherwood accompanied John Lloyd Stephens in exploration of "ruins" in the Maya region, he produced accurately scaled and detailed sketches of archaeological sites. For scale and local color, he placed Native inhabitants in the drawings, as seen in the gathering around a well (figure 2.1). With extraordinarily well-preserved one-thousand-year-old Puuc-style architecture in the background, scantily clad locals lounge and socialize at the communal well of a place Catherwood called Sabachtsche. In relaxed body positions, Indigenous peoples are portrayed as natural (as opposed to cultural and literate). Children are naked, young females are shown frontally as topless, innocently filling water jugs and apparently unperturbed by the probing eyes of Catherwood. In the background, fully clad white men (and one dark-skinned young man) ride horseback. The contrast is complete.

Figure 2.1. Catherwood (1844:Plate 18) drawing titled "Well and Building at Sabachtsche [*sic*]." Reproduced by permission of the John Carter Brown Library, Brown University.

But in reality, the contrast between the lettered city and an Indigenous and largely illiterate countryside was never absolute. Michael Huner provides a case to the contrary, which may prove the rule of this separation. In nineteenth-century wartime Paraguay, printing presses were used to circulate the story of an Indigenous Guaraní mother who instructed her children to kill the invading forces with a knife and then fight until death. Her "words" were printed in Guaraní.[32] This example—and there are others—is intriguing from the perspective of both ethnicity and gender. The fierce independence of Native persons was invoked to counter an external threat or to reinforce the idea that the nation stands ready to defend its freedom. This trope is particularly popular on currencies (see table 2.1): Tecún Umán, a young K'iche' prince who died in battle against incursive Spanish forces during the sixteenth century, occupies pride of place on the 0.50 quetzal note. Honduran currency is called the lempira, named after a sixteenth-century Indigenous Lenca ruler who resisted Spanish conquest. Prominent Indigenous heritage sites (Tikal and Copán, respectively) grace the obverse side of both paper currencies.

Indigenous women, in particular, were pressed into the service of nascent states to symbolize independence and firm resolve but in a way that could be managed by the ringleaders of independence. Hugo Achugar describes a painting of the famous liberator Simón Bolívar with his arm paternalistically around a woman who wears a headdress of feathers and sports a quiver of arrows. She is both regal and martial. Painted by Pedro José Figueroa in 1819, the composition hangs in the Casa Museo Quinta de Bolívar in Colombia.[33]

Insofar as these imagined communities of nation-states were defined and flourished in lettered cities, they existed outside the orbit of many Indigenous peoples. Perceived Native qualities of fierceness and independence were called upon as needed, and currencies provided a ready medium on which to display these imagined national characteristics.

HIGH-FLYING NATIONALISM

Flags represent a very different medium from currency. Since flags are a focus of nationalist pride, examination of these creations is informative of national ethos. For the most part, flags encode abstract ideas such as liberty, equality, and freedom and in the process can also provide a canvas for valorizing or erasing Indigeneity (see table 2.1). The flags of both Honduras and El Salvador are relatively abstract, with two horizontal bands of blue separated by a central white band. Five blue stars arranged in a quincunx pattern are centrally positioned in a field of white on the Honduran flag. The central field of the Salvadoran flag features a more complex composition that includes five volcanoes floating in a blue sea; the composition refers to the short-lived United Provinces of Central America of which El Salvador was a member immediately after its 1821 independence from

Spain. Oddly, a Phrygian cap (perhaps symbolizing freedom) hangs from a pole jutting from one of the volcanoes.

The Guatemalan flag is distinguished by blue bands arranged vertically. Inside a laurel wreath that defines a circular field within a central white band there are two crossed sabers, two crossed rifles, a quetzal bird, and a scroll containing the date of independence from Spain: September 15, 1821. The quetzal bird could be construed as a nod toward precolonial systems of value since its long green iridescent feathers were a precious item worn in elaborate headdresses by Classic Maya royalty, but here the bird symbolizes the independence, liberty, and autonomy of the nation.[34] In Wikipedia, the entry for the flag of Guatemala also shows a flag that was designed as part of the post–civil war peace accords and was adopted in 2008 (figure 2.2). Called Bandera de Los Pueblos (flag of the Indigenous peoples), the design features four intersecting triangular bands of color: red, yellow, black, and white. These four colors are linked with directionality in Maya cosmologies, but on the flag they represent four groups of nonwhite citizens of Guatemala: Xinca, Garifuna, Maya, and ladino (those of mixed ancestry). Xinca peoples are a non-Maya Indigenous group, while the Garifuna have mixed Indigenous and African ancestry. In the center of the four intersecting triangles, the classic Maya hieroglyph for earth (*kab*) is positioned. Is this glyph a reference to nonwhites of Guatemala as people of the earth (as opposed to people of the cities)? The three curls under the *kab* sign and the semi-enclosure of the glyph within a cartouche mark it as the day sign *kaban* within the Maya calendar round. *Kaban* is one of four possible days that can coincide with the seating of a new month and so also evokes a sense of renewal or new beginnings. By national decree, this flag must be present at all events in which the president is featured.

The flag of México is distinct from that of Central American countries to the south, as are the details of its precolonial and colonial history. With three vertical bands of color (green, white, and red), the central white band contains the Mexican coat of arms. Most definitely of pre-Hispanic origin, the crest features an eagle holding a rattlesnake in its mouth and claw while the other claw wraps

Figure 2.2. *Bandera de Los Pueblos*—a second Guatemalan flag designed to represent nonwhite peoples of the nation-state (from Wikipedia commons).

around a fruiting *nopal* cactus that sprouts from a rock in a lake. This image was used by Aztecs (or Mexicas) to reference the founding of Tenochtitlan in the basin of México. The colonial and contemporary Mexico City (Cuidad de México) sits directly on top of the old Aztec capital. This juxtaposition not-so-subtly hints at the manner in which Mexican nationalism borrows from older Mexica heritage.

As early as the eighteenth century, exiled Jesuit Francisco Javier Clavijero wrote *Historia Antigua de México* (ancient history of México); he is cited by Mexican archaeologist Ignacio Bernal as desiring to "advance the claims of both strands of inheritance."[35] Although this statement alludes to the racial separation between "the strands of inheritance" that gelled during the colonial period, this desire also points toward a pluralistic political entity as a goal if not a reality. Of the nations under consideration here, México is most notable for its experimentation with (or imagination of) a national identity of *mestizaje*—mixed ancestry. Called *indigenismo* in postrevolutionary México, the movement sought to homogenize the "approximately 58 different ethnolinguistic groups in Mexico," ostensibly to erase economic exploitation.[36] *Indigenismo* included the selective integration into the national consciousness of cultural practices and precolonial places of Indigenous groups, and the outcome was profoundly negative for Indigenous groups that were targeted for assimilation.[37] This postrevolutionary turn continued well into the twentieth century and succeeded in demonstrating only that forceful national rhetoric and all the Diego Rivera murals in the world could not change the fact that Mexican politics, economics, and education perpetuated a large underclass of persons of principally Indigenous ancestry.[38]

It's hard to resist a comment about the Aztec or Mexica ethnicity of the Mexican flag, which meets with a chilly reception in the Maya region, particularly on the Yucatán Peninsula. A forty-year-long insurgency led primarily by Yucatec Mayan leaders who desired succession from México just decades after its 1822 independence left bitter memories of a struggle that almost succeeded[39] as well as a legacy of crushing "war-related poverty and social dislocations."[40] Even among the nineteenth-century urban citizens of Mérida, Yucatán was perceived as a world apart from México, a *patria chica*[41] (small country or homeland).

The final and most recent flag—that of Belize, a former colony of Britain—is less abstract and more ethnic and gender exclusive than the other four. Two thin bands of red border a solid field of blue. A white disc in the center of the flag features a laurel wreath and the coat of arms of Belize: two shirtless men wearing white trousers stand side by side and face forward. The white man on the left carries an ax, while the black man on the right carries a paddle. Between them is a tree that refers to the logging industry, which was foundational to the establishment of the British colony. The free hands of each man rest on a crest subdivided into three parts: (1) a sailing ship, (2) a paddle crossed with a large hammer, and (3) an ax crossed with a two-handled saw. Beneath the men, the national motto is written: *sub umbra floreo* (loosely translated as "flourishing under the shade").

This remarkable flag indexes the nautical origins of the colony; its role in logging hardwoods such as mahogany for ship masts as well as export to the United States for furniture manufacture; the black men who did most of the lumbering, initially as slaves and after the emancipation of 1838 as poorly paid lumberjacks; and the white men who initially "owned" and then supervised them. Many Belizeans interpret the equal footing of the black and white men on the flag as a sign of racial equality between those of African and European ancestry. The sizable Indigenous Maya population of Belize (estimated conservatively to be 10 percent of the total) is absent from the imaginary of a racially blind fraternity (represented on the flag as men only) of workers toiling together. In addition to "flourishing under the shade," a more colloquial national ideology—and one that complements the flag—states: "We are all immigrants here." During a recent court case brought by Toledo Maya peoples against the government of Belize[42] in an effort to settle land claims, the state provided expert witnesses who testified that there are no people who are indigenous to Belize because all were killed or driven from the territory by early Spanish conquistadors or later British slave runners.

THE LETTERED CHURCH

Up to this point, we have not considered the role of the Catholic Church in the emerging nations of the nineteenth century. Priests and friars played an active role in the sixteenth-century colonization of Latin America and in the maintenance of colonial rule for the next three hundred years. In the Yucatán and the highlands of Guatemala especially, massive mission churches were constructed using the conscripted labor of Native populations. From these strongholds, circuits for proselytizing and maintaining "the flock" were organized (figure 2.3). In the colonies, priests were charged with (or took upon themselves) the task of recording the birth/baptism and sometimes marriage and death of all souls under their spiritual jurisdiction. Early census records often are ecclesiastical records. Significantly, a proselytizing profession demanded that missionaries be amateur linguists. Religious clergy produced the first transcriptions of Mayan languages into the European alphabet. They did so for the purpose of creating catechisms and other doctrinal materials in Mayan languages. William Hanks has written of the powerful impact of this translative process on the very fabric of Yucatec Mayan as a language and medium of cognition.[43]

One sixteenth-century Yucatec bishop—Diego de Landa—created a syllabary that translated Postclassic Maya hieroglyphs into the Spanish alphabet.[44] Working with aristocratic scribes, the bishop produced a concordance that has been called the Rosetta Stone of Maya hieroglyphs.[45] A keen observer of daily life, ritual cycles, and calendric observances, Landa apparently kept a voluminous journal that later served as the basis for writing the *Relación de las Cosas de Yucatán* (An account of the things of Yucatán).[46] Landa was called back to

Figure 2.3. Remains of the stone sanctuary for a *visita* church thought to have been constructed around 1612 at Tahcabo in Yucatán, México (photo by author).

Spain for engaging in overly zealous conversion practices that included torture and burning countless invaluable Maya codices during the infamous *auto da fé* (confession and act of faith) at Maní in 1562. Such practices would be considered religious persecution today. Nonetheless, his account of the practices and beliefs of his parishioners has been called the first Maya ethnography and is referenced extensively by Maya archaeologists to buttress interpretation.

Often members of the clergy found themselves in a conflictive relationship with colonial and then national authorities either because they protested the inhumane treatment and unfair taxation of Native peoples or because they amassed tremendous wealth and power that rivaled and challenged secular authorities. A sixteenth-century clerical figure most often cited as a defender of Indigenous peoples is the Dominican priest Bartolomé de las Casas. For part of his religious career, he was stationed in the western part of the Maya region (in the town now called San Cristobal de las Casas in Chiapas). Casas famously named the Alta Verapaz region as a place inhabited by people of "true peace." He did so to circumvent the incessant slave raiding that was taking place in that area, which bureaucratically had not been incorporated into the Spanish Empire.[47] By 1767, Jesuits were expelled from the Spanish colonies and additional repression of the activities of religious orders followed Mexican independence (under Benito Juárez in 1860) and again in 1917 after the Mexican Revolution. Later enforcement of a 1917 Mexican law that limited the jurisdiction of the church is thought by some to have sparked the Cristero insurrection (1926–1929), in which Indigenous Mexicans took up arms against the government to protest anti-Catholicism.

Given the stormy relationship between church and secular authorities, the strategy of the church in nineteenth-century Yucatán is particularly intriguing. With a kind of Catholicism practiced in the rural areas that few in Spain would recognize as orthodox, the church in Yucatán decided to focus on the urban zone and lettered city of Mérida. The first printing press to appear in Yucatán (in 1812) was used primarily for religious purposes. Rugeley suggests that the decision of the church "to engage with both the state and the public through books, newspapers, pious literature, and polemical pamphlets turned out to be one of the shrewdest decisions the Mexican Catholic church ever made."[48] But Rugeley goes on to note that the strategy of the Catholic Church concocted to survive México's turbulent and frequently anticlerical political swings through "press venues, urban societies, Catholic education, and cautious national engagement—excluded rural Mayas altogether."[49]

The arc of church engagement—in México, at least—with Indigenous peoples is long indeed and started with intense efforts at proselytism in remote areas during early colonization. Missionizing included the creation of Spanish-alphabet orthographies of Indigenous languages, avid description of cultural practices, compulsory labor conscription, residential relocation, and physical violence for noncompliance. At times, clergy were advocates for Native peoples but at other times were more interested in wealth accumulation. By the nineteenth century, missionary zeal within the Catholic Church had dampened considerably and in places like Yucatán focused on maintaining a "client base" in urban areas. At this historical moment, the church appears to have abandoned its role as interlocutor—for better or worse—between rural communities and the lettered cities where nation building was taking place.

ENTANGLED WITH BANANAS, SUGAR, COFFEE, AND HENEQUEN

Near the end of the nineteenth century, Cuban writer José Martí actively warned Latin Americans about the "expansionist nature and imperialist drive of the United States."[50] The neocolonialism of global capitalism, nineteenth-century style, was quickly expanding south of the U.S. border. These warmer climes were gazed upon as valuable and strategic zones of resource extraction, particularly for crops that do not thrive in temperate environments. In the Maya region, that included henequen (for rope and package twining), coffee, sugar, and bananas. Within a capitalist system of production, demand is the paramount precondition, and there was no shortage of demand for these commodities. In order to supply the north, entire landscapes were reconfigured to accommodate large-scale plantation agriculture, and the inequities of colonial labor practices intensified. An atmosphere of economic imperialism saturated the hot and humid neotropical landscapes. Here we are concerned with landscape reconfiguration, its impact on Indigenous landholdings, and ultimately on practices of landscape inhabitation.

The reconfiguring of landscape from the lettered cities can be studied through the self-representation of Latin American countries at world fairs, which grew in popularity through the nineteenth century. Arguably the world's first global spectacles, nations competed to represent themselves as modern, seductive, and most of all, open for business. Countries with only rudimentary infrastructure (most of Latin America) could present their landscape as a treasure trove of exotic and desirable resources. For instance, the 1883 National Fair held in Caracas, Venezuela, featured a national pavilion that harkened back to European gothic architecture in a manner that González-Stephan interprets as whitening the urban style of Caracas and masking "the continued existence of a semi-feudal, semi-enslaved workforce that enabled the high profits for foreign capital."[51] One can reasonably ask how the birthplace of the wars of independence from Spain could harbor such inequitable labor conditions well after colonial times.

Earlier, Rugeley characterized nineteenth-century Yucatán as a place of liberal positivist sensibilities pasted over unreformed colonial practices. Let's unpack this allegation a bit more. Classical liberalism of the time—a belief in individualism, limited government, private property, and, over the arc of the nineteenth century, social Darwinism—often was interlaced with positivism. This ethos coexisted with scientific problem solving, the efficacy of which was demonstrated by the Industrial Revolution. If this heady tonic is overlaid with laissez-faire economics (which by definition are devoid of any moral dimension, unless you include the protection of private property) and then contextualized within newly created and somewhat chaotic postcolonial nations (with large swaths of countryside inhabited by Indigenous rural populations with insecure land tenure), it's not hard to predict a scenario that is disastrous and painful for Indigenous peoples living in the countryside. One can almost draw a direct line from the world fairs to a Guatemalan coffee *finca* (plantation) owned and operated by foreign interests.

Significantly, the symbolic capital of these fledgling nations was imagined and crafted most actively in the lettered cities, but the tangible capital was produced in the countryside. Freed from colonial strictures against colonizing rural landscapes previously classified as part of the República de Indios, white and mestizo/ladino expansion into rural landscapes quickened throughout the nineteenth century. There were plenty of mechanisms for displacing Native peoples, including failure to pay newly levied taxes, accusation of criminal activity, and outright denial of prior land claims. The nineteenth-century myth of the land beyond the lettered city as an empty landscape waiting to be developed was not restricted to westward expansion within the United States. Through archival and archaeological research, Adam Kaeding has documented this displacement in a relatively remote area of southeastern Yucatán where nineteenth-century cattle ranching and sugarcane production expanded rapidly on Indigenous lands classified by postindependence Mexican law as *terrenos baldíos* (unclaimed land).[52]

In other areas, carving up and reshaping colonial landscapes focused on the creation of large-scale agriculture (large by nineteenth-century standards, that is). In Brazil, the reshaping process involved "parceling out neat parallel strips of fertile coastal plain for sugar plantations to be worked by uprooted African slaves."[53] *Plantation* is the operative word here, although other words, such as *hacienda* and *finca*, also were used. In the drier, western portion of Yucatán, plantations of spiky henequen plants proliferated, while in the cooler highlands of Chiapas, México, and Guatemala, coffee plantations were established. The hot and humid Pacific coast of Guatemala was planted in sugarcane. In Honduras and El Salvador, banana plantations cropped up. Such large-scale agricultural projects often were funded by foreign capital, and some were "owner-occupied" by recent European immigrants (particularly the coffee *fincas* of Guatemala[54] and highland Chiapas[55]). In many respects, plantation agriculture represented the most drastic reconfiguration of landscape and of social relations between rural and urban peoples since the wane of the Classic period one thousand years earlier. The large-scale displacement of mostly Indigenous peoples that took place at this time is poorly documented; we know much more about the urban-linked white/mestizo settlers who actively transformed landscapes and in the process erased (or attempted to erase) prior claims.

In an era that predated bulldozers and backhoes, landscape reconfiguration was labor-intensive work followed by equally labor-intensive planting, weeding, and harvesting of plantation crops. Historically, wherever plantation agriculture emerged in the Americas, slave trading of African captives soon followed.[56] But in some areas, part or all of a labor force could be amassed by persuading local, rural farmers to work and often to reside on plantations. Soon entangled in a network of debt relations with plantation owners, this arrangement became a postcolonial secular version of the predatory labor practices of the colonial period. Lacking the religious overtones of missionization and *encomienda*,[57] plantation owners were free to define the morality of the treatment of their labor force and faced few nationally imposed restrictions on labor relations. Given the laissez-faire economic climate in which plantations operated, it's not surprising that Rugeley refers to the "disguised slavery then proliferating on the [henequen] estates,"[58] which he further alleges to have embodied the "racism and violence of a plantation police state."[59]

These are strong words, and they are matched by equally compelling images of the extremely hard work that destroyed the hands of workers involved in harvesting the spiky henequen leaves—whether the image be an innocuous photograph published in *Popular Science* (figure 2.4) or a more dramatic portrayal on the painted murals of the Palacio de Gobierno in Mérida (figure 2.5). The fact that many Yucatec Mayan peoples found themselves trapped on plantations due to debt repayment continues to be part of an active social memory of the nineteenth century that generally is referred to as *tiempo de esclavos* (time of slavery). But perhaps it is not debt per se that continues to rankle descendants of henequen laborers. David Graeber argues that debt is a foundational and social strategy of human interaction;[60] rather it was the amorality of the debt relations and the disrespect for human dignity exhibited by plantation owners.

Figure 2.4. Henequen harvesting—a photo published in a 1922 issue of *Popular Science*.

Figure 2.5. Physical toll of henequen harvesting depicted in the painted murals of the Palacio de Gobierno in Mérida by artist Fernando Castro Pacheco (photo by Maia Dedrick).

Land reforms that followed the early twentieth-century Mexican Revolution focused on breaking up large plantations and restoring land to farmers, who were given ownership in a land cooperative called an *ejido*. This federally mandated reform of the 1930s presaged by only a decade or so the collapse of the henequen industry, which was killed by the advent of synthetic petroleum-based ropes and fibers in the global north.[61] In Yucatán, hard-won *ejido* lands are not a distant memory but stories told by grandparents.[62] When *ejido* lands contain archaeological sites in which the nation or foreign archaeologists take an interest, *ejido* members can exhibit reluctance to permit further investigation, fearing a repeat of the cycle of land alienation that occurred during previous generations.[63]

Even a landscape reconfigured by plantations and characterized by abusive labor practices nonetheless embodies social memories and, more literally, ancestors. Maggie Morgan-Smith has documented the process of leaving a ranching *hacienda* in the Puuc region of western Yucatán. Significantly, an Indigenous Yucatec family owned the ranch and during the nineteenth century had provided hospitality to the traveling team of explorers John Lloyd Stephens and Frederick Catherwood while they measured and drew the Classic-period "ruins" of nearby Kiuic. Descendants of those who lived at Rancho Kiuic emphasize that labor relations at the rancho were no different from those at nearby henequen *haciendas*. As opportunities for membership in *ejido* communal lands developed in the twentieth century, families left the rancho and the population dwindled. Nonetheless, the cemetery is actively maintained, and periodically new interments are added. Despite the relations of debt servitude suffered by community members, some descendants of former residents prefer to be buried with their ancestors.[64]

A narrative of postrevolutionary land redistribution is distinct to México. Analogous and tumultuous politico-economic change did not take place to the south in the Central American nations of the Maya region, where coffee, banana, and sugar plantations continued to flourish. The corrupting entanglements of U.S. businesses with inchoate national politics led writer O. Henry to coin the term *banana republic* based on his 1896–1897 experience in Honduras. In 1940s Guatemala, significant change could have occurred through national leadership but was aborted by a series of coups known to have been organized by the U.S. Central Intelligence Agency.[65] A painful civil war in which ethnically Mayan peoples were targeted and subjected to genocide erupted thirty years later, and to this day Guatemala struggles to imagine an ethnically diverse national community that includes equality and prosperity for all.

Coffee plantations expanded throughout Guatemala in the late nineteenth to mid-twentieth century and still provide one of the mainstays of the Guatemalan export economy.[66] The importance of coffee production is indicated by the depiction of a coffee plantation on Guatemalan currency (the 20-quetzal note). On the contrary, men and women (the latter in traditional Maya *traje* or costume) pick coffee berries from small trees. The women fill baskets and prepare to transport a basketload via the traditional head-carrying method. These are disciplined workers—in the manner that Michel Foucault[67] discussed—whose labor is vital to the wealth of the Guatemalan state.

Nineteenth-century plantations were seated within a larger zeitgeist of economic imperialism that permeated the landscapes of the neotropics and further alienated Indigenous peoples from their landscape. At the fin de siècle, North American companies such as the United Fruit Company and later Dole controlled major landholdings in Central America and expressed a vested interest in maintaining the status quo and promoting business as usual, which was dependent on an accessible source of cheap labor and available land. Both internal and international business interests supported the maintenance of plantation agriculture. When the perceived threat of communism became the guiding light of U.S. foreign policy during much of the twentieth century, U.S. businesses could enlist the assistance of their government to protect their international landholdings and their profits. In what has been called "bitter fruit" by Stephen Schlesinger and Stephen Kinzer,[68] the United States—particularly during the Cold War era—became an active force against democratic change in Central America. Using diplomatic and intelligence channels, the United States ensured unhindered profits for U.S. companies despite damage to the human and land rights of local laborers. Through it all, breakfast tables in the United States contained a cheap and ready supply of coffee, sugar, and bananas.

NOTES

1. Tedlock (1996:194–95).
2. As noted by Dennis Tedlock (1996:334), Tonatiuh is the name of the Aztec sun god.
3. See Stoler (2006).
4. See Tedlock (1993) for a difficult but vivid account of the importation of the Spanish Inquisition to the Yucatán.
5. See Quezada (2014) for an in-depth historical account of Spanish colonial manipulation of the power and authority of Native Yucatec aristocracies.
6. Hanks (2010:32).
7. For instance, see Sánchez de Aguilar (1639).
8. For an early example of crediting construction of Classic Maya cities to Old World influences, see Cogolludo (1688); for a late eighteenth-century example, see the account of Río (1822); and for a nineteenth-century disassociation between Native inhabitants and the old cities, see the discussion of Jean-Frédéric Waldeck in Coe (1992:77).
9. For a comparable example from the United States, see Colwell-Chanthaphonh (2005).
10. Rugeley (2009:184).
11. For more on weapons of the weak, see Scott (1990).
12. See Anderson (1991).
13. English translation: "coffee with milk"; see González-Stephan (2009:14).
14. Mintz (1985:37–50).
15. See Finamore (2008).

16. Kohl and Fawcett (1995); Trigger (2006:211–16, 235–41, 248–61).
17. Sara Castro-Klarén (2003:188) uses the term *scientific travel literature.*
18. "Coffee without milk" or dark-brown coffee.
19. Anderson (1991).
20. Anderson (1991:47–65).
21. Chasteen (2003:ix–xxv).
22. Chasteen (2003:xiii).
23. Mörner (1967:53–73).
24. Wright (2009:72).
25. Rugeley (2009:178).
26. Chasteen (2003:xi).
27. Chasteen (2003:xi–xii).
28. For further discussion of this complex issue, see Alexander (2004:151–62); also Kaeding (2013).
29. See Acree and González Espitia (2009:5) for a discussion of the role of print in building nineteenth-century Latin American nations.
30. Rama (1996:29–49).
31. See Acree and González Espitia (2009:5).
32. See Huner (2009:91).
33. See Achugar (2009:23) for a reproduction of the image.
34. *Historial de las Insignias de Guatemala* (1971:59).
35. Bernal (1980:52); see also Castro-Klarén (2003:180).
36. González (2004:143).
37. González (2004:143–44); Navarrete (2011:43–48).
38. See Bonfil Batalla (1996); also Patterson (1995:84–85).
39. See Rugeley (1996).
40. Rugeley (2009:191).
41. See Wright (2009:68–69).
42. www.law.arizona.edu/depts/iplp/international/maya_belize/documents/ReparationsChapter.pdf.
43. Hanks (2010).
44. This syllabary appears in versions of Diego de Landa's *Relación de Cosas de Yucatán,* a remarkable compilation of ethnographic and linguistic material based on Landa's observations as a bishop and a zealot in sixteenth-century Yucatán. Alfred Tozzer's 1941 translation, *Landa's Relación de las Cosas de Yucatán,* is a commonly referenced source. Restall and Chuchiak (2002) provide critical historiographic commentary on the manuscript.
45. See Coe (1999).
46. A commonly used translation of Landa is the heavily footnoted Peabody Museum version by Tozzer (1941). Restall and Chuchiak (2002) provide additional commentary on the questionable integrity of the original text.
47. Wagner and Rand (1967:138–42).
48. Rugeley (2009:187).
49. Rugeley (2009:192).
50. See Lapolla Swier (2009:228) on the life and times of José Martí.
51. González-Stephan (2009:111, 121).
52. Kaeding (2013:158–206).

53. Chasteen (2003:xiv).

54. See Grandia (2012:36–45) for a detailed treatment of the displacement of Indigenous people from lands that were turned into coffee plantations in the Alta Verapaz Department of Guatemala and the subsequent attempts to indenture Q'eqchi' peoples as laborers on coffee plantations. Also see Clarence-Smith and Topik (2003:191).

55. Rus (2003).

56. Restall (2009). Table 1.5 lists slave-owning societies in eighteenth-century American colonies. In places such as the southeastern United States and Brazil where large-scale plantations had been established, up to 54 percent of the population consisted of slaves of African descent.

57. An *encomienda* was a grant by the Spanish crown to the labor and products of Native peoples within a specified area. Theoretically, *encomiendas* could not be inherited, and the *encomendero* was officially obliged to promote and fund Christianization efforts.

58. Rugeley (2009:185).

59. Rugeley (2009:179); see also Joseph (1982) for more on the "plantocracy" that remained firmly in control of Yucatán even after the Mexican Revolution had reconfigured landscape and power relations elsewhere in México.

60. Graeber (2011).

61. Land reform, including the redistribution of land to former henequen *hacienda* indentured servants, was enacted in Yucatán primarily during the 1930s, with some notable exceptions (Breglia 2006:137, 150).

62. See Breglia (2006:135–70).

63. An example of this dynamic occurred at the archaeological site of Chunchucmil when archaeologists tried to persuade *ejido* members to go along with a development plan for the site, which is located on *ejido* lands. For a detailed discussion, see Breglia (2006:135–205) and Rodriguez (2006).

64. Morgan-Smith (2014).

65. See Blum (2004) or Schlesinger and Kinzer (1990) for an analysis of the involvement of the U.S. military and Central Intelligence Agency in discrediting the social-democracy movement growing in Guatemala and engineering the successive coups of Presidents Juan José Arévalo (1945–1951) and Jacobo Árbenz Guzmán (1951–1954).

66. Between 1881 and 1885, the average yearly production of coffee beans in Guatemala was 18.18 thousand metric tons, topping México and all other Central American countries.

67. Foucault (1979).

68. Schlesinger and Kinzer (1990).

3

◦◦◦

Disciplining the Past

The presence of foreign nationals conducting business within the young nations of the Maya region resulted in a particular constellation of opportunities for nineteenth-century science-travel writers and for the archaeologists who followed thereafter. Logistical support, camaraderie, and the ability to explore plantation holdings (and extract antiquities for shipment back to the global north) were just a few of the advantages. The North American and European audience of readers and buyers of printed materials took a keen interest in what lay beneath the forest canopy—or was exposed during clearing for plantation development. Connections formed between plantation owners and explorers of the past, which often resulted in the transport of massive amounts of archaeological materials (portable artifacts as well as massive carved monuments) to the United States via the banana boats that traveled between Caribbean ports and U.S. cities. Major U.S. research institutions were founded, such as the Middle American Research Institute at Tulane University, which was endowed in 1924 by Samuel Zemurray (nicknamed "Sam, the banana man"), president of the United Fruit Company—more on the entanglement of bananas with academic archaeology shortly.

TRAVEL WRITERS, SPIES, AND MACHETE-WIELDING EXCAVATORS

Sara Castro-Klarén suggests that the postcolonial ruling elites of Latin America were "intellectually and emotionally underequipped to begin to reconnoiter the multiple dimensions of the inherited space-time of which they understood little."[1] After independence, there were new nations, but what of the cultural heritage of these emergent political entities? Castro-Klarén argues that nineteenth-century science-travel writers and then archaeologists played a large role in crafting a temporal dimension to Latin American national cultures: "The past, as the time of dead ancestors, will first appear in the discourse of the nation as the work of archaeology. The nation then slowly emerges as an archaeospace that both marks and erases the distance from the past."[2] For Peru, Castro-Klarén finds it impossible to separate the history of archaeology from that of "scientific travel and exploration" conducted during the first part of the nineteenth century.[3] The same can be said for the Maya region, where nineteenth-century explorers John Lloyd Stephens and Frederick Catherwood (among others)[4] left a trail of descriptions and drawings that later archaeologists followed.

Science and travel writers—such as Humbolt, Prescott, and others—produced publishable manuscripts quickly after completing their travels. There was a ready audience in the global north for their firsthand descriptions of places, plants, and people presented as hyperexotic. The authority of their voices was amplified by scientifically accurate illustrations produced on the spot by accompanying draftsmen (Catherwood, for instance, drew for Stephens). Readers purchased richly illustrated books that could be experienced with a "double vision"[5]—attending to text or image or both. Drawings of tropical plants might be interleaved with drawings of Native inhabitants in traditional dress or the architectural remains of cities, as observable in many of Catherwood's drawings (see figure 2.1). By nineteenth-century Eurocentric sentiments, all were considered part of nature rather than history.[6] Archaeologists would later amend this ahistorical perspective by characterizing the archaeology of the Americas as prehistoric—a framework that would only be challenged for the Maya region when hieroglyphic decipherment began to yield dynastic chronicles in the 1980s.

Before the nineteenth century, exploration of archaeological sites in the Maya region was sporadic. One of the earliest on record occurred in 1576 when a member of the colonial Audiencia de Guatemala, Diego García de Palacio, wrote a letter to King Philip II of Spain describing the archaeological site of Copán. Then in 1787, "European antiquarianism spurred King Charles III to send Antonio del Río to explore Maya sites in his colonial possessions."[7] Del Río traveled to Palenque, where he thoroughly investigated the site and in his report to the king suggested that Phoenicians, Greeks, or Romans must have "pursued their conquests even to this country, where it is probable they only remained long enough to enable the Indian tribes to imitate their ideas and adopt, in a rude and awkward manner, such arts as their invaders thought fit to inculcate."[8] The drawings of del Río's illustrator—Ricardo Almendáriz—are still considered accurate and useful. Unfortunately, Jean-Frédéric Waldeck, a French explorer of the early nineteenth century, is infamous for "adapting" the illustrations from del Río's trip for an 1822 publication. Because Waldeck believed that the origins of Maya peoples should be traced back to the biblical Chaldeans and Phoenicians and even to Hindus, he "interpreted" Classic Maya royal portraiture and hieroglyphs according to the artistic canons of the Near East and even inserted elephants into his renderings.[9]

Throughout the nineteenth century and even into the twentieth, travel writers continued to weigh in on the link between Native peoples of the Maya region and the builders and carvers of the abandoned cities. Colonial Juan Galindo (born in Dublin, Ireland) visited Palenque in 1831 and, contrary to del Río, published a report that proposed a connection between present Indigenous inhabitants and those who had built Palenque.[10] Three years later, Galindo visited Copán and there pointed out the close resemblance between the carved-stone hieroglyphic blocks at Palenque and Copán.[11] The "debate" over the identity of the builders of Palenque, Copán, and other Late Classic Maya cities, in retrospect, was a thinly veiled attempt to sever the linkage between Indigenous peoples and their past, and it foreshadows a continuing estrangement that serves the interests of political and economic sectors that would not be well served by yielding patrimonial rights to Indigenous peoples.[12]

In the Maya region, exploration codified in travel writing arguably began with the accounts of John Lloyd Stephens and Frederick Catherwood, who disembarked from a steamship in British Honduras in 1839.[13] From there, they used all available modes of transportation, including mules, to travel through the Maya region. A beautifully illustrated account of their travels (*Incidents of Travel in Central America, Chiapas, and Yucatan*) was published in 1941 to great acclaim and has been republished again and again.

Given the political volatility of this region, it's amazing that Stephens returned to tell his tale. Experiencing firsthand the chaos of postindependence México and Central America, Stephens described the disintegration of the United Provinces of Central America, which formed and dissolved between 1821 and 1840.[14] The team traveled overland through Yucatán during the first *Incidents of Travel* and again in the autumn of 1841, just six years before the eruption of the so-called Caste War (which Yucatec Maya people refer to as *Guerra Social* or the Social War). Stephens and Catherwood spent significant time in rural Yucatán—traveling between archaeological sites, drawing and mapping found locations, and relying on the hospitality of *hacienda* owners and the labor of their indentured servants. Stephens provides an excruciatingly blasé yet violent and racist description of Yucatec servants living under the yoke of Don Simon, owner of the *hacienda* of Uxmal: "In general they are mild, amiable, and very docile; bear no malice; and when one of them is whipped and smarting under stripes, with tears in his eyes he makes a bow to the major-domo, and says 'buenos tarde, señor;' 'good evening, sir.'"[15]

Small wonder that Yucatán was a smoldering powder keg of discontentment among Native peoples, although, enigmatically, many Yucatecs in the western part of the peninsula—where Uxmal is located—were classified as "indios pacificos" during the Caste War because they did not take up arms.[16] Regarding the putative link between contemporary peoples and those who built the Classic Maya cities, Stephens—in the end—argues that "they were constructed by the races who occupied the country at the time of the invasion by the Spaniards, or of some not very distant progenitors."[17]

Like the neocolonial business entrepreneurs who were setting up shop in Central America, Stephens was perfectly willing to take advantage of the chaotic postcolonial situation. He reports that he was able to purchase the archaeological site of Copán (now a UNESCO World Heritage site) for only $50 and planned to dismantle it, float the architectural elements down the Río Copán, and ship the entire site to the United States.[18] Although this plan did not come to pass, Stephens did arrange for the removal of stelae and carved stone from sites when he thought they were particularly interesting. Catherwood illustrated the removal of a large, heavy stela from Kabah by local laborers working only with rudimentary ropes and poles under the supervision of a white, bearded man (perhaps Stephens) who holds a gun or a stick in an active pose (figure 3.1).

Despite the neocolonial posture of these science-travel writers, their illustrators (for the most part) provided scaled and accurate drawings that vividly demonstrated the architectural and sculptural prowess of pre-Columbian civilizations. There is no denying the popularity of their accounts in the nineteenth-century global north. While exoticizing the Maya region, their publications also created a new space—an archaeospace, as Castro-Klarén calls it—that both accentuated and eradicated distance from the past, depending on the perspective of the writer.

Aspiring archaeologists soon populated the archaeospace and brought along not only skilled illustrators but also large-format cameras. More than explorers, late nineteenth-century travelers from the global north were self-styled professionals equipped to document in exquisite detail the primarily eighth-century

Figure 3.1. Catherwood (1844:Plate 15) drawing of the removal of a monument from Kabah, a Puuc site in northern Yucatán. Reproduced by permission of the John Carter Brown Library, Brown University.

hieroglyphic texts and programs of royal iconography carved on stelae, door-jambs, lintels, and other architectural spaces. Naturalistic portraiture carved in stone appeared in the lens of large-format cameras. Between 1880 and 1900, Englishman Alfred Maudslay visited, photographed, and made plaster and papier-mâché casts of carvings at numerous sites throughout the Maya region. The casts (rather than the artifacts) were shipped to museums in the United States and England. In 1902, Maudslay published an amply illustrated five-volume work titled *Biologia Centrali-Americana*, which is still considered a valuable and useful source.[19] Maudslay's expeditions were self-financed, as were those of his Austrian colleague Theobert Maler.

Maler first came to México in the 1860s as a soldier in the forces of Emperor Maximilian, whose army occupied México in a futile European effort to establish a second Mexican empire. After surrendering to forces of the Mexican Republic, Maler stayed in México and eventually became a Mexican citizen. As invader-turned-archaeologist, Maler made detailed sketches and took measurements of structures at Palenque, Tikal, Uxmal, Chichén Itzá, and many more sites. His photographs are still highly regarded because many of the newly discovered carvings he photographed had not yet been subjected to the severe chemical weathering (or looting) that occurs after a stone monument has been exposed. After 1884, Maler settled in Ticul, Yucatán, and learned to speak Yucatec Mayan. Throughout his career, Maler was an avid conservationist and despised the customary nineteenth-century habit of dismantling sculptural elements from archaeological sites for museums in the United States and Europe. Maudslay and Maler represented the best of the late nineteenth-century explorers who worked in a milieu that predated academic training and institutional backing. In the manner described by Castro-Klarén, they contributed to the creation of an archaeospace that crosscut the newly created national boundaries of an area that would come to be called the Maya region—a space that embodied an exotic otherness in the episteme of the nineteenth century.[20]

By the early twentieth century, the Peabody Museum of Harvard University was in the business of Maya archaeology, and due to the energetic campaigning of Sylvanus Morley, the Carnegie Institution of Washington, DC, would soon follow suit.[21] The Maya past was meshing with the young discipline of archaeology. Morley was Harvard educated but at odds with the power structure of the Peabody Museum. As a research associate of the Carnegie Institution, Morley was free to plan archaeological expeditions to remote corners of the Maya region to study hieroglyphs—his passion. He commenced Carnegie projects in 1915 with a long-term project through the 1920s at Chichén Itzá. The Chichén Itzá project included massive excavation and reconstruction, which has been characterized by some Latin American archaeologists as a highly controversial "ideological manipulation."[22] As the menace of World War I began to cast a long shadow over the Americas and rumors of German submarine bases off the Caribbean coast of México and Central America intensified, Morley offered to collect and transmit covert information while in the field to the U.S. Office of Naval Intelligence (ONI).[23] His offer was accepted, and in some circles he is considered the "finest American spy of World War I."[24] With Morley, we consider a different kind of entanglement: archaeology with espionage, not with the overt imperial capitalism of foreign businesses with Central American landholdings but a covert imperialism that strengthen the U.S. political position via intelligence gathering.

Morley was not the only anthropologist or archaeologist who became an ONI special agent during World War I. He was joined by other luminaries of the time, such as Herbert Spinden (Agent No. 56), John Alden Mason (Agent No. 157), Samuel K. Lothrop (with ONI and then the U.S. Military Intelligence Corps), and Thomas Gann (Agent No. 242).[25] For these special agents, patriotism had called, but Franz Boas (a German American and founding figure within American anthropology) saw it differently. In a letter to the *Nation*, Boas accused Morley and others of using academic cover to conceal their intelligence operations for the U.S. Navy.[26] The young field of American anthropology was not ready to consider the darker side of nationalism as a violation of professional ethics. In response to the accusation by Franz Boas, Boas himself was expelled from the American Anthropological Association.[27]

Today, Morley's espionage activities would be severely censured within the American Anthropological Association as a breach of ethical conduct, but there is no denying that he played a key role in the development of Maya archaeology and its distinctive place within American archaeology. He was a prolific writer and keenly aware of the distinctiveness of Maya hieroglyphic script. He penned the original version of *The Ancient Maya* (1946), a 520-page text probing the deep history of this region. The book is still published today (now in its sixth edition and substantially revised).[28] In the first edition, Morley set out his ideas about Classic Maya society (the "Old Empire," as he called it) and borrowed heavily from ethnohistorical documents (such as the account by Bishop Diego de Landa) that referred back to the "New Empire" or Postclassic period. Soon thereafter, English archaeologist J. Eric Thompson, who was equally enthralled by Maya hieroglyphs, proposed that Classic Maya society had been a peaceful theocracy concerned primarily with calendrics and time and thus very different from known civilizations of the Old World. This *otherness* was accentuated by Thompson's notion that Classic Maya dynastic centers (in reality, small cities) lacked a residential component and were what came to be called vacant ceremonial centers.[29]

Arguably, Morley and Thompson were the first of a breed of Maya archaeologists who were knowledge specialists uniquely situated to apply the methods of archaeology to discipline the past. They understood enough of the hieroglyphic script to present themselves as authorities on Classic Maya society—and they wrote books that were read by students and laypersons alike. For the Maya region, the mantle of scientific authority was enhanced and richly embroidered with the romance of an undeciphered script. Morley and Thompson both spent considerable time with Native communities in the Maya region. Yucatec descendants of Caste War veterans famously courted Morley as a possible source for guns and ammunition to continue the struggle.[30] Thompson, because of his archaeological fieldwork experience in southern Belize, became an astute observer of Mopan Maya cultural practices. In his *Ethnology of the Mayas of Southern and Central British Honduras*, published in 1930, Thompson suggested that archaeological and epigraphic questions might be answered through analogy with ethnographic practices—the first explicit statement of ethnographic analogy as a method for interpreting the Maya past. This would become a primary role of Indigenous peoples in reference to the past (in addition to the heavy physical work of clearing trails and sites and moving stones). Their cultural practices became the subject of observations, which in turn were deployed to interpret artifacts and structures from earlier times. This modus operandi presupposed that local Mayan-speaking peoples were the descendants of those who built the thousand-year-old pyramids and palaces, that their cultural practices were not significantly changed by centuries of colonialism, and that the cultural practices of contemporary Maya peoples were relevant to Classic Maya nobility—who were largely the focus of early archaeological investigations.

These early Maya archaeologists cultivated a sense of mystery about the Classic period and particularly its endpoint, which undeniably exoticized the past. They developed an expert knowledge of Maya glyphs—a knowledge that was very distant from the daily experience of Indigenous (and sometimes indentured) Maya peoples in the early to mid-twentieth century.[31] But they maintained relationships with descendant communities and aggressively linked things of the past with people of the present.

As a Maya past increasingly was defined through expert knowledge—and subjected to the discipline of archaeology—it became increasingly estranged from Indigenous peoples, many of whom lacked access to basic education, much less classes in epigraphy.[32] The creation of an archaeospace was an extension of the lettered city into the countryside. Unlike the Mexican highlands in which colonial capitals—such as México City—were built on top of subjugated pre-Columbian capitals, many classic Maya cities were located in places such as El Petén that were not intensively resettled prior to the twentieth century. Throughout the twentieth century, the spidery web of connectors between Maya archaeological sites and lettered cities intensified as nation-states moved to control access to these cultural resources and to profit from a new form of extraction—that of heritage tourism. This complexity can be seen as the culmination of what Castro-Klarén characterizes as a "finely attuned and yet dissonant concordance . . . [and] a growing sense of the past as 'other.'"[33]

NATIONALIZING THE ARCHAEOSPACE

We have already considered the time beyond the nineteenth century in terms of Maya archaeologists, but what of changes to imagined communities in relation to an emergent archaeospace? And what of the continued global entanglements of plantation agriculture? Certainly, twentieth-century nations of the Maya region began to embrace the past created by archaeological research—the archaeospace, as it were. The rapaciousness with which explorers and then archaeologists sought to dismantle and export elements of this archaeospace spurred the establishment of regulatory agencies to curtail the hemorrhaging of nationalized cultural heritage. México led the way in 1939 by establishing a national agency—the Instituto Nacional de Antropología e Historia (INAH, the acronym for a national institute of anthropology and history)—to initiate and regulate the investigation of archaeological sites and other fields of cultural study.[34] Guatemala followed suit in 1946 with IDEAH (Instituto de Antropología e Historia), then Honduras in 1952 with IHAH (Instituto Hondureño de Antropología e Historia), and El Salvador in 1991 with the establishment of CONCULTURA (Consejo National para la Cultura y el Arte), which was replaced in 2009 with the Secretaría de Cultura a la Presidencia—a cabinet-level position. In El Salvador, a lower-level position, director of cultural patrimony, was in existence by the 1980s and continues today.[35] In Belize, a "full-service" Department of Archaeology was founded in 1957 and later transformed into the current Institute of Archaeology within the National Institute of Culture and History (NICH).

All of the institutes are founded on the principle of safeguarding the antiquities of the nation, which by national decree belong to all citizens of the nation. Each institute interfaces with their publics, attempts to curb looting and destruction of archaeological sites, creates rules and regulations for foreign investigators, and selects sites that are groomed for tourism. These sites undergo excavation, consolidation, stabilization, and varying amounts of reconstruction—a labor-intensive and job-producing process. Site selection is highly politicized and often includes the consideration of economic benefits to a surrounding and usually rural Indigenous population.

México was the first to develop the touristic potential of their precolonial heritage. INAH initiated ambitious projects of site reconstruction beginning in the 1940s. At Palenque, a Classic Maya site in Chiapas, Mexican archaeologist Alberto Ruz Lhuillier undertook consolidation of the Temple of the Inscriptions (so called because of the large stone panels carved with 617 glyph blocks—the second-longest text known from the Maya region).[36] In 1949, as Ruz cleared off the flagstone floor of the temple that was situated on top of a tall pyramidal platform, he discovered twelve stone-plugged holes in one of the floor slabs. He cleared out the holes and lifted the flagstone to find a rubble-choked stairway that led to the base of the platform and the tomb of a Classic Maya ruler, now known aa K'inich Janaab' Pakal I.[37] Before this discovery, Mesoamerican pyramids were considered distinct from Egyptian pyramids. The former were thought to be temples, while the latter were mausolea for deceased rulers. Now it was clear that some Mesoamerican pyramids were both.

LOOTERS, COLLECTORS, AND THE PEOPLE IN BETWEEN

In retrospect, the discovery of the royal tomb of K'inich Janaab' Pakal of Palenque was a harbinger of both good and bad things. It initiated the intense fascination of Maya archaeologists with Classic Maya royals—their names, the details of their lives, and their ultimate places of interment after death. For Classic Maya peoples, death marked the beginning of a passage for which one needed to be equipped. Royals were interred in lavish style, with food and drink placed in beautiful pottery vessels often painted with hieroglyphs and palace scenes. Their bodies were adorned generously with jadeite and intricately worked marine-shell jewelry. The fact that royal tombs embodied the wealth that rulers had accumulated during their lives was not lost on archaeologists or looters. For the latter, pyramidal forms now were envisioned as a skin covering tombs filled with valuable objects that could be sold to acquisitive museums and private collectors.[38]

During the last half of the twentieth century, looting activity accelerated, particularly in the more remote parts of El Petén (Guatemala), Belize, Honduras, and El Salvador.[39] The political turmoil and violence experienced during this time in Guatemala and El Salvador exacerbated the looting problem. As heritage tourism and field research ramped up during the latter half of the twentieth century, so did looting.[40] A fascination with an exotic past and a desire to own a piece of it apparently are not disconnected. The archaeospace was under siege. Archaeologists and government bureaucrats found common ground and allied under the banner of conservation. But national governments—housed in the lettered cities—had limited reach into the rural areas where looting and other forms of site destruction took place. Small communities proximate to looted sites came under suspicion of collusion with middlemen who combed the countryside in search of looted antiquities for which there was a ready market in the north.

Some asked if rural peoples were looting sites proximate to their communities. Archaeologists privately noted that looting activity at sites under investigation accelerated, rather than diminished, after a field season with a large local labor force. Trenches dug at looted locations often mimicked the axial trenches that archaeologists liked to place on the center line of structures in order to intersect burials and tombs. After decades of funding archaeological field research in the Maya region and witnessing the acceleration of destructive looting, the National Geographic Society began to wonder aloud and continues to wonder if archaeologists are unwittingly exacerbating the looting problem.[41] Perhaps archaeologists should be asking themselves if more energy needs to be invested in dialogue with local communities about the purpose of archaeological research, how it differs from looting, and the long-term advantages of conservation. As field activity quickened through the second half of the twentieth century, working with archaeological projects became a significant source of revenue in rural areas, but the relationship between archaeologists and their rural workforce, for the most part, replicated the hierarchy of colonial and postcolonial economic practices.

On the southeastern edge of the Maya region, Darío Euraque brought attention to the negative effects of the fascination with all things Maya to the ethnically diverse nation of Honduras.[42] With a small Ch'orti' Mayan population living in western Honduras and a national campaign to Mayanize Honduras for the purposes of tourism at Copán, those whose ethnic identity sat elsewhere were effectively disenfranchised from the national conversation. The commodification of heritage tourism by way of advertising campaigns in glossy travel magazines that contain dubious assertions in order to sell a product (in this case, a vacation to visit an archaeological site) is evidence of another kind of entanglement.[43] Fredric Jameson characterizes the cultural logic of late capitalism as one in which all forms of cultural production can be commodified.[44] Beyond the problem of commodifying the past, the Honduran situation invokes unsettling questions. Do putative links to the past on a national scale within an ethnically diverse citizenry do more harm than good? We will return to this question in later chapters.

On January 1, 1994, the United States, Canada, and México enacted the North American Free Trade Agreement (NAFTA). Although controversial in the United States (for fear that manufacturers would move south of the border, which they did), the agreement sparked a major insurgency in the mountainous region of Chiapas. There, Indigenous peoples had tolerated abusive labor arrangements on coffee plantations for over a hundred years,[45] and the land reform that followed the Mexican Revolution earlier in the twentieth century had never quite reached Chiapas. The Zapatista Army of Liberation (Ejécito Zapatista de Liberación Nacional) perceived NAFTA as another assault by neocolonialists. In a prepared statement, a spokesperson for the Zapatistas expressed this sentiment with the following words: "Years have passed, since about 1974, when we began trying to get land, dwellings, roads, rural clinics, but without any success. The only response was trickery and false promises."[46] Mexican federal forces and tanks were deployed to the mountains of Chiapas—to the land behind the tourist mecca that Palenque had become. The world turned briefly to see stunningly high rates of poverty and an appalling lack of access to education for Indigenous peoples.

The Zapatista insurgency was exacerbated by the tumultuous situation in highland Chiapas caused by the decade-plus flow of refugees from the civil war and genocide in adjacent Guatemala.[47] The thirty-six-year violent conflict, which pitted rural communities against the Guatemala state and military, ended in 1996 with a signing of peace accords.[48] The accords suggested the possibility of greater participation of the majority Indigenous population in the political process. In 1992, a K'iche' Maya woman named Rigoberta Menchú who survived the civil war and lived to write about it won the Nobel Peace Prize.[49] It seemed that space in the political arena was opening for Maya peoples. Perhaps the imagined communities of these nation-states would find a space in which nationalism and ethnic diversity might coexist.

According to Ernest Renan, the core principle of nationalism, in the end, turns out to be the shared possession of a rich legacy of memories and the desire to live together.[50] The first criterion certainly exists in the Maya region, but the second is a more tentative proposition. In the chapter to follow, the field of focus shifts from the desire to live together to the desire to work and learn together. We examine how archaeologists ply their trade in a world in which the aftershocks of colonialism, nationalism, and globalism continue to reverberate darkly through the lives of Native peoples.

NOTES

1. Castro-Klarén (2003:179).
2. Castro-Klarén (2003:182).
3. Castro-Klarén (2003:184).
4. For instance, see the account of the 1839 Walker-Caddy expedition from Belize City to Palenque undertaken in order to describe (and illustrate) Palenque before Stephens and Catherwood could file a report (Pendergast 1967).
5. Castro-Klarén (2003:188–89).
6. Castro-Klarén (2003:187).
7. Yaeger and Borgstede (2004:262).
8. Río (1822:19).
9. Coe (1999:76–77).
10. Coe (1999:75).
11. Coe (1999:75–76).
12. As referenced in chapter 1, questioning whether an Indigenous population could be linked to precolonial constructions was strongly paralleled in the United States. See the discussion in Thomas (2000).
13. Stephens (1993:11).
14. Stephens (1993:111–27).
15. Stephens (1993:240).
16. Patch (1985:47).
17. Stephens (1993:258).
18. Stephens (1993:41–46).
19. For more on Maudslay, see Graham (2002).
20. See Yaeger and Borgstede (2004:262) for a commentary on nineteenth-century archaeological explorations in Mesoamerica as fostering a fetishism of the exotic and enabled by the neoimperialist policies of the United States.
21. Charles Harris III and Louis Sadler (2003) provide a page-turning account of Sylvanus Morley and his association with the U.S. Office of Naval Intelligence.
22. Politis and Pérez Gollán (2004:357).
23. Harris and Sadler (2003:46).
24. Harris and Sadler (2003:xiii).
25. Harris and Sadler (2003:figs. 7–10).
26. Harris and Sadler (2003:218).
27. Harris and Sadler (2003:218).
28. Sharer and Traxler (2006).
29. See Thompson (1966), especially pages 302–6.

30. See Sullivan (1989).

31. For an expanded discussion, see Sabloff (2015).

32. For an analysis of a comparable situation of heritage estrangement in the United States, see Colwell-Chanthaphonh (2005).

33. Castro-Klarén (2003:173).

34. Bernal (1980:140, 186–87); see also Navarrete (2011).

35. I am indebted to Payson Sheets (personal communication, 2015) for clarifying changes within the administrative structure of the Salvadoran national agencies that manage cultural resources.

36. Martin and Grube (2008:168).

37. Martin and Grube (2008:165).

38. For an account of the illicit art market of the first half of the twentieth century, see Coe (1993).

39. See Parks, McAnany, and Murata (2006).

40. For a detailed analysis of the interconnectivities among looting, international diplomacy and trade, and archaeological research, see Luke (2006).

41. Vance (2014).

42. See Euraque (1998, 2004) and Joyce (2003).

43. See Ardren (2004).

44. See Jameson (1991).

45. See Rus (2003).

46. *Tiempo*, February 5, 1994; translation from Collier and Lowery Quaratiello (2009:66).

47. See the discussion in Collier and Lowery Quaratiello (2009:84).

48. For accounts of the impact of the Guatemalan civil war, genocide, and subsequent peace accords on Indigenous communities in both the highlands and the lowlands, see Manz (2004), Sanford (2003), and Warren (2002:176).

49. Menchú (1984).

50. Renan (1990:19).

4

Rethinking Business as Usual

Sadly and unfortunately, the history of our people has also been colonised. That is, the history of the Mayas has been distorted and is told by others.

—Avexnim Cojti Ren[1]

K'iche' writer Avexnim Cojti Ren expresses the sentiment that experts have colonized the Maya past; in the previous chapter, we met a few of those experts. From this perspective, archaeological research is seen as analogous to the appropriation of land for coffee *finca*s or banana plantations, only more personal because it cuts to the heart of identity, social memory, and self-representation.[2] Cojti Ren articulates what is generally called a *postcolonial critique*, which oftentimes is voiced by descendants of those who were colonized during the post-fifteenth-century expansion of European nations. Uncomfortable material for those who benefitted from colonization, nonetheless these voices sound a clarion call for more thoughtful and inclusive ways of reckoning with collective history, ethnic diversity, and the disparities in wealth and access to education that stubbornly linger through postcolonial times.

This chapter takes a close look at postcolonialism, particularly as it pertains to anthropological research in the Maya region. I propose that the postcolonial critique lays the foundation for a serious engagement with multivocality. The community heritage programs described in chapters 7 through 9 provide examples of efforts to work toward such multivocality within archaeology—a discipline that matured within a colonial context and benefitted from the powerful imperial gaze upon peoples, places, and histories that were extraordinarily different from those of Europe. The response within academia to the postcolonial critique—a relational turn to cultural studies that are perceived as transcultural and participatory—brings new opportunities and new challenges to the social sciences, and we turn to this trend in the latter half of the chapter.

THE POSTCOLONIAL CRITIQUE

Archaeologist Tom Patterson describes postcolonialism as "an umbrella term . . . [that] refers to the cultural effects of colonization as well as to the interactions and representations engendered in societies that were former colonies of European states."[3] Responding to a perceived hegemony of Western culture, literary traditions, and science, the critique directly confronts stereotypical notions about the inferiority of colonized peoples. Touchstone texts such as Gayatri Spivak's "Can the Subaltern Speak?" (published in 1988) gave voice to a new kind of scholar whose origins lay outside the global north and whose scholarship grapples with the authoritarian voice that emanates from that heady conflation of political power, prolific intellectual production, and capitalist economic interests.[4]

Spivak elaborated a standpoint arguably established a decade earlier by Edward Said in his book *Orientalism* (1978). Said argued that the West created "the Middle East" through a discourse that fabricated and imposed stereotypical polarities, such as masculine versus feminine and familiar/rational versus exotic/irrational.[5] Making a powerful argument for how the category of *other* (as in not like me or us) became an instrument of colonial representation and repression, Said meshed together the literary with the political, the cultural with the imperial.[6] Although Said has been criticized for painting too starkly a portrait of polarities, his emphasis on the entangled nature of knowledge exposed the larger network of power relations that stands behind seemingly nonpolitical acts such as archaeological excavation and report writing. As noted by Patterson, Said importantly suggested that Orientalism was not necessarily self-perpetuating but contained an internal dialectic of change "because not all of the participants in the formation of the discourse are necessarily contributing to its reproduction."[7]

Distortion in the representation of others—especially colonized others—is a strong theme of postcolonialism and provides the subtext for the opening epigraph by Cojti Ren. Homi Bhabha, the third author of the triad of influential postcolonial writers, challenges the polar representations of the colonial discourse by stressing hybridity—which Matthew Liebmann characterizes in this context as "new transcultural forms produced through colonization that cannot be neatly classified into a single cultural or ethnic category."[8] Significantly, both the colonized and the colonizer are hybridized by the encounter, which often transforms foundational elements of identity such as cuisine, clothing, or language. In this way, active agency resides with both parties, and the end result—hybridity—challenges binary categories. The concept of hybridity is relevant to the different kinds of identities and relationships with the past that exist throughout the Maya region—explored in further detail in chapter 5.

How colonized peoples are represented perhaps is less important than the fact that subalterns often lack a voice of self-representation and self-determination (as expressed by Cojti Ren in the opening quotation).[9] The refracted mirror of colonialism has been pervasive and intransigent. A strong theme of postcolonial studies is the assertion that colonial relations, discourse, and standpoints have not faded despite the dissolution of most European and U.S. colonial holdings.[10] As we learned in chapter 2, colonial relations of power and abuse often intensified rather than lessened in the aftermath of imperial control. The intransigence of coloniality has given rise to calls for purposeful attention to a process called *decolonization*. Like desalinization, in which salt is removed from water, decolonization aims to rebalance what were unidirectional power relations and augment multivocality. But rebalancing the distribution of political power is more challenging than removing saline content from a fluid. In 1999, Maori social scientist Linda Tuhiwai Smith called for a complete overhaul of the epistemological and methodological basis of research with Indigenous peoples.[11] The on-point criticism hit a nerve, and *Decolonizing Methodologies* became a best-selling academic book. The tightly reasoned treatise issued a clarion call to change business, and this call sounded closer to the home of anthropology because Smith is a social scientist.

As one might imagine, postcolonial scholarship as well as advocates of decolonization exist amid a swirl of controversy, critique, and allegations that the postcolonial perspective overly homogenizes the colonial experience and fails to account for the impact of capitalist modernity (to name a just a few criticisms).[12] We are concerned here with how the practice of archaeological anthropology cross-threads with currents of postcolonialism and decolonization. Such currents can become tidal waves in *settler societies* (such as the United States, Canada, Australia, New Zealand, and others). In these contexts, archaeologists most often self-identify with the settler society—often settled for hundreds of years—and may engage in the pursuit of a past that is claimed by the nation-state but is not part of the shared group identity of the archaeologist. This situation closely describes the practice of Maya archaeology, to which we return after considering more broadly the reception of postcolonialism within anthropology and archaeology.

ANTHROPOLOGY DURING POSTCOLONIAL TIMES

In what has been called a crisis of representation, post-1970 sociocultural anthropology faced a challenge to its authority to represent social realities—especially those of previously colonized peoples. The work of Edward Said and others of the postcolonial school of thought was highly critical of anthropology, partly because of its privileged position within colonial regimes. One influential response to this crisis was to recast the business of sociocultural anthropology as cultural critique at any time and any place.[13] In 1986, George E. Marcus and Michael M. J. Fischer published *Anthropology as Cultural Critique: An Experimental Moment in the Human Sciences*. Maintaining the basic structure of the ethnographic method—which had gone viral in the fields of literary and cultural studies—Marcus and Fischer argued for the continued relevance of anthropology, "which plays off other cultural realms against our own in order to gain a more adequate knowledge of them all."[14] The increasingly globalized nature of cultural realms, however, means that "most interesting processes of social and cultural formations are translocal, operating across any distinct cultural boundaries."[15] In order to reposition anthropological research, Marcus and Fischer emphasized *multisited ethnographic research* and recast fieldwork as the investigation of "a complex web of interactions . . . located in a variety of often contrasting settings" with an eye to "track connections amid networks, mutations, influences of cultural forces and changing social pressures."[16]

An important facet of the new *experimental moment* in anthropology included an explicit emphasis on collaboration and dialogue with those who previously had been positioned as informants or objects of anthropological inquiry. Collaboration was projected to create "novel research landscapes, agendas, and relationships."[17] But for anthropologist Charles Hale—a proponent of methodological activism—the nod toward collaborative research seated within the niche of cultural critique did not hold the potential for truly transforming anthropological method or theory.[18] Citing fieldwork that involved participatory mapping with Afro-Caribbean and Indigenous peoples for legal land claims in Nicaragua as an example, Hale argued that anthropological fieldwork should be more engaged with real-world problems and that ethnography should include the messy and politically compromising business of advocacy in collaboration with local communities. Alleging that cultural critique was not methodologically transformative, Hale referred to the many central topics of anthropology—including hegemony, race, class, and gender—that had matured theoretically within activist scholarship rather than growing from the more detached analysis of cultural critique.[19]

Not only does Hale advocate that anthropologists roll up their sleeves and become active participants in human struggles—particularly for social, economic, and environmental justice—he also suggests that collaboration imbue the research process from the bottom up. In Hale's words, "By activist research, I mean a method through which we affirm a political alignment with an organized group of people in struggle and allow dialogue with them to shape each phase of the process, from conception of the research topic to data collection to verification and dissemination of the results."[20] In practical terms, this statement means that anthropologists cede some control of and authority over the research endeavor. Where the rubber meets the road, this space of compromise in which anthropologists share authority with coresearchers who generally are not trained social scientists has proven to be a very contentious space within anthropology. At the same time, for those who practice activist research, the abilities to share authority, to listen and formulate plans in terms of community desires, and to negotiate how, where, and if results will be published are consistently cited as key elements leading to the success of a project (more on this in reference to community archaeology in chapter 6). Although not framed within the model of political transformation proposed by Hale, applied anthropology was a well-established subdivision within sociocultural anthropology, whose practitioners concerned themselves with real-life problems and already had moved toward more collaborative endeavors.

Within the current era of declining enrollment in anthropology programs and a decrease in federal spending for social science research, the call for engagement with pressing social issues has only strengthened. Setha Low has called for anthropologists to engage with the spatial inequality and social exclusion that exist within U.S. cities, gated communities, and urban tracts that lack open green spaces for community integration and recreation.[21] Jerry Sabloff laments the absence of public intellectuals—in the tradition of Margaret Mead—within contemporary anthropology and urges anthropologists to engage with the national policy-making process and exhibit leadership that is nationally recognized in a public forum.[22]

Coming from a Latin American perspective, Roberto González maintains that theory and practice—in Mexican anthropology—have always been united and focused on the resolution of real-world problems.[23] The position of anthropologists within the republic of México pivoted dramatically throughout the twentieth century—from working through nation building, acculturation (via *indigenismo*), and Marxism to current grassroots collaboration with Indigenous movements such as the Zapatistas.[24] Through this dynamism, a concern to improve the livelihood of underrepresented Indigenous peoples has been a constant.

Latin American anthropologists from South America Eduardo Restrepo and Arturo Escobar are critical of the "picture of a simple anthropological tradition emanating from the West that defines anthropology as a modern form of expert knowledge."[25] Restrepo and Escobar urge the discipline to take seriously the theory and practice of anthropology in places outside of the West (to create a plural landscape of world anthropologies) and to reckon with the privileged economic and political contexts in which anthropologists from the West operate. Citing the call in 2000 from Walter Mignolo for *epistemic transformation* (change in how we know what we think we know), Restrepo and Escobar advocate a broadening of the sanctioned corridors of knowledge production within anthropology.[26] This call to "de-naturaliz[e] the *doxa* of 'dominant anthropologies'"[27] is of interest here because the challenge comes from anthropologists who are Latin American (specifically from Colombia) and who align themselves with subaltern discourse not because they identify as Indigenous or because their ancestors were colonized but because they perceive their standpoint to be peripheral to the juggernaut of intellectual production in the dominant centers of the global north. The complexity of the postcolonial world—in which power relations are so starkly implicated in the production of knowledge—provides a challenge to more participatory modes of research because the specter of radical imbalance in political relations (and wealth) is never far from the surface. This imbalance casts a long shadow and can be paralyzing. This fact was never far from our minds as we worked on the design of the heritage programs presented in chapter 7. For these initiatives, working with local organizations to develop ideas and then to operationalize them helped to balance the power differential.

The soul searching and repositioning that has occurred within sociocultural anthropology within the past several decades is deeper and more complicated than we have time to cover here. I have described a discipline in transition by reference to key thinkers who addressed issues of relevance to our concern: how Maya archaeologists and Indigenous communities engage with the past. Archaeology, as a discipline that operates under the umbrella of anthropology (within the Americas at least), also entered a period of reflexivity, but it was different for archaeology, which finds itself in a triadic relationship with both places/things of the past and people of the present who exercise a claim on the past through physical proximity, ethnic identity, or other common denominators.

Within archaeology, the crisis of representation is enlarged temporally and materially because archaeologists investigate (and take responsibility to curate) material remains of the past in order to create representations of the past in the present. As you might imagine, interested descendant communities or those otherwise affiliated with materials linked to the past might desire input on this process. On the one hand, archaeologists are trained in the theory and methods of sleuthing the past, but on the other hand, excluding the voices and participation of others in the interpretive representation of the past can do violence in the present and may not be the most enlightened way to study the past even from a scientific viewpoint.

ARCHAEOLOGY WITH A POSTCOLONIAL SENSIBILITY

The different ways in which archaeologists encounter postcolonialism led Chris Gosden to note its two basic forms: "the investigation of histories of colonialism from an archaeological standpoint, often driven by Native peoples in collaboration with non-Native archaeologists; and investigating the colonial histories of archaeology . . . to discern hitherto unrecognized tropes of colonialism in our studies and to start to rethink the discipline along new lines which admit a greater plurality."[28] The part about thinking along new lines and admitting greater plurality leads us back to the crisis of representation and to multivocality within the practice of archaeology. How would/could those with expert knowledge about investigating the past work alongside those with other kinds of knowledge of the past based on oral history, landscape experience, language, or some other domain of cultural knowledge that connects with the past? Many archaeologists had ideas about how this could be done. Jane Lydon and Uzma Rizvi collected many of these ideas and approaches into the *Handbook of Postcolonial Archaeology*, published in 2010, which details case studies of a new style of collaborative, postcolonial archaeology.[29]

Among Native American peoples of the United States, postcolonial sensibilities can be traced back to the Red Power movement of the 1960s and the challenge that Native American author Vine Deloria issued to U.S. anthropology in his now classic *Custer Died for Your Sins: An Indian Manifesto*, published in 1969.[30] Forty years later, Native American archaeologist Joe Watkins spoke directly to the relationship between archaeologists and Native Americans and intimated that it was possible to forge a new kind of archaeology—an Indigenous archaeology—that would incorporate both scientific practice and Native American values.[31]

Between these key publications by Deloria and Watkins, the U.S. Congress passed into law the Native American Graves Protection and Repatriation Act (NAGPRA) in 1990. Analogous change (although not always originating with federal legislation) in the political sphere occurred in Canada, Australia, and New Zealand. These countries all contained large colonizing populations—mostly European derived—that coexisted uneasily with Indigenous peoples. To my knowledge, no legislation similar to NAGPRA has been proposed for any Latin American or Caribbean nation, although there have been challenges to the authority of the republic of México—specifically INAH—to hold human remains from excavation without consultation with Indigenous peoples.[32] Within the United States, NAGPRA requires that federally funded museums and institutions holding Native American human remains, associated burial items, and sacred artifacts consult with and potentially return such cultural patrimony to Native American groups if their return is desired. Called *repatriation* (meaning, significantly, to return to *patria* or country of origin), this law set into motion a process of consultation between institutions holding Native American materials and tribal groups.[33] The law also impacts the archaeological excavation of Native American remains and further sets into motion a field-based consultation process between archaeologists and Native Americans.

Some would say that the law humanized North American archaeology and began to undo or decolonize the heritage alienation forced upon Native Americans through land appropriation, compulsory boarding school education, harsh retribution for speaking a Native language, and earlier broken land treaties (to name a few injustices). Decades of twentieth-century archaeological practices in which research goals were based on either inductive culture-historical classification of artifacts or the deductive testing of theoretical constructs has not included much dialogue with Native populations beyond extracting ethnographic information.[34] NAGPRA asserted the rights of Native American tribes to control the disposition of the remains and things of their ancestors. The law also opened the door to a deeper relationship between archaeologists—gatekeepers of the past—and Native Americans—descendants of those who lived that past. Some archaeologists saw this as a unique opportunity to enrich the study of the past through greater inclusivity while also effecting a necessary rebalancing of the power relations embedded within the practice of archaeology. Chip Colwell-Chanthaphonh and T. J. Ferguson wrote of the *collaborative continuum*; at one end, archaeologists merely obeyed the letter of the law by consulting in a pro forma manner with affiliated Native Americans, while on the other end, Native Americans became collaborative partners with archaeologists, and together they studied and inter-preted the past.[35]

Conducting archaeology with a postcolonial sensibility to the circumstances of recent history, an ear to multivocality, and a fairness of representation seemed un-scientific to some archaeologists, who voiced objections to collaborative research, fearing that it undermined the scientific basis of archaeology and the authority of archaeologists.[36] Although NAGPRA doesn't extend beyond the United States, it is a critical piece of legislation for understanding the collaborative trend within archaeology and also because it has been woven into the discussion of ethical research in many academic programs within the United States. Advanced under-graduate and certainly graduate courses often include coverage of the law and a discussion of how it challenges the "representational authority"[37] of archaeologists. Through this pedagogical stream, issues of representation and control of ancestral remains impacts the research practices of U.S.-trained archaeologists who are permitted to conduct archaeology south of the U.S. border. Professional archae-ologists who self-identify as Native American—Sonya Atalay, Dorothy Lippert, Joe Watkins (mentioned previously), and Michael Wilcox, to name just a few and in alphabetical order—called for a different kind of archaeology that incorporated Native American voices.[38] Working in the Canadian province of British Columbia, George Nicholas and T. Andrews called this new practice Indigenous archaeology (IA) and described it as practiced by, for, and with Native American communi-ties.[39] In the long run, how these changes will manifest south of the U.S. border has yet to be determined. But few U.S.-trained archaeologists can deny the fact that there is a clear dissonance between ethical practices in the United States in refer-ence to Indigenous peoples and field practices within Latin America.

Regardless of whether one practiced archaeology in North America or else-where, we entered a new era, particularly in countries with large Anglo-derived colonial populations, such as Canada and Australia.[40] But the call for an embrace of archaeological practices that diminished the estrangement of Indigenous peoples from their past and promoted collaborative research was not positively received by all archaeologists, and many continued to pursue business as usual. Non-Indigenous archaeologists, such as George Nicholas and Stephen Silliman, have appealed to the archaeological community for general acceptance of a new kind of archaeological practice; they argue that IA represents a necessary reform and not a new and optional specialty.[41] Matthew Liebmann notes the overlap between IA and postcolonialism—joined by a shared commitment to decolonize archaeological practices—while Robert Preucel and Craig Cipolla point to the crucial problem of IA as practiced in the United States, that it challenges "the dominant Western paradigm."[42] Critics, such as Robert McGhee, allege that the Western paradigm is just fine as it is and that IA represents a new kind of rac-ism—which McGhee called *aboriginalism*—which marginalizes archaeological scientists.[43] In response, Chip Colwell-Chanthaphonh sums up the position of many advocates of IA when he writes that "Indigenous archaeology's common denominator is not racial constructs, but rather the colonial context that has empowered scientists to define the 'Other,' control heritage resources, and interpret the past."[44]

The back-and-forth within North American archaeology points to the difficulty of "understand[ing] and work[ing] through the complex effects of colonialism."[45] These new approaches, including postcolonial archaeology, Indigenous archaeology, and community archaeology, all have in common a commitment to reflexivity of a kind that is a bit foreign to archaeology. Most archaeologists see themselves as friends and advocates of Indigenous peoples even though research plans seldom include local peoples in any way but as guides and "silent laborers."[46] To be accused of perpetrating epistemic violence on Native Americans was shocking and hurtful to many archaeologists. But archaeologists are mindful of the fact that interpretation stems from a process of reasoning. So when philosopher of science Alison Wylie began to write about changes in the epistemic basis of archaeological knowledge, archaeologists took note.[47]

In 1995, Wylie wrote about a more inclusive archaeology as representing epistemic disunity but political integrity.[48] Serving an a discussant for a group of papers that would later be published as *Making Alternative Histories: The Practice of Archaeology and History in Non-Western Settings*,[49] Wylie noted that "the common thread in these analyses is a concern to articulate an account of knowledge production that recognizes its own contingency and standpoint specificity, that repudiates any quest for a unitary ('master') narrative and any faith in context-transcendent 'foundations,' and that yet resists the implication that any comparison or judgment of credibility is irreducibly arbitrary, that 'anything goes.'"[50] *Repudiation* is a strong word. What is being repudiated? Unitary narratives and comparative generalizations are linchpins of the Western paradigm—a framework of reasoning that Preucel and Cipolla previously suggested is under attack from advocates of IA. But there also is an assertion that not just anything goes. In other words, the turn toward alternative histories is not a wallow in relativistic nihilism. And what about acknowledging standpoint specificity? Accounting for where you "come from" when offering a reading of the past sounds like an intellectually honest way to proceed.

Thirteen years after *Making Alternative Histories* was published, Alison Wylie reflected in greater depth on alternative ways of creating histories, the importance of standpoint analysis, and the potential of multivocality. Serving once more as a discussant but this time for a series of papers that considered the evaluation of multiple narratives[51] (a predictable outcome of multivocality), Wylie sought constructive ways in which archaeologists might reckon with the history of their discipline, build working partnerships with communities involved in the archaeological process, and negotiate multiple narratives about the past. Borrowing from philosopher Helen Longino, Wylie outlined guidelines to empirical and conceptual integrity in archaeological research: tempered equality of intellectual authority (taking others seriously); recognized avenues of criticism, uptake of criticism, and grounded reflexivity or "a commitment to deploying the insights of standpoint analysis in the design and practice of archaeological research, and in the adjudication of the explanatory, interpretive understanding it produces of the cultural past."[52] The last point is pretty opaque, but we can take it to mean that we should take seriously the contingency of knowledge production and that we should be prepared for adjudication among multiple narratives. Finally, and in no uncertain terms, Wylie recommends that "inquiry must be democratized."[53]

The philosophical insight and recommendations of Alison Wylie and others does not mean that archaeological research cannot seek to dimensionalize an understanding of the past through comparative analysis, only that such comparisons ought to be grounded contextually. While some archaeologists continue to voice concerns about the compatibility of the science of archaeology with the heritage concerns of Native Americans and local communities, most feel that the ship has sailed. Although we have launched into largely uncharted waters, we are free to navigate a new course and over the past decades or so have been rethinking the practice of archaeology.[54]

POSTCOLONIAL ARCHAEOLOGY SOUTH OF THE U.S. BORDER

The newly charted terrain in which North American archaeologists find themselves ends at the southern U.S. border, which is defined partially by the Río Grande and almost totally by an increasingly formidable border wall.[55] The political will that built the border wall forcefully accentuates the asymmetrical economies of the north-south divide. Although poverty assuredly exists north of the border, it takes on monstrous proportions south of the wall—confirmable from a glance toward Juárez, México, from Interstate 10 just north of El Paso, Texas. South of the border, archaeology, as well as the struggles of Indigenous peoples for self-representation and multivocality, takes place in the context of grinding poverty. Unfortunately but not unexpectedly, Indigenous peoples suffer poverty in disproportionate numbers in Latin America, as they do also in the United States.[56]

As mentioned previously, no legislation comparable to NAGPRA has been enacted south of the border. Archaeologists who are citizens of (or trained in) the United States negotiate with federal agencies that have been charged with conserving national patrimony and regulating archaeological investigations— particularly those conducted by foreign archaeologists. Federal agencies, such as INAH in México, are vested in the centralized control of national patrimony and not in returning funerary bundles to Indigenous peoples or sharing management of places termed sacred by Native peoples. Archaeologists trained in the United States have come to understand that reburial may be a necessary part of scientific investigation when human remains are involved, but they can run afoul of regulatory agencies if such protocols are initiated outside of the United States.

Randall McGuire relates how a planned reburial of ancestral Tohono O'odham individuals exhumed during archaeological excavation in Sonora—just south of the border—was cancelled because of objections from INAH authorities.[57]

On the other hand, and as Thomas Patterson brought to the attention of the Anglo-speaking world in 1994, *arqueología social* (social archaeology) has a deeper history in Latin America than in the global north.[58] Construed much differently from the social archaeology manifesto of Anglo archaeology, which privileges contextualized singularities, agent-structured symbols, and historical action,[59] *arqueología social* concerns itself with Marxist forces and relations of production as they played out in the past as well as in the current highly racialized and unequal social contexts in which Latin American archaeologists practice their profession.[60] This standpoint translates into a concern for and commitment to community that is only a weak trend within the Anglo-speaking world of archaeologists. Proponents of *arqueología social* seek transformative change for impoverished and underrepresented communities—a sustaining plank of a Marxist platform.

Writing from the vantage point of self-proclaimed "strategic marginality," O. Hugo Benavides notes that "in the last two decades . . . a community of archaeologists . . . have disengaged themselves from pretended scientific neutrality and actively connected their professional work with their political involvement."[61] Citing the 1981 publication of *La arqueología como ciencia social* (Archaeology as social science), written by Peruvian archaeologist Luis Lumbreras as a highly influential text, Benavides freely states that *arqueología social* privileges "why we do archaeology rather than how we do it."[62] So the practice of *arqueología social* translates into more of an emphasis on social theory and less on archaeological methods—whether practiced strictly within a scientific community or in collaboration with communities outside of academic archaeology.

Over time, Latin American archaeologists became more reflexive about *arqueología social*. For instance, Mexican archaeologist Patricia Fournier has noted the disjuncture between rhetoric and methods.[63] Despite less emphasis being placed on methods—which are an important part of how the business of archaeology is accomplished and retooled—the commitment to transformative change among proponents of *arqueología social* provides a window of possibilities.

These possibilities—hard-won collaborations that provide opportunities for self-representation and multivocality—are increasingly realities throughout Latin America, regardless of whether local groups self-identify as Indigenous or "distinctive," the latter a term preferred by Oaxacan archaeologist Nelly Robles.[64] In 2004, Gustavo Politis and José Antonio Pérez Gollán wrote that "there is nothing that can be labeled as an 'indigenous archaeology'" in Latin America.[65] They followed that statement, however, by citing at least five collaborative projects between Indigenous groups and archaeologists or museum specialists: a community-designed local museum in Santa Ana del Valle (Oaxaca, México) created in collaboration with INAH and ENAH (National School of Anthropology and

History); a cooperative excavation in Añelo (Neuquén), Argentina, involving Mapuche people and archaeologists who worked side by side to excavate and conserve cultural remains and to create a community museum; the ceding of a Mapuche sacred site to the custody of the Ñorquinco Mapuche community (also in Argentina); the creation of space for multivocality in museum spaces of the Ethnographic Museum at the University of Buenos Aires; and sustainable development plans for archaeological areas of the Serra do Capibara National Park in Brazil.[66]

Although modest in number and scope, during the ten years that have elapsed since these efforts were reported by Politis and Pérez Gollán, more critical attention has been devoted to the power dynamics between Latin American archaeologists and Indigenous peoples.[67] Many more collaborations have sprouted. The community museum in Santa Ana, Oaxaca (Museo Shan-Dany) proved to be a trendsetter, and by 2006 at least sixteen other community museums that house items of deep heritage and highlight local cultural practices had been established in Oaxaca.[68] Likewise, community museums in Peru, Bolivia, and Ecuador had been conceived and constructed by 2006.[69] Heritage programs had begun to sprout in Mesoamerica as well and are discussed in detail in chapter 6.

In reference to Ecuador, Benavides notes the change that has occurred since the 1970s as a self-styled *Indianismo* movement, organized and run by Indigenous communities, replaced an earlier *Indigenismo* movement, which had been organized outside of Indigenous communities.[70] This distinction—between organization within and organization imposed from outside and usually through authoritarian channels—is critically significant, especially for archaeologists who seek to partner with Indigenous groups. Autonomy of voice and self-representation for Indigenous communities is a first principle of collaboration. Without that, we are simply repeating history—albeit in a gentler fashion.

The lack of autonomy of voice and self-representation undergirds the epigraph at the beginning of this chapter, in which Avexnim Cojti Ren alleges that Classic Maya history has been distorted and told by others. Self-representation is particularly a problem in the Maya region, where tourism fosters distorted representations of contemporary Maya peoples[71] and fascination with the Classic period leads to both valorization and denigration (as in lessons in what not to do in the present).[72] This fascination—with an apocalyptic edge—characterized the events of 2012, when the old dynastic calendar shifted to a new *bak'tun* (a bundle of time equal to about four hundred years). Matthew Restall and Amara Solari have argued that this shift would have been perceived as an auspicious time of renewal during Classic times, when the long-count calendar was actively maintained, and not interpreted as an apocalyptic end of time.[73] Pablo Mis, a Q'eqchi' leader and advocate of self-governance for the Toledo District of southern Belize, had this to say about 2012: "For us it's not about catastrophe but about renewal. It's a time to reflect on the path we have walked. It is a positive time when Maya people are becoming actors—no longer passive. Many things are changing now. We want to embrace the change and channel it."[74]

In chapter 5, we take a closer look at how people who self-identify as Maya engage and activate the shadow of the *ancient Maya*—a monolithic term that masks the considerable ethnic and linguistic variation that pervaded this tropical landscape in the past.

To return to the metaphor that I used in chapter 1, postcolonial archaeology south of the border is a complex endeavor that truly can be characterized as a busy intersection. By shifting our standpoint from U.S. archaeologists to Latin American archaeologists, and to Indigenous persons, we begin to glimpse the complexities, challenges, and opportunities that lie ahead. Maya archaeology is a particularly distinctive kind of postcolonial animal, if the term *postcolonial* can be used in reference to the theory and methods of Maya archaeologists.[75] In the Maya region, for a shift is to occur toward research strategies that are more collaborative with Indigenous and local communities, archaeologists will need to rethink the terms of engagement[76] and—particularly when working with Native communities—yield space for self-representation.

ARE HUMAN RIGHTS AT STAKE?

Should control over the representation of your identity and your past as well as the disposition of the remains of your ancestors be considered a basic human right? The 1990 passage of NAGPRA into law within the United States brought to front and center these very issues. Increasingly, issues of cultural heritage are linked to human rights by virtue of a powerful precedent. Much earlier (in 1948), in the wake of universal horror over the genocide perpetrated on European Jews during World War II, the United Nations passed a Universal Declaration of Human Rights in an attempt to establish basic principles of human dignity that should never be violated. In a 2007 introduction to *Cultural Heritage and Human Rights*, Helaine Silverman and Fairchild Ruggles discuss the highly politicized terrain of human rights in relation to Indigenous peoples, intellectual property, national decisions regarding what is memorialized as opposed to forgotten, and the determination of access to sacred sites. They ask who has the right to study, manage, and benefit economically from tangible cultural heritage.[77]

Convention No. 169 of the International Labor Organization (ILO) represents another quasilegal instrument that has shaped the discussion of cultural heritage and human rights. Adopted in 1989, the ILO convention established ground rules for ethical interaction between Indigenous peoples and nation-states and referenced the following human rights: respect for Indigenous spirituality; allowance of public religious ceremonies; and honoring of cultural traditions, expressions, and traditional lands. Compliance with international agreements such as ILO Convention No. 169 is voluntary, and large wealthy nations, such as the United States and Canada, have refused to sign on to the convention. But for developing nations, failure to ratify ILO 169 can have major consequences in terms of international aid, trade agreements, and other economically vital resources.[78] Of the five nations that are home to Maya peoples, only three have ratified the convention: México in 1990, Honduras in 1995, and Guatemala in 1996.[79]

Setting aside universal declarations and conventions, we can see that questions abound regarding the role of human rights in relation to cultural heritage.[80] Discussing multivocality and the challenge of negotiating among many voices of interpretation (and prioritizing some over others), Ian Hodder asks whether those "who have suffered loss of heritage under colonial rule have special rights . . . ? In the end it seems more likely to me that rather than defining universal rights to heritage it would be better to embed rights to cultural heritage within wider considerations of human rights."[81] For Hodder, cultural heritage and human rights are inseparable issues and should not be considered in isolation from one another. But for others, the thought that Indigenous peoples might have special rights to places that are recognized globally as valued sites of human heritage is fraught with difficulties. When the United Nations designates an archaeological site as significant to world heritage, that action can exacerbate the conflict between local rights, access, and benefit, on the one hand, and appreciation and conservation of world heritage, on the other.

In an effort to work through the polarizing discourse of human rights in reference to the cultural heritage of descendant communities, Chip Colwell-Chanthaphonh and T. J. Ferguson suggest that while many people may exert a claim on the past, descendent communities possess "more complex and compelling *interests* than other communities, including the archaeological community itself."[82] According descendants a priority of rights over cultural heritage might frame a complex issue too narrowly, but a case can be made that local communities—many of which self-identify as descendants of the people who built the cities, towns, and farmscapes of precolonial times—do possess a long-standing and compelling entanglement with the tangible heritage located in their "backyard."

The universality of the global often is cast against the distinctiveness of the local and in many ways recapitulates the tension between modernism and the postmodern. The former is construed in universalist terms, while the latter more frequently is characterized as diverse with connecting threads of commonality. But stark polarities—when applied to human rights, cultural heritage, and indigeneity—can mask the importance of tacking back and forth between the global and the local. In a study titled *Human Rights and Gender Violence*, Sally Engle Merry provides an example of how international law emanating from the United Nations can be translated into local justice for victims of gender violence.[83] Merry finds that U.N. decrees often are criticized as too universalist and culturally tone deaf—similar to critiques of UNESCO World Heritage Site designations and conventions promoting human rights for Indigenous peoples. While these criticisms are valid, U.N. decrees inevitably open space for local negotiation of critically important issues and injustices that sometimes can be resolved in locally contextualized solutions.[84] But exactly how does one "open space" for dialogue? This challenge is considered from a societal perspective before delving into the nuts and bolts of building dialogue in chapter 6.

THE RELATIONAL TURN

In a fit of pique, philosophers Gilles Deleuze and Félix Guattari complain: "We're tired of trees. We should stop believing in trees, roots, and radicles. They've made us suffer too much."[85] What do these two Continental philosophers mean by the expression "believing in trees"? Who *believes* in trees anyway? They exist as majestic forms with sturdy trunks and branching limbs. In fact, it is precisely the single sturdy base from which arboreal shoots trace their origins that disturbed Deleuze and Guattari. As a metaphor of the Western intellectual tradition and also of hierarchical power relations in many different contexts, Deleuze and Guattari find the arborescent metaphor to be too restrictive and exclusive. Instead, they propose a model that centers on the humble rhizome—a nodal root mat that expands horizontally to create a loosely structured network. The rhizome is argued to provide a relational (rather than hierarchical) model that opens new spaces.[86] Unsettling arborescent models is no easy feat, as Deleuze and Guattari admit, but the expanded arena of participation that results from cultivating rhizome-like networks can be transformative for all participants.

A relational turn can be understood as a turn toward decentering and flattening existing hierarchies—as a decolonization of knowledge production for the specific case in hand. While certainly not problem free, a relational model of rhizome-like connections does accurately model the complex trajectories of contemporary archaeological ethics and responsibilities. Contributing authors to *The Ethics of Archaeology* note the multiple responsibilities of the discipline toward the curation of places and things of the past *as well as* accountability to people of the present.[87]

The changes in *business as usual* that are introduced in this chapter and explored in further detail in the chapters to come accent the differences between the practice of archaeology and that of sociocultural anthropology. For the latter, a relational turn led to multisited studies that follow pathways of power through a globalized world with less focus on a single community. In contrast, a relational turn within archaeology tends to intensify relations between archaeologists and communities residing around archaeological sites of interest. As a result of this engagement, we focus more intently on the impact of archaeological research on the well-being of proximate communities. The temporal dimension and materiality of this engagement undergirds the search for balance between scientific research and community heritage interests. In this way, the relational turn does not follow the path of sociocultural anthropology but rather propels us into new terrain—albeit one in which ethnographic methods have a role to play.

Community archaeology—as a kind of relational archaeology—is an enterprise that is distinct from multisited sociocultural anthropology, although similar tensions exist within the two approaches. As discussed previously, sociocultural anthropologists debate whether social realities are more closely comprehended through the analytical gaze of cultural critique (as George Marcus and Michael Fischer suggest) or through direct engagement with the real-life social problems encountered by anthropologists (a path pursued by Charles Hale and others). Sociocultural anthropologists agree on the real-world problems that need to be addressed but differ in *how* those problems are best addressed.

Archaeologists also tend to fall into two camps: those who feel that the past can be understood as an entity that is independent of contemporary social reality and those who believe that our understanding of the past is embedded in our cultural context and intellectual traditions. Both camps support the empirical reality of a past, and the former often espouse the idea that findings about the past will be relevant to planning a course of action for the future.[88] From this perspective, grand challenges to archaeology are restricted to the realms of social theory and analytical methods and need not involve a transformation in the social context of knowledge production. This group espouses a notion of relevance that is linked to positive change in social policy and planning.

Views on how the past is relevant to the present drill to the core of these two different approaches. The latter camp views the link between the past and present in epistemological terms that include consideration of knowledge production.[89] For this group, a significant challenge to archaeology is the exclusivity of the social context within which archaeology takes place, particularly in reference to underrepresented Indigenous communities whose past has been intensively studied in the Americas.

Archaeologists in Australia have wrestled with these ethical and procedural issues proactively. In reference to research partnerships established with Yarrawarra people of New South Wales, Wendy Beck and colleagues have this to say about the relational turn in archaeological practice: "We must not underestimate the complexity of 'decolonising' archaeological theory and practice. It is a long slow process, which only happens by doing it."[90] In chapter 7, we turn to "doing it," the relational process of building bridges. This work opens the practice of archaeology to new participants by implementing methods that are participatory and collaborative. Though shaky at first, over time new bridges can provide the foundation for an epistemological transformation in our study of the past.

Before we turn to bridge building, it is vital to consider the lived experiences of people inhabiting the Maya region—those whose "backyards" have been excavated to provide the raw material from which archaeologists create the *ancient Maya*. We are interested particularly in how the monolithic term—the Maya— fits the diverse experiences of local inhabitants. Do people today see themselves as heirs to a Classic-period legacy or as cohabiting a landscape that is unconformably and uneasily imbued with a distant and unrelated past? We tackle these questions and others in chapter 5.

NOTES

1. Cojti Ren (2006:10).
2. For an analogous perspective from Australia, see McNiven and Russell (2005).
3. Patterson (2008:21).
4. Spivak (1988). Matthew Liebmann (2008:9) sources the term *subaltern* (meaning one of inferior position) to Antonio Gramsci, who is also known for popularizing the term *hegemony* to refer to oppressive political authority.
5. Said (1978).
6. See also Said (1996).
7. Patterson (2008:27).
8. Bhabha (1994); Liebmann (2008:5).
9. For essays on Indigenous self-determination, see chapters in Woons (2104).
10. For instance, see Pagán Jiménez and Rodríguez Ramos (2008:54, 69).
11. Smith (2012).
12. See Liebmann (2008:10–13) for a well-referenced review of the critiques of post-colonialism.
13. See Marcus and Fischer (1999).
14. Marcus and Fischer (1999:x).
15. Marcus and Fischer (1999:xviii)
16. Marcus and Fischer (1999:xviii–xix); see also Marcus (1995).
17. Marcus and Fischer (1999:xxii).
18. Hale (2006).
19. Hale (2006:108).
20. Hale (2006:97); see also Low and Merry (2010) for a discussion of engaged research and Schensul (2010:307), who discusses participatory research using the rubric of "third-sector science."
21. Low (2011).
22. Sabloff (2011).
23. González (2004).
24. González (2004).
25. Restrepo and Escobar (2005).
26. Restrepo and Escobar (2005:113); see also Mignolo (2000) for further thoughts on *critical border thinking.*
27. Restrepo and Escobar (2005:118).
28. Gosden (2012:253).
29. See Lydon and Rivzi (2010).
30. Deloria (1969).
31. Watkins (2000).
32. See the discussion in Navarrete (2011).
33. Much has been written about the challenges of NAGPRA; excellent references include Bray and Killion (1994), Killion (2008), and Thomas (2000).
34. Trigger (2003:410).
35. Colwell-Chanthaphonh and Ferguson (2008); see also Dongoske, Aldenderfer, and Doehner (2000).
36. See particularly Clark (2000) and McGhee (2008).
37. Wilcox (2010b:223).

38. Atalay (2006, 2008, 2012); Lippert (2008); Watkins (2000, 2005); and Wilcox (2009, 2010a, 2010b).

39. Nicholas and Andrews (1997a).

40. In particular, see contributions in McNiven and Russell (2005), Nicholas (2011), and Smith and Wobst (2005).

41. Nicholas (2010); Sillliman (2008).

42. Liebmann (2008:17); Preucel and Cipolla (2008:131).

43. McGhee (2008).

44. Colwell-Chanthaphonh (2012:279).

45. Gosden (2012:255).

46. Colwell-Chanthaphonh (2012:269).

47. Wylie (1995, 2008, 2015).

48. Wylie (1995).

49. Schmidt and Patterson (1995); the title is a veiled tribute to a 1984 article published by Bruce Trigger, "Alternative Archaeologies: Nationalist, Colonialist, Imperialist."

50. Wylie (1995:270).

51. See Habu, Fawcett, and Matsunaga (2008). This book is yet another veiled tribute to the 1984 article published by Bruce Trigger, "Alternative Archaeologies: Nationalist, Colonialist, Imperialist."

52. Wylie (2008:208–9).

53. Wylie (2008:208–10).

54. For more on the paradigm shift within archaeology, see Atalay (2012:53–54), McAnany and Rowe (2015), and Thomas (2008).

55. McGuire (2013).

56. See Hall and Patrinos (2006).

57. McGuire (2008:180–86); for a discussion of Papago requests for reburial of ancestral remains, see Navarrete (2011:49).

58. Patterson (1994).

59. Hodder and Hutson (2003).

60. Benavides (2001:358–60); see also McGuire and Navarrete (2005).

61. Benavides (2001:356, 357).

62. Benavides (2001:358–59).

63. Fournier (1999); also see the discussion in Politis and Pérez Gollán (2004:360–61).

64. Robles (2010:277).

65. Politis and Pérez Gollán (2004:364)

66. Politis and Pérez Gollán (2004:364–65).

67. For instance, see Gnecco and Ayala (2011).

68. For an in-depth discussion of community museums in Oaxaca, see Hoobler (2006) and also comments by Robles (2010:285).

69. Silverman (2006).

70. Benavides (2001:365).

71. Ardren (2004).

72. Most notably in Diamond (2005).

73. See the further discussion and contrast of precolonial conceptions of time with missionized conceptions of the colonial period in Restall and Solari (2011).

74. Pablo Mis, personal communication, 2011 (see also the discussion in McAnany 2014).

75. Pyburn (2004) questions the "post-ness" of the present state of Maya archaeology.

76. Along these lines, see McAnany (2014) and Pyburn (2003).

77. Silverman and Ruggles (2007).

78. Niezen (2003:36–50).

79. http://en.wikipedia.org/wiki/Indigenous_and_Tribal_Peoples_Convention,_1989 #Ratifications.

80. See Langfield, Logan, and Nic Craith (2010) for case studies.

81. Hodder (2008:199).

82. Colwell-Chanthaphonh and Ferguson (2008:8), italics in the original.

83. Merry (2006).

84. Helen Human (2015) provides a sobering account to the contrary in reference to local vernacularization of the UNESCO site inscription process when Turkish authorities thwarted community participation during the inscription of Çatalhöyük as a World Heritage Site.

85. Deleuze and Guattari (1987:15).

86. Deleuze and Guattari (1987:11, 21).

87. See Scarre and Scarre (2006) and also Sabloff (2008).

88. See Kintigh et al. (2014) for a relevant example of this approach.

89. McAnany (2014).

90. Beck et al. (2005:239).

5

⌒

Engaging the Shadow
of the "Ancient Maya"

Maya culture has been shaped by the favorable and unfavorable circumstances
under which we Maya have lived throughout our history, yet it remains the same
culture developed over thousands of years by our ancestors in the territory that
is today Guatemala. The form of our culture has changed, but not its essence.

—Raxche' aka Demetrio Rodríguez Guaján[1]

This statement of cultural identity and survival draws upon ancestral connections to a distant past in a direct fashion. Running contrary to theorizations
of situated or constructed identities that are vogue within contemporary cultural
studies, assertions such as that of Raxche' are labeled by some social scientists
as strategic essentialism or ethnopolitics.[2] There is no doubt that invocation of
a straightforward identity with multigenerational continuity from a storied past
augments current struggles for ethnic revindication in the face of strong and
historically grounded racism and discrimination.[3] For Maya cultural activists in
Guatemala, the long shadow of the ancient Maya provides a touchstone employed
to galvanize "self-determination, cultural pride, and pan-Maya unity."[4]

Pan-Maya unity—in either the past or the present—is not a problem-free
construct. Across the Maya region today, there is tremendous variability in how
people relate to the past (if at all), to the imprint of the past on the inhabited
landscape and the degree to which the past is deployed for economic purposes or
held sacred. And—most importantly for this study—whether self-identification
emphasizes links with a deep past. A person may identify in any number of
ways: with a local community, as a speaker of a particular language (Spanish or
a Mayan language), with a nation, or in reference to the history of colonization
as an Indigenous, Original, or Native person. One thing is certain, however, the
monolithic entity termed the *ancient Maya* by archaeologists casts a very long
shadow over the Maya region. The shadow penetrates the lives and livelihoods of

69

rural and urban dwellers alike whether or not a self-reflexive identification with the deep past is present. The purpose of this chapter (as well as chapters 8 and 9) is to examine this shadow as it is shaped and reconstituted in endlessly variable ways. While this chapter focuses on shadow shaping in relation to coloniality and nationalism, chapters 8 and 9 discuss how local communities and specific persons dialogue with and subtly craft the past. But before we delve into this key topic, a word about the monolithic impulse in Maya archaeology.

THE IMPULSE TO REIFY

Issues of ethnic identity, continuity with a past, or homogeneity across the Maya region today are difficult to divorce from archaeological frameworks. Historians and cultural anthropologists alike are fond of pointing toward archaeologists and linguists as instigators of a reified notion of a monolithic Maya identity.[5] Indeed, the frequently employed tree diagram showing a proto-Mayan language family that diversified into many branches, with the limbs becoming the languages that are spoken today (such as Yucateko, Tzeltal, Mopan, K'iche', Ch'orti', and so forth), provides an excellent example of the powerful arborescent metaphor that so irked Gilles Deleuze and Félix Guattari. (Furthermore, archaeologists have been hard put to provide on-the-ground evidence in support of the glotto-chronological sequence and rate of linguistic diversification proposed by linguists.) Deleuze and Guattari might label the linguistic dendrogram an example of the tyrannical authority of Western intellectualism—another imposing tree that must be felled to yield a more relational understanding of linguistic diversification. Beyond the challenge of understanding the origin of Mayan languages, there exists tremendous linguistic diversity within the Maya region. Although this situation is not atypical for tropical regions worldwide, it does cast doubt upon the reality of a monolithic Maya identity at any time within the past three thousand years.

In the title of this chapter, the "ancient Maya" is placed within quotation marks to indicate the extraordinary nature of this monolithic category. What do we mean by this term and to whom does it refer? Does it encompass all of the ancient peoples who lived in what is now called the Maya region, which is a palimpsest of the geographical extent of spoken languages that can be classified within the Mayan language family plus large archaeological sites that served as political capitals between 500 BCE and 1500 CE? There is no analytical reason to fuse historical linguistics with archaeological patterns, but since earlier scholars perceived a concordance, a marriage formed that has proven very durable.

Are archaeological remains of diverse size and time periods subsumed under the rubric of the "ancient Maya"? Theoretically, yes, but in terms of museum exhibits and public curiosity, no. In reality, the two-hundred-year span between 600 and 800 CE—the time of royal courts—dominates the stage and provides the criteria for the definition of the "ancient Maya." Perhaps this is not so surprising since elites and royals of most times and places thrive on visually distinctive, far-flung, and sharply defined networks that yield a monolithic identity, awesome artifacts, and (they hope) indisputable authority; Pierre Bourdieu and others call it orthodoxy.[6] The tremendous diversity across time and space that character-izes the two-thousand-plus years of Maya civilization tends to be collapsed (in the popular imaginary at least) into two hundred years during which a type of pottery was produced that contains polychrome painted scenes of royal courts augmented by hieroglyphic calligraphy. But it is highly improbable that ordinary people, who likely spoke several different languages across the region—as is the case today—considered themselves part of a large, homogeneous ethnic bloc. Increasingly, epigraphers suggest that the widely spoken languages of the Classic period stood apart from court language(s), which were read and written by a very small percentage of the overall populace.[7] Reification of the authoritarian appa-ratus of the rich and powerful of times gone by is not unique to Maya archaeol-ogy, but it does shape the shadow cast on the present. This impulse also makes for strange bedfellows as archaeologists analogically deploy postcolonial cultural practices to better understand powerful authority structures of the distant past.

ISSUES OF CONTINUITY AND ETHNOGENESIS

Peter Hervik decries the trope of mystery that often cloaks discussion of Classic Maya society in the pages of *National Geographic* magazine and in some scholarly publications as well.[8] He is equally perplexed by the constant drumbeat of cultural continuity that pervades scholarly writing. But Hervik avoids discussing human rights discourse among Maya cultural activists, which also emphasizes continuity. Employing a parallel to Viking reenactments in his home country, Hervik writes: "I anticipate that most readers will agree it would be meaningless, if not absurd, to understand the cultural identity and social activities of contemporary Danes [including Hervik], Norwegians, Finns, and Swedes as meaningful in relation to the era of the Vikings. Indeed, hardly anyone does represent contemporary reconstructions of ancient ways as signs of cultural continuity."[9]

Hervik goes on to explain the difference between the two places by reference to poverty and the third-world status of México in contrast to the postindustrial nations of Scandinavia.[10] But a more compelling, if less proximate, explanation would point to the aftermath of European colonization, which led to a loss of political autonomy and thus the political muscle and authority required to man-age cultural representation by others. For Hervik, *National Geographic* evokes a "timeless Maya" in order to sell magazines and because it has the authority to freeze-frame the cultural practices of Indigenous peoples.[11] Hervik suggests that anthropologists—both archaeologists and ethnographers alike—have colluded in perpetuating this perception. While this serious accusation cannot be completely denied, goals and motivations differ.

For archaeologists, cultural continuity facilitates analogy. If the shadow of the past is not so different from the present, then contemporary or historical cultural practices might be used as a key to unlock the meaning of archaeological materials. Unlike *National Geographic*'s desire to tell a story cloaked in mysterious continuities in order to sell magazines, archaeologists impute continuity as a point of method—a prelude to building narratives of the past.[12] Whether such analogies are methodologically and ethically defendable is another matter altogether.

The most significant rationale for invoking continuity relates to Maya cultural activists such as Raxche', who was quoted in the epigraph. As Kay Warren has written, "Continuity in descent, culture, and language is being constructed as a challenge to histories of conquest and assimilation."[13] This engagement with the past is not atemporal—that is, an assertion of continuity without change—but rather asserts active links with a deep history that, until the 1980s, had been the exclusive domain of academics. Recall the nineteenth-century trend discussed in chapter 3 of folding the Maya past into the emergent discipline of archaeology. Explorers and archaeologists assumed control of narratives about the impressive old places in the Maya region. Warren describes meeting with a group of prominent linguists—all with ethnic taproots in highland Guatemala—who gathered together to study passages from the *Annals of the Kaqchikels*, including the chapter on genealogy in which the family name of one of the participating linguists figured prominently.[14] Warren notes the new and insightful perspectives that emerge from reading old texts with new eyes and with a firm grasp on the language in which the text was composed. As perspective begins to shift, received wisdom about conquest and assimilation narratives does not appear so solid.

The survival of Mayan languages has always been a cornerstone of cultural resilience (more on this shortly), but linking language to Classic Maya hieroglyphic texts is another matter altogether. The success of late twentieth-century decipherment by epigraphers was due in large part to the acceptance of a phonetic component to hieroglyphic writing and the acknowledgment that Mayan languages could play a role in aiding decipherment. If knowledge of Mayan languages is critical to decipherment, then it stands to reason that native speakers might have considerable insight about the structure and content of hieroglyphic writing. From the early 1990s, there has been keen interest in ancient Maya writing among descendant populations, particularly in Guatemala, where the University of Texas hieroglyphic conference now takes place every other year in Antigua.[15] In the spirit of Linda Schele (one of the pioneers of the late twentieth-century decipherment), her former student Bruce Love formed a group called MAM, which is devoted to sponsoring workshops in communities across the Maya region in order to provide Indigenous Maya peoples with an opportunity to study and translate hieroglyphics.[16]

Engagement with hieroglyphic writing as well as ethnohistoric texts is a way in which contemporary descendants can reshape the shadow of the ancient Maya— by translating the words of those who wrote before the three-hundred-year "hiatus in Mayan writing and self-representation during colonial and postcolonial periods."[17] This activity facilitates several goals: reclaiming representations of the past, emphasizing the continuity of linguistic forms of expression, and learning the words and texts of distant ancestors. Similar curiosity about ethnic histories perceived as proximate in a genealogical sense fosters a strong interest in Viking archaeology among U.S. college students as well as the trend among Latin American students who attend U.S. universities to choose Latin American studies as their major. There is an added potency and excitement to acquiring knowledge about a past with which you personally identify. Thus, the powerful impact of Juan Canul, a retired Yucatec tour guide who in 2014 spoke a lyrical Yucatec Mayan translation of a hieroglyphic text at Ek' Balam for a group of students from the nearby town of Tahcabo (figure 5.1). Few students had ever visited the site despite the fact that it is located less than thirty-five kilometers from their hometown. There is a cultural fit to these activities that makes such events appear natural and the way that things should always have been.

A similar experience occurred while we were writing the script for *On the Road of Our Ancestors* (Spanish: *En el Camino de Nuestros Ancestros*, Yucatec: *U be'jil k-úuchben k-ch'i'ibalo'ob*), a puppet-performed video. More details about the video are provided in chapters 7 and 9; briefly, the production explores Yucatec cultural

Figure 5.1. Tour guide Juan Canul translates the hieroglyphic text of a mortuary dedication at Ek' Balam to students from Tahcabo, Yucatán, and staff of Proyecto Arqueológico Colaborativo de Oriente de Yucatán (PACOY), June 2014 (photo by author).

heritage through the eyes of two young siblings and their friend. One of our collaborating partners (Tomás Gallareta Negrón) wanted to include an episode that was modeled after glyph classes taught in a small school in Sisbicchen, Yucatán, by the extraordinary teacher, Professor Crisanto Mukul. We commissioned the fabrication of a puppet modeled after the teacher; the puppet-mentary director, Sergio García-Agundis, staged the scene in a local classroom (figure 5.2). The scene appears quite ordinary unless you know that in reality rural schoolchildren rarely have the opportunity to learn Maya history, much less Maya hieroglyphs.

Yadira Vargas employed a similar trope when scripting radio *novelas* for a Petén rural audience. Set in the small, fictional town of San Gerónimo, Petén, episodes included dialogue within a school where a teacher taught Maya history and was able to take students on a field trip to Tikal. In reality, both are rare occurrences. But exposure to such a world, even if it is fictional, changes the dynamic and allows students and adults alike to imagine a different kind of learning.

Making the extraordinary ordinary is the subtext of the emphasis on continuity among Maya cultural activists who speak of Maya revindication, renaissance, and revitalization.[18] For Maya cultural activists, reshaping the shadow of the past is an integral part of reshaping the present and future. From this perspective, the Viking example provided by Hervik takes on new meaning. Danish schoolchildren learn about their Viking heritage in history class and may decide that Vikings

Figure 5.2. Still frame from puppet-mentary on Yucatec Maya cultural heritage, *U be'jil k-úuchen k-ch'i'ibalo'ob*, showing a Maya professor teaching hieroglyphs.

lived a very long time ago and much has changed since then. If similar curriculum existed in the tragically underfunded rural schools where the bulk of Indigenous children learn Eurocentric history rather than Maya history, the discourse on continuity might take a different tack.

Ever since Fredrik Barth wrote about ethnicity and its corollary—ethnic boundaries—anthropologists have been exploring the conditions under which human difference is emphasized or minimalized.[19] When do "we" become an exclusive and bounded group juxtaposed against others? Does a prior condition of inequality, hegemony, or violence need to exist? And how do self-ascribed ethnicities relate to language? As discussed previously, archaeologists and ethnographers have come under fire for deploying terms such as *ancient Maya* and *modern Maya* that intimate the existence of a homogeneous ethnic bloc of self-ascribed Maya people who existed in the past and persist culturally and linguistically into the present.

On the ground, of course, we find that identities are (and probably were in the distant past as well) very local—sometimes restricted to a single community.[20] In an effort to forge consensus, cooperation, and political action on a larger scale, Maya cultural activists in Guatemala emphasize commonalities across the ethnolinguistic boundaries shown on every map of highland Guatemala. Thus, the origins of the so-called pan-Maya movement or Movimiento Maya,[21] which, as Kay Warren writes, was controversial and critiqued from both the left and right ends of the political spectrum.[22]

An assertion of a supraethnic identity that transcends traditionally recognized linguistic and ethnic boundaries—to foment societal change—is dramatically different from the situation in the northern lowlands, where a large bloc of people speaking Yucateko or *maya t'aan* exist and until recently were not vested in the discourse of ethnic continuity or indigeneity. Analysis of Yucatec historical sources by both Matthew Restall and Wolfgang Gabbert led each to argue that there is no historical evidence to suggest that the oppositional framing and self-referential naming that accompanies ethnic identification existed before the nineteenth-century Caste (or Social) War.[23] Given the relentless exploitation of the *maya t'aan*–speaking population up to the Mexican Revolution of the early twentieth century—which came to Yucatán later than other parts of México—this assertion stretches the imagination. That is, it is difficult to imagine that Yucatec Native peoples survived four hundred years of political tumult and subjugation while maintaining their language as well as many cultural practices without adopting a mind-set of ethnic identity. But then again, things are never as they seem in Yucatán, where counterintuitive facts are everyday occurrences.

In Yucatán, ethnic markers have a way of dissolving upon closer scrutiny. For instance, during the nineteenth century Yucateko became a lingua franca and was widely spoken by persons of European heritage.[24] Today, *mestiza* is a term used for a female wearing the traditional dress of a white *huipil* with an elaborately embroidered square neckline.[25] Furthermore, Fernando Armstrong-Fumero notes, "Yucatán is remarkable for the relative lack of grassroots organization based on indigenous identity."[26] The kind of cultural activism that reverberates through the highlands of both Guatemala and Chiapas is rarely encountered in Yucatán; in fact, it is a place where many Native peoples emphatically resist the label *Indigenous*.[27] On the other hand, language revitalization and bilingual schools (Spanish and Yucateko) are actively promoted in Yucatán, where there is a strong sentiment among descendants that language loss is an ongoing and tragic development.

INTANGIBLE HERITAGE AND THE
STRUGGLE FOR LANGUAGE SURVIVAL

As an integral gear of cultural representation, language assumes a privileged position, and rightly so. But regardless of the commanding role of language in expressive culture, human speech is a fragile thing. Types of speech—languages, that is—are dependent on intimate and practically one-on-one modes of transmission. A break in the transmission—usually between mother and child—for just one generation across a population can result in significant language loss. When a language is stigmatized and not a lingua franca (which is the case for most Mayan languages today), then parents are placed in a difficult position. Do they teach a child their native language so that the child can be culturally proficient even though to be successful in school and survive economically a child needs to be bilingual or trilingual?

Fernando Armstrong-Fumero, who spent time learning *maya t'aan* or Yucateko in communities located in the *oriente* of Yucatán, discusses this conundrum within a vernacular context.[28] As he conversed with a local artisan and maize farmer from Pisté, the man referred to the difficulty of "communicating jokes and parables to his younger children [who were not proficient in *maya t'aan*]. He noted that 'the fact that Maya is being lost is very sad. [The children] must learn Spanish to defend themselves, but Maya is also beautiful.'"[29] The artisan spoke in *maya t'aan*, which is reproduced here. The original words are demonstrative of an ongoing controversy within the *maya t'aan* revitalization movement—what to do about the admixture of Spanish in spoken Yucatec:

> Jach tríiste le ku sa'atal le maayajo'. K'abeet u kaanko'ob eespanyol tial u defendert[i] kubao'ob, pero jatsuts le maaya xan.[30]

For this parent, children must learn Spanish to defend themselves, to make their way in a world in which there are significantly fewer opportunities for monolingual speakers. The multiculturalism that is celebrated (officially, at least) in México since the end of the *mestizaje* era has yet to grapple with linguistic plurality.

On the other hand, since the 1960s there has been a sea change throughout the Americas in reference to the linguistic rights of Indigenous peoples, First Nations, Native Americans, *Originales*—whichever self-referential term is preferred. Slowly and with great difficulty, the settler nation-states of the Americas are moving toward pluralism and abandoning the mirage of a monoethnic state. To accept language plurality on a national level is to acknowledge that a wider spectrum of cultural representations—and cultural logics—can be accommodated within the boundary of a nation-state.

Guatemala, in particular, has a painful history of grappling with the plurality of its peoples. Recognition of the many Mayan languages that are spoken within the boundaries of the state is central to creating a truly plural society. In 1986, a governmental entity titled Academia de las Lenguas Maya de Guatemala (ALMG) was established to codify the writing of Mayan languages (previously the domain of missionaries and a few linguists).[31] In 1996, Demetrio Cojtí Cuxil urged the Guatemalan government to fulfill its commitment to fund ALMG and outlined linguistic "demands of the nations of the Maya People."[32] These included "emergency programs to rescue linguistic communities in danger of extinction" as well as "the development and use of Mayan languages in education," public affairs, courts of justice, and mass media.[33] These demands for greater inclusivity and self-representation through the vehicle of language revitalization have been acknowledged partially at best by the Guatemalan state.[34]

A significant term used above by Demetrio Cojtí Cuxil is "the nations of the Maya People," which constructs a similarity between the First Nations of Canada or the Indian Nations of the United States and the twenty-three ethnolinguistic communities identified by Cojtí Cuxil for Guatemala.[35] At the heart of the matter, the crisis of representation is one of political sovereignty. Within the highlands of both Guatemala and Chiapas, where ethnic identity is more polarized and geographically defined than in parts of Yucatán,[36] a model of nationalism is conceivable, albeit not based on treaty diplomacy or an internal mechanism of recognition, such as exists within the U.S. Bureau of Indian Affairs.

Recent scholarship by a younger generation of Guatemalan Maya intellectuals who came of age during the civil war—such as Emilio del Valle Escalante—opt for the term *Maya nationalisms* (over earlier pan-Maya constructs) to refer to "how indigenous intellectuals are not only reimagining Guatemala but also developing proposals and political strategies to reconstruct the nation within and outside the indigenous movement. . . . I consider it important not only to analyze the relation between those who defy Maya nationalist proposals but also to consider the nationalist contradictions within the indigenous movement itself."[37] In a postcolonial world of plurality and contradiction, cultural heritage—both tangible and intangible—is powerfully instrumental. Because it is capable of both forging unity and creating fragmentation, cultural heritage resides perennially in a powerful and equivocal place.

Such is the case for language and cultural practice, which convey vividly what Armstrong-Fumero calls "vernacular multiculturalism."[38] For the cultural heritage initiatives discussed in chapters 7 through 9, we were particularly sensitized to the intersection of vernacular multiculturalism with the tangible heritage of archaeological sites. Since most of our educational programs focused on children in grade 4 or higher, we decided to create coloring books for younger children that would include cultural practices, local archaeological sites, and short passages in local Mayan languages as well as a lingua franca (Spanish or English). We worked with ALMG linguists to create Mayan language translations for three of the four different coloring books (figure 5.3). This project is discussed in greater detail in chapters 7, but I mention it here because of the way in which the project sensitized us to vernacular multiculturalism. Initially, we thought that we could use a stock set of images of cultural practices and change out the archaeological sites and language captions for each of the four versions, but of course dress and cultural practices among Ch'orti' people in Honduras look very different from those of Yucatán. Only a few pages could be used in more than one coloring book. The books and the accompanying heritage programs highlighted significant local variation in perceptions of the past and ideas about the uses to which the past could be put.

Figure 5.3. Page from a coloring book with text in Q'eqchi' and Spanish that was distributed by the Maya Area Cultural Heritage Initiative (MACHI) within the Petén Department of Guatemala.

Lajeek'aal rox oq'ob'eb' re ula'eb' re chijunli ch'ol re ruchich'och' nakechalk sa' Watemaal re chi rilb'aal li ochochil tusb'il pek ut rochochil li xe'jolominkre li najter tenamit li xexb'anu qaxe' qaton. lRuk'in li nab'aal qaq'etq'etil kak'uteb' chi ru qaoxloq'il na'leb' li ula'eb'l

Miles de visitantes de todas partes del mundo vienen a Guatemala a ver los templos y palacios que construyeron nuestros antepasados. ¡Con mucho orgullo les mostramos nuestra cultura a los visitantes!

24

WAYS AND MEANS OF DEPLOYING THE PAST

In the region we are considering, the shadow of the "ancient Maya" often seems both distant and proximate, a shadow that is barely observable at one moment and looming large the next. Formerly, the shape of the shadow changed as archaeologists revised narratives about the past on the basis of new evidence and new theoretical bents. But increasingly, the shadow is reshaping in reference to the struggles of local peoples who exercise agency in order to secure greater self-determination within nation-states and globally. Here we examine this politics of the past with special reference to the following movements: (a) the discourse of sacred sites within Guatemala and the Ch'orti' area of western Honduras; (b) the invocation of ancestors to secure land rights among Q'eqchi and Mopan peoples in southern Belize; (c) calling to ancestors and Mexican revolutionary heroes in highland Chiapas in the struggle for a more secure livelihood; and (d) invocation of "postpeasant"[39] heritage rights in reference to the lucrative tourist zone of Chichén Itzá. In each area, the past is deployed in distinctive ways. People who have lived for centuries, if not millennia, on top of and around remains of the "old Maya" differentially perceive their value and relevance in relation to the challenges of a postcolonial world.

A salient feature of the postcolonial world includes a sea change in identity, both self-referential as well as academically ascribed. For example, the homogenizing term *peasant* is rarely uttered or written by anthropologists today in contrast to its use in just about every ethnographic study conducted in México between the Mexican Revolution and the late 1970s. Today, ethnographic studies of rural communities stress the ethnolinguistic identity of those living in a place with a history. Likewise, the more self-referential but similarly homogenizing term *campesino* holds less appeal today for farmers in México, who are more likely to refer to themselves as *ejidaterios* (vested members of an agricultural cooperative) in a given town. The luster of gross, class-based social categories has dulled. The decay process arguably was accelerated by assimilationist models for dealing with "the Indian problem," which proved both ineffective and harmful.

The "postpeasant" world is one of fine-grained identities that are grounded in place and arced in time to both distant and not-so-distant pasts. There is an active shaping of the past in reference to the present and future. Armstrong-Fumero addresses the complications of the transition from a peasant to a post-peasant reality in Yucatán, where schoolchildren learn of the liberating activities of the Mexican revolutionary heroes in ways that blur "the boundaries between struggles based on class and ethnicity to such a point that it becomes difficult to distinguish claims made for indigenous rights from those of a more general Mexican nation."[40]

In nations to the south of México, there have been no revolutions of similar scope or with an impact that led to significant rebalancing of access to land. The 1960–1996 civil war in Guatemala can be characterized as a class-based insurgency, and the impact on Indigenous peoples—especially in terms of the death toll—was devastating. Unfortunately, a national referendum held in 1999 that would have led to sweeping changes somewhat analogous to the aftermath of the Mexican Revolution did not pass. Presently, societal change within Guatemala tracks opportunities afforded through the pathway of human and Indigenous rights discourse rather than a class-based discourse.

Sacred Places Seen and Unseen

Chip Colwell-Chanthaphonh and T. J. Ferguson write that Indigenous peoples possess "more complex and compelling interests" in reference to the past than do other communities, including the archaeological community.[41] In Guatemala and western Honduras, this compelling interest is expressed in the idiom of sacred sites, which include both natural and constructed places. Sacred sites are linked to contemporary Mayan peoples by virtue of a multifaceted connection that is akin to a covenant. The right to pray, to conduct healing ceremonies, to make offerings and construct fire hearths at sacred sites are rights accorded Mayan peoples by the 1996 peace accords. In the central plazas of once-powerful ancestral places such as Kaminaljuyu, Iximché, or Tikal, smoldering fire hearths attended by one or more spiritual healers are invariant features (figure 5.4). Archaeologists have always acknowledged that such places were powerful and sacred in the past and

Figure 5.4. Tikal, view of modern fire pit in central plaza with Temple 1 in background (photo by author).

have worked for over a hundred years to understand how that power and sacrality were constructed. But to perceive the old places as powerful and sacred today is another matter. Yet this is exactly how the meaning of such places is being actively reshaped through contemporary ritual practice that might be understood as a "politics of recognition" according to Nancy Fraser.[42]

In 2002, the Guatemalan minister of culture Otilia Lux de Cotí issued a decree that spiritual guides and their followers were free to enter (with no restrictions or fees) sacred sites under the jurisdiction of the Ministry of Culture.[43] The decree defines sacred sites as "those spaces—monuments, parks, complexes or archaeological centers—[that are] considered [a] source of cosmic energy, life and knowledge, for the spiritual communication with the Superior Being or Ajaw and its cohabitation with nature, for strengthening and linking the present with the past and the future."[44]

In 2010, on behalf of the activist organization Oxlajuj Ajpop, Felipe Gomez summarized the stalled progress on a proposed national sacred sites law.[45] The proposed law was envisioned to act as a legal incentive to "create jurisprudence in other areas rooted in Mayan identity, such as education, health and justice."[46] Under the proposed law, sacred sites would be administered by the Ministry of Culture along with the National Council of Sacred Sites. Furthermore, a Council of Principals would be formed, which together with the Ministry of Culture would "form the highest authority of the National Council of Sacred Sites."[47] Of the fifty-two representatives serving on the Council of Principals, twenty-four would come from "each of the linguistic communities of Maya, Garifuna and Xinca origin, and 28 representatives [would be] appointed in proportion to the size of each linguistic community."[48] Resistance to the proposed law has delayed its passage, but it's not difficult to envision how the presence of a Council of Principals might reshape not only the shadow of the past but the current and future practice of archaeological research.

In small communities (locally called *aldeas*) of western Honduras, Ch'orti' Maya peoples also employ a sacred/ancestral site discourse in reference to the World Heritage Site of Copán. Elsewhere, Shoshaunna Parks and I have discussed the complexities of this "heritage-scape"[49] in reference to Indigenous identity and heritage programs that our collaborating organization created for primary schools of the *aldeas*.[50] Honduran Ch'orti' peoples live proximate to the Guatemalan border and to the larger Ch'orti' population that resides on the other side of the national boundary. Although ethnographic analogies between Ch'orti' cultural practices and the deep history of Copán pervade archaeological narratives of Copán[51] and recent epigraphic studies point toward the endangered Ch'orti' language as the closest relative of the Classic court language in which the hieroglyphs were written,[52] access to Copán for Ch'orti' peoples has been a hard-fought battle. Repeated strikes at the entrance to Copán mobilized by an Indigenous organization (Consejo Nacional de Indígenas Maya Ch'orti' Honduras) and demands for land reform led to government concessions but rarely with follow-through.[53]

Darío Euraque has critiqued the Mayanization of Honduran identity (created mostly for the purpose of tourism) and the unwillingness of the state to grapple with true ethnic plurality,[54] but Ch'orti' peoples are still struggling for rights accorded over a decade ago to their cousins across the border.

Imagining Autonomy

In 1994, many were shocked when the implementation of the North American Free Trade Agreement (NAFTA, which created a free-trade zone among Canada, the United States, and México) sparked an insurgency in the highlands of Chiapas. Masked, self-styled Zapatistas (many of whom were local Indigenous peoples who spoke highland Chiapas Mayan languages such as Tzeltal, Tzotzil, and others) were coordinated by a non-Indigenous person, also masked, called *Subcomandante* Marcos. Although recognition and self-determination loomed large in the communiqués issued by Ejército Zapatista de Liberación Nacional (EZLN, Zapatista Army of National Liberation), their goals and methods differed and continue to differ remarkably from those of cultural activists in the highlands of Guatemala.

Embracing the class struggle and liberation discourse of heroes of the Mexican Revolution such as Emiliano Zapata, Zapatistas reminded those who now "rule" the republic of México that there is much unfinished work left to do. Owners of large estates in Chiapas, much like Yucatán, managed to avoid or delay many of the postrevolutionary land reforms that rebalanced access to resources in other regions of México.[55] The shadow of the Mexican Revolution—and its long-term impact on the redistribution of resources to the underclass—loomed large on the agenda of Zapatistas and was linked successfully to ethnopolitics.[56] As Gary Gossen observes, the well-publicized communiqués issued by the EZLN featured a similar innovative fusion of poetic elements characteristic of Maya oration melded with the romanticism of Western-style revolutionary rhetoric. Consider this passage that was translated by Ronald Nigh:

> When the EZLN was only a shadow, creeping through the mist and darkness of the jungle, when the words "justice," "liberty" and democracy" were only that: words; barely a dream that the elders of our communities, true guardians of the words of our dead ancestors, had given us in the moment when day gives way to night, when hatred and fear began to grow in our hearts, when there was nothing but desperation; when the times repeated themselves, with no way out, with no door, no tomorrow, when all was injustice, as it was, the true men spoke, the faceless ones, the ones who go by night, the ones who are in the jungle. . . . Another word came from afar so that this government was named and this work gave the name "democracy" to our way that was from before words traveled.[57]

At the decisive 1996 National Indigenous Forum in San Cristóbal, Chiapas, demands for cultural autonomy were laid out:[58]

We are not asking anyone to grant us autonomy. We have always had it and we have it today. No one can "give" us the capacity to be ourselves, to think and act in ways that are governed by our own way of looking at the world. However, we have not been free, either during the Spanish colonial regime or under the post-Independence Mexican states, to exercise freely our separate identity as a people. Throughout our long struggle of resistance, we have always been obliged to express our identity against a repressive backdrop of Mexican state representatives and Mexican state institutions.

Basta! We have had enough of this.

As a result of the forum and in order to move toward a peace accord with the Zapatistas, in 1996 the Mexican government agreed to a number of reforms, including (a) greater political autonomy and representation for Mexico's Indigenous peoples and (b) the right to a multicultural education taught in an Indigenous language.[59] In terms of the struggles of Indigenous peoples for revitalization of Native languages and greater self-determination, Zapatistas achieved a victory, even though funding of the proposed reforms was not included in the peace accord. Real change in the distribution of landholdings has been equally elusive.

A discourse of sacred sites did not feature prominently in the communiqués of the Zapatistas, although prominent landscape features do figure prominently in twentieth-century ethnographic studies conducted in the highlands of Chiapas.[60] A conflict over the disposition of a Classic Maya carved-stone monument from El Cayo did arise in 1997, when archaeologists Peter Mathews and Mario Aliphat attempted to move the monument—under a directive from the Instituto Nacional de Antropología e Historia (INAH) and with prior community support—to a secure location where it would not be endangered by looting.[61] Claiming autonomous rule, a large group of men arrived at the site and insisted that the monument be buried in place under concrete. After a life-threatening ordeal, the archaeologists escaped. Later, the local Lacandon Maya community issued a statement labeling the group of men invasive bandits.[62]

In the 1990s, Chiapas was a tumultuous place, trying to accommodate a large refugee population from the Guatemalan civil war as well as Zapatista insurgents (some of whom were one and the same). While the ordeal of the archaeological party should not be trivialized, the incident proves revealing on several levels. First, the manner in which the group of men invoked a discourse of autonomy only one year after the Indigenous Forum held in San Cristóbal; second, the demand that the monument be sealed under concrete rather than transported away from El Cayo; and third, the response of the Lacandon community—decrying the lawlessness of the area and largely supporting the archaeologists. In a later interview, Peter Mathews summarized his thoughts on the ordeal: "I think the incident was 90 percent banditry and 10 percent patriotism. They did not want to give up their artifacts."[63]

Reasserting autonomy and the right to determine the disposition of sacred spaces and charged objects from the past (such as El Cayo Altar 4) is distinct from asserting *continued* autonomy and management of sacred places, which is closer to the perspective voiced by Lacandon Maya with whom archaeologist Joel Palka has worked.[64] Long inhabiting the interstices between colonially and then state-controlled spaces, Lacandon Maya peoples continued to ritually use classic Maya sites—such as Palenque and Yaxchilan, which are located in Chiapas near the Usumacinta River—until the late twentieth century. Then "the presence of guards and tourists" became overbearing, and religious artifacts left at the old places "were broken or taken by outsiders."[65] Today, the ritual landscape of Lacandon peoples is focused on the more remote Sierra Lacandon, although the Southern Lacandon control tourist access to the sites of Bonampak and Lacanja through claims of ancestry.[66]

Land with "No Marketable Title"

Southern Belize is not densely populated; about fourteen thousand people— mostly Q'eqchi' and Mopan Maya—inhabit the land between the Maya Mountains and the Caribbean Sea.[67] Early Spanish accounts describe a population of Manché Chol whose numbers dwindled catastrophically through the colonial period. During the nineteenth century, communities such as Pueblo Viejo and San Antonio were established by Q'eqchi' and Mopan peoples who were pushed off their traditional-use lands by the development of coffee *fincas* in the nascent state of Guatemala. Offered few alternatives other than entering into a debt-peonage relationship with *finca* owners, many moved their families east, where land remained available.[68]

During the second half of the nineteenth century, the British Empire extended colonial power south of the Sibun River (which is located in the central part of Belize) and brought what is now the Toledo District of southern Belize under the administrative jurisdiction of British Honduras. This southern area had never been colonized by Spanish settlers, so colonial officials forged an uneasy truce with the inhabitants so that British logging concessions might be granted and safely worked. Joel Wainwright cites an 1868 dispatch from colonial Lieutenant Governor Longden, which states that "the villages and a sufficient surrounding space should be reserved in the hands of the Crown for the use of the Indians—no marketable titles being issued to them to enable them to dispose of such lands— but the land being divided amongst them."[69]

Thus, the Indian Reserve Lands came into existence and survive—in the Toledo District—until this day. Set-aside lands would seem to be a good thing except that, without title, the crown and now the state are free to lease or sell sections of the reserve lands. This began to happen with increasing frequency in the latter third of the twentieth century—timber and oil exploration leases and the outright sale of land tracts. Currently, a latticework of private leases and purchases subdivides the large tracts of reserve lands.[70] During the 1990s, local Q'eqchi' and Mopan peoples organized resistance to this land encroachment through peaceful marches and petitions to the government. In response to these requests, Toledo

Maya peoples were increasingly characterized nationally as not native to Belize (many have close relatives who live in Guatemala, and the international border between Guatemala and Belize has yet to be agreed upon by both sides). In effect, the government of Belize challenged the assertion that "we have always been here" as a legitimate defense of Indigenous land rights. Recourse to distant ancestors—to justify claims to the Indian Reserve Lands—fell on deaf ears.

A group from the Geography Department of the University of California, Berkeley, sought to employ Indigenous countermapping (in the tradition of Edward Said[71]) in order to solidify the land claims of Toledo peoples, thus turning the tables on the usual modus operandi in which cartographic projections engender and justify colonial usurpation of land. Completed in 1997, the *Maya Atlas* was a collaborative project among geographers from the University of California, Berkeley; the Toledo Maya Cultural Council; the Toledo Alcaldes Association; Maya Mapping Project administrators and coordinators; and a community researcher from each village in Toledo.[72] The handsome, colorful publication details the resources and use areas of each community within the "Maya Homeland," a term used in the *Maya Atlas* in conjunction with a vernacular drawing of a classic Maya temple (figure 5.5). Unfortunately, the massive effort expended on making the atlas "failed to shift the political terrain in the struggle for Maya land rights."[73] Within a year of its publication, the primary leader of the movement—Julian Cho—died under mysterious circumstances in December of 1998.

Figure 5.5. The *Maya Atlas* (p. 7) in which a Maya homeland is discussed and juxtaposed with a vernacular drawing of a precolonial pyramidal shrine.

The movement lives on through the efforts of Cho's sister-in-law—Cristina Coc.[74] During the making of the *Maya Atlas*, the Indian Law Resource Center in Helena, Montana, was asked "to file a lawsuit challenging the government's right to grant concessions on our land, and to assist in gaining legal security for our ancestral land."[75] Although litigation has been punctuated by repeated victories for the people of Toledo, appeals filed by the government of Belize managed to forestall official recognition of land rights, including the right of villages to hold communal land title. On April 22, 2015, the court of last resort—the Caribbean Court of Justice—ruled against an appeal filed by the government of Belize and in favor of the land rights of Toledo Maya peoples.[76]

For people of the Toledo District—the poorest district in Belize—cultural and linguistic rights are not front-burner issues. Children generally grow up in Q'eqchi'- or Mopan-speaking households and learn English in school or through interactions outside the community. Although many local persons comment on the loss of traditional cultural practices (see chapter 8), the Deer Dance is still the performance de rigueur for any truly significant occasion (such as the legal victory in land rights litigation that was celebrated on June 28, 2010). It is land usurpation—a process repeated throughout the Americas since the sixteenth century—against which Toledo Maya people are trying to hold the line. Constructing a "Maya Homeland" by reference to their cultural heritage as pyramid builders is a way in which Indigenous peoples of the Toledo District reshape and lay claim to the shadow of the ancient Maya.

Chichén Itzá as *Nohoch Kiuic*

The struggle for land rights is a driving force of Indigenous movements worldwide and often is accompanied by calls for political autonomy, self-determination, and language revitalization. Unfortunately, the struggle for land practically defines *Indigenous*, and the litigation pursued by Toledo Maya peoples in Belize provides a relevant case in point. In México, many would contend that the perceived success of the revolution was due, in large part, to the follow-up creation of the *ejido* system (lands deeded and held cooperatively), which alleviated the problem of the "landless peasant." But what of those who live in a postpeasant world and make their living crafting or selling objects for the tourist trade or performing custodial work at archaeological sites that have been groomed for tourism?

Perhaps the first anthropologist to take seriously the manner in which artisans and vendors of Chichén Itzá make use of the past was Quetzil Castañeda, who discovered that the lived experience of Yucatec peoples in Pisté (a town close to Chichén Itzá) had radically transformed since the days of the storied ethnographic accounts of Robert Redfield and Alfonso Villa Rojas.[77] Economic pursuits and power struggles were focused around opportunities afforded by tourism at Chichén Itzá. Employing a Foucauldian lens, Castañeda toured us through the panopticon[78] of the *nohoch kiuic* (Yucateko for "giant marketplace") that Chichén Itzá has become.

During the second half of the twentieth century, the number of vendors selling local and not-so-local crafted items in and around Chichén Itzá grew dramatically until it reached crisis proportions in the 1980s.[79] The flood of vendors was a problem to be solved by federal and state authorities in conjunction with the Barbachano family, who until 2010 owned the ground on which Chichén Itzá is located. Various methods and new spaces were conceived to control the flow and number of vendors but to little avail. The vendors and many of the artisans are of local Maya ancestry and "have asserted their rights to sites of sale in the ruins of Chichén Itzá as descendants of its ancient builders."[80] As recently as the summer of 2014, vendors remained locked in a hostile and conflictive relationship with the State of Yucatán (the post-Barbachano owner of the site) over rights to vend artisan crafts within the site boundaries.

Site guards (who are unionized and employees of the INAH) likewise safeguard their position as gatekeepers and controllers of the flow of traffic within Chichén Itzá (and other archaeological sites in Yucatán) by invoking a patrimonial discourse that emphasizes site conservation.[81] I once visited Chichén Itzá shortly after world-renowned opera singer Luciano Pavarotti performed there and was treated to a long lecture by a second-generation site guard who heartily disapproved of the impact of holding large music concerts within the archaeological site.[82]

Unlike Guatemala or Honduras, site guards, artisans, and vendors were not invoking a sacred-site discourse in reference to this World Heritage Site, but they do assert custodial and economic-transactional rights to the space based on ancestry. These rights are not those generally associated with Indigenous issues.[83] Representatives of the State of Yucatán have gone on record characterizing the handicrafts market at Chichén Itzá as a "quintessentially inauthentic cultural phenomenon."[84] In reference to this cauldron of vernacular heritage politics, Armstrong-Fumero notes that this struggle between local vendors and the State of Yucatán deviates in an important way from a discourse of multivocality that situates "the creation of 'inclusive' heritage practice primarily in the democratization of the right to tell stories about the past, saying little about other kinds of activities with which people may have interacted with ancient objects."[85] In other words, crafting and selling objects that are inspired by past artisans can be labeled "inauthentic" precisely because the crafter does not invoke a sacred-sites discourse or provide alternative narratives about the past. Once again, the Original peoples of Yucatán give us a glimpse of the complexity of agency in a postcolonial world.

A MULTIPLICITY OF MAYAN VOICES

If we set aside the discourse-centered aspect of multivocality for the moment and simply focus on voices and dialogue, we hear in this chapter the "multiplicity of

Mayan voices" to which Jakaltek Maya intellectual Victor Montejo refers.[86] For Montejo, engaging with the shadow of the ancient Maya serves "not to embellish ourselves with a romantic past or to wrap ourselves in ancient Mayan garb but to revitalize our Mayan identity and weave back in the sections worn away by centuries of neglect."[87] From Montejo's perspective, to assert continuity is not to assume a uniform continuity of Maya lived experiences but rather to provide a wellspring of pride, strength, and resilience in the face of those who "continue to insist that what we have or what we are is not Mayan."[88]

First and foremost, the words of Victor Montejo invite inclusivity and dissuade the kind of stereotyping that historically has denigrated Maya identities. Earlier in this chapter, I brought up the topic of a monolithic Maya and discussed a critique of *National Geographic* magazine as well as of archaeologists and ethnographers who stand accused of portraying Indigenous Maya peoples as timeless and plugged into the past in a seamless fashion. I hope this chapter has demonstrated that, on the contrary, Maya peoples draw upon their deep history in many different ways—using different means—although often for similar reasons: to fortify their struggle to survive and to leave their children a better world in which to reside. In this struggle, touchstones that *National Geographic* and archaeologists find so compelling—pyramidal temple shrines and hieroglyphic texts, for instance—can also be used to emphasize Indigenous self-determination and longevity of inhabitation.

We could think of this past as a blessing and burden of the ancestors. It's a blessing because who wouldn't mind having an ancestry that is celebrated globally as an extraordinary contribution to human history? It's a burden because every action, cultural practice, and statement uttered by someone who self-identifies as Maya invites comparison with a past that is always present. Walter Little has written about the burden of heritage tourism in Guatemala, which rests particularly heavily on females who are entangled in the gendered production and sale of textiles.[89] Touristic schemes such as La Ruta Maya or Mundo Maya promise prosperity for all but inevitably reward international travel agencies, bus companies, and hotel chains disproportionately. Decoupling a celebration of Maya cultural heritage from heritage tourism as a development strategy would alleviate some of the burden and permit the conceptualization of other kinds of activities and livelihoods that while in dialogue (or not) with the legacy of the ancient Maya would not be confined by it.[90] In order to explore this uncharted terrain in greater depth, the heritage programs envisioned and collaboratively implemented here were decoupled from heritage tourism and focused instead on education and a celebration of local cultural expression.

In the next chapter, we turn to partnerships between archaeologists and communities that bridged heritage and archaeology. These efforts generally are decoupled from tourism and focus on dialogue and process rather than tourism as a development product.

NOTES

1. Raxche' (1996:7).
2. See Logan (2009), among others.
3. See Cojtí Cuxil (1996:19–50) for expanded treatment of the human rights and territorial, political, jurisdictional, and linguistic demands of ethnic revindication from the perspective of an active participant in the Guatemalan Movimiento Maya.
4. Fischer (1996:64).
5. For instance, see Hervik (1999).
6. See Bourdieu (1977:164–66).
7. Stephen Houston and Takeshi Inomata (2009:45) refer to the presence of a court language that is distinct from that spoken by the populace as "diglossia"; for more on Classic Maya court language, see Law et al. (2009).
8. Hervik (1998).
9. Hervik (1998:167–68).
10. Hervik (1998:168).
11. For more on *National Geographic*'s representation of Indigenous peoples, see Gero and Root (1990) and Lutz and Collins (1993).
12. Arguably, Evon Vogt set the stage for this approach with his 1964 publication promoting "The Genetic Model and Maya Cultural Development."
13. Warren (1996:101); see also Borgstede and Yaeger (2008:105).
14. Warren (1996:98).
15. For more on this topic, see Sturm (1996); Schele and Grube (1996); and www.utmesoamerica.org/maya/ for the University of Texas Maya Meetings organized by David Stuart and held biennially at Casa Herrerra in Antigua, Guatemala.
16. MAM maintains an active website at http://discovermam.org/.
17. Montejo (2002:131).
18. For more on this topic, see Parks and McAnany (2007).
19. Barth (1969).
20. See Borgstede and Yaeger (2008:96) for further coverage of this topic. Here I provide an excerpt from their discussion of continuity and identity, which contains useful references: "Even those who speak *Maya t'aan* [Yucatec] do not use the term self-referentially (Gabbert 2004; Schackt 2001). Instead, the community most often forms the basis of self-identification, with more extensive and inclusive identities built around community (e.g., Fischer 2001; Hervik 2003). As with many concepts, the importance of community identification has been variously interpreted as pre-Conquest (Hill and Monaghan 1987), a consequence of the Conquest (Wolf 1957), or a syncretic combination of the two (Farriss 1984)."
21. Bastos and Camus (2004).
22. Warren (1998).
23. Gabbert (2004); Restall (2004).
24. Gabbert (2004:95).
25. Armstrong-Fumero (2013:7).
26. Armstrong-Fumero (2013:11).
27. Castañeda (2004:38); also personal communication, July 2013, with Ivan Batun Alpuche, whose disdain for the term *Indigenous* is linked to its closeness to the pejorative term *indio*. He prefers *Native* or *Original inhabitant*.

28. Armstrong-Fumero (2013:7).
29. Armstrong-Fumero (2013:153–54).
30. Armstrong-Fumero (2013:154).
31. Cojtí Cuxil (1996:36).
32. Cojtí Cuxil (1996:29–39).
33. Cojtí Cuxil (1996:36–38).
34. For more on language revitalization, particularly in Guatemala, see Bastos and Camus (2004), England (1996), and Maxwell (1996), among others.
35. Cojtí Cuxil (1996:36).
36. See Castañeda (2004:52) for further discussion of ethnic polarity.
37. Valle Escalante (2009:6–7).
38. Armstrong-Fumero (2011:69).
39. Armstrong-Fumero (2013:114).
40. Armstrong-Fumero (2013:98).
41. Colwell-Chanthaphonh and Ferguson (2008:8).
42. Fraser (1996).
43. Ivic de Monterroso (2004:304).
44. Ivic de Monterroso (2004:304–5).
45. Gomez (2010).
46. Gomez (2010:27).
47. Gomez (2010:29).
48. Gomez (2010:29).
49. See Di Giovine (2009).
50. McAnany and Parks (2012).
51. Maca (2009).
52. Law et al. (2009).
53. See Mortensen (2009); also McAnany and Parks (2012: 81–84).
54. Euraque (1998).
55. Nigh (1994:12).
56. Lynn Stephen (2002) notes that the Zapatistas distinctively managed a synergism between the class-based agenda of the Mexican Revolution and the ethnopolitics of more recent times.
57. Nigh (1994:12); translation cited by Gossen (1996:532–33).
58. Translation by Gossen (1996:530).
59. Gossen (1996:530).
60. For instance, see Vogt (1976), among others.
61. Hoopes (1997).
62. Hoopes (1997).
63. www.mayaexploration.org/pdf/interview_mathews_elcayo.pdf.
64. Palka (2005).
65. Palka (2005:273).
66. Joel W. Palka, personal communication, August 15, 2014.
67. Toledo Maya Cultural Council (1997:14).
68. Wainwright (2008:44).
69. Wainwright (2008:51).
70. Wainwright (2008:fig. 5.4).
71. Said (1996:27–28).

72. Toledo Maya Cultural Council (1997:1).

73. Wainwright (2008: 250).

74. See a short biography of Cristina Coc in McAnany (2010:166–67).

75. Toledo Maya Cultural Council (1997:1).

76. https://law.arizona.edu/iplp-wins-landmark-human-rights-case-belize.

77. Castañeda (1996).

78. Popularized within the social sciences by Michel Foucault's sociohistorical analysis of the late eighteenth-century design of large prison buildings, a panopticon is a structure engineered to observe the movements and behaviors of inhabitants without being observed oneself. See Foucault (1979).

79. Castañeda (1996:232–34).

80. Armstrong-Fumero (2013:3).

81. For more on patrimonial discourse among INAH site guards at Chichén Itzá, see Breglia (2005, 2006).

82. Under the tenure of the State of Yucatán, the number and frequency of large music concerts at Chichén Itzá has increased.

83. Armstrong-Fumero (2013:148).

84. Armstrong-Fumero (2013:172).

85. Armstrong-Fumero (2011:74).

86. Montejo (2002).

87. Montejo (2002:129).

88. Montejo (2002:130–31).

89. Little (2008); see also Ardren (2004).

90. For an excellent example of the burden of performing cultural heritage, see Taylor (2014) for a discussion of heritage tourism as the propagation of "otherness" at Ek' Balam.

PART II

Connecting with Communities around Heritage Issues

This section moves from background and theory to tackle on-the-ground implementation of more inclusive and participatory modes of understanding the past. In chapter 6, bridges between archaeology and community—especially Indigenous communities—are reviewed. Community archaeology, as one of the most codified methods within the discipline of archaeology, receives particular attention. How partnerships can be forged around heritage issues also is examined.

In chapter 7, the Maya Area Cultural Heritage Initiative (MACHI) is introduced, and the circumstances under which it came into being are presented. Each of the programs operationalized within this multisited initiative are discussed, as well as the local, collaborative partners who worked to make the programs happen. The transition of MACHI into InHerit: Indigenous Heritage Passed to Present is discussed within the framework of expanding the geographical scope of heritage programs.

6

⤚⤙

Bridges to Community Partnerships

I bet that we're the first Caddos in a thousand years to see these objects.

—spoken by Bobby Gonzalez to Dorothy Lippert[1]

As an archaeologist who is a member of the Choctaw Nation, Dorothy Lippert describes her position at the National Museum of Natural History in Washington, DC, as working to build "a bridge to cross a thousand years."[2] That's heavy lifting and made all the more so by the complex relationship between Native Americans and their past as curated by the U.S. government. For Lippert, the act of hosting a consultation in which Caddo descendants enter a collections facility in order to see objects crafted by their ancestors opens a path between the present and the past—"a chance to narrow this gap."[3] The gap that Lippert refers to separates archaeologists (who value objects for their scientific and interpretive value) from the heritage value ascribed to things by descendants. Lippert suggests that if archaeologists can acknowledge that things of the past possess different kinds of value to different people, we will be on our way to repairing the "bridge between the past and present."[4] For Lippert, the polyvalence of artifacts can help to bridge the arc of time and reestablish links between people and their past while also forging a rapprochement or reconciliation between archaeologists and descendant communities.

Let's consider this proposition in light of the busy intersection of cultural heritage interests introduced in chapter 1. Envision a rotary in which many roads converge and for a while, vehicles run parallel. But running parallel does not change the fact that those traveling along convergent roadways come from very different perspectives and generally value the past for different purposes. If I am a genetic, cultural, or ideological descendant, then I likely will value objects from a related past differently than if I am a tourist seeking to experience a place or an object from the past or an archaeologist seeking to interpret the significance of objects in order to create a historical narrative. These constituencies of the past, if we can call them that, share in common only their interest in the past and little else. Bridges of communication, collaboration, and trust need to be constructed, especially with constituencies who have not had a voice in creating the past even though their ancestors may have lived it. This bridge, precarious because it is still under construction and never a fait accompli, is the connective arc between archaeologists and communities that have a vested interest in tangible heritage.

Shaky bridges and community partnerships form the grist of this chapter, which takes us into the realm of people, place, archaeology, and heritage. First, we consider broadly the topic of community archaeology (an enterprise that specializes in shaky bridges) and then applications of community archaeology and other kinds of heritage-related endeavors with local groups within the Maya region. In the chapter to follow, I introduce the communities and organizations with which we worked to build bridges and develop cultural heritage programs through an organization called the Maya Area Cultural Heritage Initiative (MACHI), which later transformed into InHerit: Indigenous Heritage Passed to Present. Community voices responding to these heritage programs form the substance of chapters 8 and 9.

THE CONNECTIVE ARC BETWEEN
ARCHAEOLOGY AND COMMUNITY

Within the field of archaeology, there is growing recognition that the study of the things of the past cannot be decontextualized from contemporary society. In large part due to their alterity, foreign landscapes—conjured by archaeologists and historians alike—hold allure for many interested groups (thus the metaphor of a busy intersection). The past provides a wellspring of identity for descendants and, for better or for worse, for nation-states. The past is a source of fascination for tourists as well as collectors of illegally excavated antiquities. Its resonance with a variety of constituencies indicates that the past is actively present among us.[5] Related issues of rights, responsibilities, and accountabilities are seated within a larger historical and political milieu that we ignore at our own risk. In chapter 4, we considered whether access to one's cultural heritage is a basic human right. In this chapter, we move to more pragmatic concerns in order to consider how and why archaeologists might seek common ground with communities around the topic of heritage archaeology.

Archaeologist Yvonne Marshall suggests that community archaeology represents a fourth kind of archaeology—beyond the nationalist, imperialist, and colonialist archaeologies discussed by Bruce Trigger.[6] Multivocality, a concept introduced in chapter 4, forms the nucleus of community archaeology in which "at every step in a project at least partial control remains with the community."[7] Although a daunting thought to many archaeologists, decentralization of authority has become the litmus test of whether or not community archaeology is actually happening.[8] The subtitle of the recent book by Sonya Atalay draws upon an earlier codification by George Nicholas and colleagues of the equal-partnership approach as "research with, by, and for Indigenous and local communities."[9]

We can track the emergence and maturation of community-based archaeology and its cousin "public archaeology" to the early 1990s. Across the world, there is tremendous variation in this mode of research due to the legal apparatus of different nation-states, ethnic relations, affinities with heritage, and the perceived urgency of attending to heritage issues involving architecture, ecology, or other kinds of heritage altogether. We examine key publications that are relevant to our main concern: building bridges between archaeologists and communities in the Maya region.

In 2000, three archaeologists (Kurt Dongoske, Mark Aldenderfer, and Karen Doehner) working under the auspices of the Society for American Archaeology (SAA) gathered together articles and commentaries on community archaeology that had appeared in the *SAA Newsletter* or the *SAA Archaeological Record*. Titled *Working Together: Native Americans and Archaeologists*,[10] the collection featured primarily U.S. projects but did include a few contributions from beyond U.S. borders. An article by archaeologist Elizabeth Brumfiel presented work with the basin of México community of Xaltocan that aimed to produce a history at a place that during pre-Columbian times had very complicated political relations with the Aztec Empire.[11] This article highlighted the political complications and potential compromises entailed in community-based research. Brumfiel's students have carried on her legacy of community engagement, most recently with an on-site symposium featuring local speakers who were crew members during archaeological excavations.[12]

In 2002, Yvonne Marshall edited a special issue of the journal *World Archaeology* and prefaced the issue with an article titled "What Is Community Archaeology?" Beyond the emphasis on research partnerships and shared authority (meaning less control of the research agenda by archaeologists), Marshall noted that although community archaeology could be traced back to the Ozette project in the United States, more of this fourth kind of archaeological research seemed to be ongoing in Australia and New Zealand.[13]

The special issue of *World Archaeology* included an article by Traci Ardren about a community-focused archaeology project in towns surrounding the Classic Maya Yucatec site of Chunchucmil, México.[14] Ardren was guardedly optimistic about the possibilities of collaborating with local communities to develop a living museum on *ejido* land. Although the project would not come to completion, the dialogue initiated between archaeologists and local community members represented an important step toward community engagement in the Maya region.[15] As Ardren points out, dialogue about the past takes on increased urgency when one considers that heritage tourism is a multibillion-dollar-per-year business that provides extremely limited benefits for impoverished local communities.[16] The sheer economic injustice of the situation calls for greater inclusivity.

Marshall concludes the special issue of *World Archaeology* with this observation about community archaeology: "We need it, not because it is politically correct, but because it enriches our discipline. Community archaeology encourages us to ask questions of the past we would not otherwise consider, to see archaeological remains in a new light and to think in new ways about how the past informs the present. . . . There is a widespread belief among the authors of this volume that the kind of collaborative research fostered by community archaeology will be crucial if archaeology is to have a future."[17]

We are now over a decade past Marshall's statement that the future of archaeology as a discipline may be jeopardized if archaeologists do not figure out how to work collaboratively with communities. Yet community archaeology—among archaeologists trained in the United States—enjoys far from universal acceptance and some outspoken critics.[18] Within the United States, community engagement is more common among historical archaeologists, who were featured prominently in a later 2003 SAA publication titled *Archaeologists and Local Communities: Partners in Exploring the Past.* Perhaps because their fieldwork often takes place within contemporary communities (and sometimes also in the context of long-term urban cycles of decay and renewal), many historical archaeologists have embraced community-based archaeology as a platform for social activism.[19] Also, many historical archaeologists directly engage with publics in reference to the creation of state and national parks and monuments.[20] They do not have the luxury of being analytically aloof.

Anne Pyburn has written of the new "rules of engagement" entrained with community archaeology.[21] More significant engagement with people as part of the research process brings archaeological research closer to the ethnographic research of sociocultural anthropologists and its associated ethical concerns. One guideline of ethnographic research—adopted from IRB (Institutional Review Board) protocols—cautions researchers to "do no harm" to involved communities. Whether or not archaeologists are involved in engaged research with communities, we inevitably become entangled in the lives of people living proximate to the archaeological sites that we study. We engage in hiring and managing personnel; we depend on the goodwill and hospitality of local communities; and increasingly we solicit oral histories. In reality, we have already entered the realm of IRB-monitored activities.

When it comes to the issue of site conservation, archaeologists are quick to realize that community support is crucial. Although this embrace of community engagement has been critiqued as servicing archaeologists' desire to conserve treasure chests of data, useful conversations often begin with a conservation agenda and deepen into meaningful collaboration that is highly beneficial to both parties. This is illustrated by the work of three archaeologists in Honduras. Karla Davis-Salazar, E. Christian Wells, and José Moreno-Cortés discovered an Ulua-style marble vase—the first of its kind to be systematically excavated rather than looted.[22] Concerned that news of this discovery would spark renewed looting near Palmarejo, Honduras, the excavators pondered whether or not to share the discovery with the community. Ultimately, they decided that community engagement was the only way to solve "the problems that led to the destruction of these resources in the first place. An applied approach may at least partially resolve the dilemma posed by discovery of the vase by tying conservation efforts directly to research questions and to issues meaningful to the residents of Palmarejo."[23]

In the United States, Indigenous archaeology and community-based archaeology developed apace with each other, but as scholars have observed they emerged from different traditions, and Indigenous archaeology dealt with a distinct set of problems.[24] While both approaches aim to democratize the production of knowledge, Indigenous archaeology focuses specifically on the integration of Indigenous concepts and knowledge into the research process and also accepts the burden of colonialism and heritage alienation as historical freight to be borne through the collaborative process. In order to frame this complex entity called Indigenous archaeology, Dorothy Lippert borrowed the concept of "deep play" from Michael Fischer,[25] who, of course, had borrowed it from Clifford Geertz.[26] Deep play can be used to describe "sites where multiple levels of structure, explanation, and meaning intersect and condense, including the cultural phantasmagoria that ground and structure the terrain on which reason, will, and language operate but cannot contain."[27] From the perspective of deep play, we begin to glimpse the complex terrain over which Indigenous archaeology takes place. By the mid-2000s, this complexity was increasingly evident. Simply holding out a hand with an invitation to Indigenous communities to participate in scientific discovery was not sufficient or even desirable. As Robert Preucel and Craig Cipolla noted, "The key point is that indigenous archaeologies involve Native peoples not as subjects but as collaborators."[28] Although still shaky, the bridge was becoming a more elaborate edifice that needed integrative epistemologies. In one approach to melding science with Indigenous values, George Nicholas discussed how cultural differences were negotiated in his Indigenous archaeology program on the Kamloops Indian Reservation in British Columbia.[29] Noting that Indigenous archaeology required archaeologists to become culturally sensitive anthropologists—not necessarily a role for which archaeologists receive training in pedagogically segregated anthropology departments—Nicholas highlighted the social interaction involved in transcultural field schools. Even more importantly, he stressed that ethnographic methods provide an important pathway to understanding and articulating "community-based conceptions of cultural heritage."[30]

Working ethnographically with Hul'qumi'num-speaking peoples who live in the Pacific Northwest, Julie Hollowell and George Nicholas note, for instance, that Hul'qumi'num peoples do not see artifacts as belonging to people (in the sense of Western notions of private property); rather people belong to things.[31] In the course of dialogue with Hul'qumi'num individuals, three "laws" of archaeological heritage were recognized: (1) an inherited right to care for the dead; (2) nondisturbance of the remains of deceased ancestors; and (3) avoidance of burial grounds. Hollowell and Nicholas contrast SAA ethics with the Hul'qumi'num way of managing the past[32] and conclude the following: "Archaeologists desperately need ethnographic examples of community-based conceptions of heritage management to expand their awareness of the complex webs of obligations and responsibilities spun on what they and the state have termed 'archaeological resources.' Critical and participatory ethnographic approaches go far in helping to define more effective and often more rewarding research methodologies."[33] In chapters 8 and 9, we examine community conceptions of heritage management and conservation by way of responses to questionnaires. With a focus on the Maya region, critical ethnographic approaches to archaeology that often include Indigenous perspectives have also been explored.[34]

Participatory approaches that attempt to balance (but more often contrast) Indigenous perspectives with those of Western research have a life outside archaeology and cultural heritage. In a multicultural study, Anne Ross and colleagues detail the many distinctions between Western and Indigenous knowledge in reference to environmental stewardship, particularly in Australia.[35] Significantly, the authors distinguish between "*epistemological* problems associated with the recognition of Indigenous knowledge and *institutional* issues typically connected to the economically and politically marginal status of Indigenous communities."[36] Indigenous stewardship and comanagement programs might founder because Indigenous ecological concepts are lost in translation or because they are incommensurate with those of the nation-state (or representatives of the state, such as the scientists with whom collaboration is taking place).

Paul Nadasdy provides a vivid example of incommensurability in his discussion of the epistemic limits to wildlife comanagement of Dall sheep in the Yukon territory of Canada.[37] Indigenous Kluane peoples sought to manage the herd with a simple quota system that would preserve the elder rams seen to play an important role in teaching and socializing within the herd. But wildlife biologists—who were more concerned with propagating herd numbers and satisfying trophy hunters desirous of a mounted sheep head with full-curl horns (i.e., an elder ram)—"decreed that hunters could only take old rams."[38] In this case, there was no rapprochement or transcultural space in which traditional ecological knowledge (TEK) and the Western science of wildlife management could coexist. In the end, the hegemonic power of the state overruled the incorporation of TEK. This example raises the specter that common ground may not always be found—like two ends of a bridge span that start on opposite sides and do not meet in the middle but rather pass each other. We return to the problem of incommensurability in chapter 10.

By 2009, the words *community* and *heritage* had seen much use and abuse within archaeology. Responding to a perceived lack of rigor, Laurajane Smith and Emma Waterton announced that community was a reified notion—something warm and fuzzy—that disintegrated upon closer scrutiny.[39] The authors proposed that heritage be understood as a process or performance of meaning making:

"Heritage, therefore, becomes not a thing or a place, but an intangible process in which social and cultural values are identified, negotiated, rejected or affirmed. It is thus what is done at, or with, heritage sites that is significant, rather than the places themselves."[40] This relational turn has been aggressively critiqued by Bjørnar Olsen, who advocates an approach that he calls *symmetrical archaeology*.[41] Following the lead of Bruno Latour, Olsen argues that an iconic heritage locale such as Stonehenge is more than a "collection of rocks in a field" and that "things are valuable in and of themselves and should be respected for their otherness and integrity.[42] Both approaches resonate with responses that we received to questions about the meaning and conservation of heritage places.

At this point in time, there is a social constructivist approach to heritage (represented by Smith, Waterton, and others) and a "thing-theory"[43] approach to tangible heritage in which things are considered to possess agency in their own right, or at least affordances and competences with which humans interact. The relational approach to heritage is not that different from the Hul'qumi'num way discussed previously. By urging archaeologists to look beyond tangible forms of heritage and to focus more on how and why places are valued, Smith and Waterton move away from a Western focus on property per se and toward modeling the relational process that links people with things and places. This approach is more flexible and can expand to include a wider diversity of stakeholders.[44] On the other hand, results of questionnaires presented in chapters 8 and 9 indicate a great respect for the alterity of archaeological monuments and a predisposition to accord these old places agency in and of themselves.

Bridging collaborations are delicate and shaky enterprises that can be derailed due to institutional (usually power-related) problems that frustrate the will and desire to find common ground. In reference to the UNESCO site of Anuradhapura in Sri Lanka, Sudharshan Seneviratne discusses those challenges and emphasizes that collaboration requires inclusivity and focus on a shared historical legacy (echoing the words of Ernest Renan in reference to nationalism).[45] The will to establish common ground appears to be the first goalpost of building community partnerships. Will and acknowledgment of the larger contexts and power relationships within which archaeology is practiced are cited by many as central to this kind of endeavor.[46]

Although community partnerships are founded on commonalities, those who are collaborating need not sacrifice their distinctive perspectives on the past. In a comprehensive study of community-based participatory research (CBPR) as it applies to archaeology, Sonya Atalay introduces the metaphor of braided knowledge—distinct strands that are woven together to create something that is greater than the sum of its parts.[47] Atalay observes that "while CBPR may complicate issues of rigor, it can also enhance rigor when it braids different perspectives and knowledge systems together in skillful ways."[48] The dilemma to which Gayatri Spivak refers in her famous article on whether the subaltern can speak should never be dismissed, but Atalay's approach to braided knowledge suggests that collaboration can occur even when the collaborating groups come from very different places, share a haunting colonial history, or represent asymmetrical power relations. Atalay echoes the sentiment of Yvonne Marshall in suggesting that braided knowledge through collaborative research is one of the few pathways toward a sustainable archaeology.

In the Maya region, the pathway of braided knowledge is not completely unblazed, but it's fair to say that it is a seldom-traveled path. Steps toward collaboration between archaeologists and communities have occurred at Xcalakdzonot and Chunchucmil, México;[49] Cancuen[50] and Candelaria Caves in Guatemala;[51] El Pilar,[52] Albion Island, and Chau Hiix[53] in Belize; and the western Maya highlands of Guatemala,[54] to name a few published examples of efforts at collaborative research in which community voices were heard and heeded. Heritage initiatives discussed below encouraged more such collaborations between Maya archaeologists and local communities.

FORGING PARTNERSHIPS AROUND HERITAGE ISSUES

Chapter 1 opened with this question from a young Yucatec Maya Belizean girl: "Why did all the Maya have to die?" That question stayed with me because of its sadness and what it revealed about colonial mythologies and the lack of access to information about the past. In the years that followed, I became increasingly concerned about the vulnerability of Indigenous Maya children, who grow up feeling like second-class citizens in their own homeland and experience discrimination because of the way they look, the clothes they wear, or the maternal language they speak (or are discouraged from speaking). Living in rural districts, many children lack access to schools with an enriched curriculum at which they might learn about their distant ancestors rather than a history that begins with European colonization. The structural inequalities of growing up with three strikes against you and few opportunities to change a preordained script were very much on my mind in 2005.

At that time, I had received a fellowship from the National Endowment for the Humanities to write a book about the embedded nature of precolonial Maya economic arrangements.[55] I was absorbed with archaeological evidence and social theory when I received word that the director of a family foundation was interested in speaking with me about funding programs in the Maya area that would curb looting and also be beneficial to local Maya populations. Initially, I thought I would take a pass on the opportunity since applied research had never been part of my professional activities. I was concerned about social justice intellectually but at the time did not feel compelled to link that concern with the practice of archaeology—a space within which I sense many of my colleagues dwell today.

But as I thought over the possibilities, I realized that I had been offered a once-in-a-lifetime opportunity. The director was persuasive and supportive, and soon I was tasked with writing a proposal that outlined a plan of action. But what kind of action could make a difference? I had just completed multiple years of fieldwork in the Sibun Valley of Belize and was entering an analysis and writing phase. There were fascinating and diverse communities living in and near the valley: Creole (Afro-European Belizeans), Anglo-Belizeans, U.S. and European expatriates, Chinese Belizeans, refugees from the Salvadoran civil war, and retired *chicle* harvesters. Interesting and important community archaeology certainly could happen in this location. But earlier fieldwork in northern Belize and Yucatán had sensitized me to the compelling issues embedded within the linkage between ethnolinguistic Mayan communities and archaeological sites located within the ambient heritage-scape. Despite the colonial-period presence of Mayan peoples (probably Yucatec speakers) in the Sibun Valley attested by ethnohistoric research,[56] such communities no longer existed.

As I mulled over a course of action, one of my Boston University graduate students and research assistants—Shoshaunna Parks—suggested that we take a multisited approach to Maya cultural heritage. As discussed in chapter 4, multisited ethnography—introduced by sociocultural anthropologist George Marcus in the 1990s—provides a comparative means of studying positional identities and the cross-threading of transnational power relationships.[57] Marcus particularly stressed the "construction of identities in global-local frames."[58] At a time and place at which Maya cultural activists sought to knit together Maya communities across ethnolinguistic and national boundaries (discussed in chapter 5) and globalized heritage tourism increasingly impacted local livelihoods, a multisited approach made a lot of sense.

I thought further about the contrastive social and political terrain within the Maya region—for instance, between the Native peoples of Yucatán and the Q'eqchi' and Mopan residents of the Toledo District in southern Belize. Regardless of the fact that both areas contained impressive Late Classic Maya archaeological sites and communities that spoke one or more Mayan languages, they were worlds apart. Not only had peoples in these two areas experienced colonization in very different ways, they now are incorporated into very different nation-states. As discussed earlier, México pivoted in the late twentieth century to acknowledge the diversity of the approximately fifty-eight ethnolinguistic groups that reside within the boundaries of the republic of México.[59] The material legacy of the first peoples of México is under the control of the Instituto Nacional de Antropología e Historia (INAH); however, management jurisdiction increasingly is relegated to state governmental representatives of INAH.

Belize, in contrast, is a much smaller and younger nation, with an ethnic diversity that includes a large percentage of Afro-Caribbeans. National identity is vested in the notion that "we are all immigrants" and the fluidity of movement of local ethnolinguistically Mayan peoples across a disputed Belize-Guatemala border used as supportive evidence that Toledo Mayan people pose no exception to the national slogan and should not be accorded special rights, particularly in reference to land. As discussed in chapter 5, many court cases—tried and won in the Supreme Court of Belize and the Caribbean Court of Justice—are challenging the government to recognize the land rights of Toledo Maya peoples.

Mayan-speaking peoples in Toledo, Belize, and in Yucatán share First Peoples status but since the sixteenth century (and probably for a millennia before) had very different lived experiences. It seemed important to understand how those different experiences affect the perception and performance of cultural heritage because, over the long run, collaborative research would be constructed in relation to such perceptions. As George Marcus wrote, "In projects of multi-sited ethnographic research, de facto comparative dimensions develop . . . as a function of the fractured, discontinuous plane of movement and discovery among sites as one maps an object of study and needs to posit logics of relationship, translation, and association among these sites."[60] A multisited cultural heritage project had the potential to map how the past is experienced today across the historically deep but fractured plane of colonialism and nation building.

NOTES

1. Lippert (2005:438).
2. Lippert (2005).
3. Lippert (2005:438).
4. Lippert (2005:438).
5. See Sabloff (2008), among others.
6. Marshall (2002:218).
7. Marshall (2002:212); see also Rizvi (2008) on collaboration and building multivocality into research and Lilley (2008) on the willingness to relinquish authority to speak and act for the past.
8. For a critical appraisal of community archaeology that focuses on decentralization of power, see La Salle (2010).
9. Atalay (2012).
10. Dongoske, Aldenderfer, and Doehner (2000).
11. Brumfiel (2000).
12. See Overholtzer (2015).
13. Marshall (2002:212).
14. Ardren (2002).
15. For an in-depth discussion of how the effort went awry, see Rodriguez (2006).
16. Ardren (2002:385).
17. Marshall (2002:218).
18. Most notably, Shannon Lee Dawdy (2009), who is deeply suspicious of attempts to democratize the research process; Marina La Salle (2010), who questions whether it is really a departure from business as usual; and Robert McGhee (2008), who considers Indigenous archaeology to be reverse racism (against scientists). For a general discussion of participatory methods in development theory and governance—both pro and con—see Cooke and Kothari (2001) and Hickey and Mohan (2004).

19. For a more recent compilation, see Stottman (2010).
20. See Little and Shackel (2014).
21. Pyburn (2003).
22. Davis-Salazar, Wells, and Moreno-Cortés (2007).
23. Davis-Salazar, Wells, and Moreno-Cortés (2007:196–97).
24. See the seminal treatment of Indigenous archaeology in Watkins (2000) and also Atalay (2012:39), Colwell-Chanthaphonh et al. (2010:228), and Silliman (2008:3).
25. Fischer (2003:30–31).
26. Geertz (1973:chap. 15).
27. Lippert (2008:123); see also Fischer (2003:31).
28. Preucel and Cipolla (2008:131).
29. Nicholas (2008); see also Nicholas and Andrews (1997a, 1997b) for the seminal theory and practice of Indigenous archaeology.
30. Hollowell and Nicholas (2009).
31. Hollowell and Nicholas (2009:150).
32. Hollowell and Nicholas (2009:150–54).
33. Hollowell and Nicholas (2009:154).
34. See Castañeda and Matthews (2008), Edgeworth (2006), and Mortensen and Hollowell (2009).
35. Ross et al. (2011).
36. Ross et al. (2011:29).
37. Nadasdy (2005).
38. Nadasdy (2005:226).
39. Smith and Waterton (2009).
40. Smith and Waterton (2009:44).
41. Olsen (2012).
42. Olsen (2012:219–20).
43. Brown (2001).
44. For an example of the relational approach, see Maldonado (2011), who examines how local residents relate to nearby archaeological sites in Honduras without reference to an Indigenous narrative.
45. Seneviratne (2008).
46. Barbara Little and Paul Shackel (2014:17) discuss their civic engagement in terms of personal motivation, as do George Nicholas and Thomas Andrews (1997a, 1997b).
47. Atalay (2012:76).
48. Atalay (2012:82).
49. See Armstrong-Fumero and Hoil Gutierrez (2010) and Ardren (2002); see also Magnoni, Ardren, and Hutson (2007).
50. Del Cid and Demarest (2004); Demarest and Barrientos (2004).
51. Del Cid and García (2005).
52. Ford (2006, 2011).
53. Pyburn (2003); Pyburn and Wilk (2000).
54. Borgstede (2010); Fruhsorge (2007).
55. McAnany (2010).

56. Grant Jones (1989) provides documentation of an early colonial mission called Xibun in the mid-valley. Steven Morandi, with assistance from the 2001 and 2003 Xibun Archaeological Research Project (XARP) students and staff, excavated an early colonial structure with associated midden material at Cedar Bank—where the coastal lowlands meet the karst formations of the mid-valley. A full account is given in Morandi (2010).

57. Marcus (1995), see especially pages 98, 105; see also Falzon (2009).

58. Marcus (1995:105).

59. González (2004).

60. Marcus (1995:102).

7

The Maya Area Cultural Heritage Initiative

The Maya Area Cultural Heritage Initiative (MACHI) took shape as a multi-sited program in 2006 at Boston University (BU), where I taught until 2008. Working with BU graduate students Shoshaunna Parks and Satoru Murata (figure 7.1), and soon thereafter a recent UC-Riverside PhD, Reiko Ishihara-Brito, we were committed to grassroots collaboration with local communities. We envisioned cultural heritage programs that could provide a vehicle of social and economic justice for vulnerable populations, particularly Indigenous children. As academics in the business of education, we reasoned that one way to effect change was to create classroom-based programs of heritage education—to talk about Maya cultural heritage during schooltime (chapter 8). While this may not sound radical, Indigenous identity and history are seldom part of school curricula, which focus on history since European colonialism and on national identity. We also envisioned a second way to move heritage to the front burner through performance—puppet shows, plays, radio series, and community mapping projects that would bring issues of cultural heritage to the attention of a broader swath of community members in a less didactic fashion (chapter 9).

Initially, we focused on three things: capacity building, enhancing opportunities for learning about Maya archaeology, and creating a forum for dialogue about cultural heritage. Embracing the liberation pedagogy of Paulo Freire and others,[1] we sought to create an interactive educational experience—particularly for children—that deviated significantly from the rote memorization of lesson plans as currently taught in underfunded rural schools. The latter dominated the formal education afforded Indigenous children in rural parts of the Maya region. These were solid goals but more top down and less collaborative than later programs implemented by MACHI and its successor, InHerit: Indigenous Heritage Passed to Present, which was launched in 2011 at the University of North Carolina at Chapel Hill. These programs were the bridges constructed to arc the colonial and nationalist periods across which the social memory of distant times had been actively discouraged and often aggressively erased. The programs also bridged

Figure 7.1. Maya Area Cultural Heritage Initiative (MACHI) launched in 2006 from an archaeological lab at Boston University: (left to right) Satoru Murata (then a graduate student), Patricia A. McAnany, and former graduate student Shoshaunna Parks (photo by Paul Zimansky).

two perspectives on the past: those of archaeologists and of local communities. As a multisited program that used a survey instrument for evaluation, MACHI and then InHerit ran the gauntlet of the Institutional Review Board (IRB) for all program evaluations. Because the purpose of our surveys was to solicit feedback on program efficacy rather than collect sensitive information such as detailed personal medical histories, we generally qualified for expedited review and approval. In general, the review process was positive because it challenged us to think about the goals of the initiative.

PROYECTO MAYA WITH ARTE ACCIÓN (COPÁN RUINAS, HONDURAS)

With a commitment to a multisited approach, we cast a wide net for community partners (figure 7.2). In Copán Ruinas, Honduras, we partnered with Arte Acción Copán Ruinas, an art cooperative directed by Carin Steen—an energetic and creative artist—who believed in artistic expression as a vehicle of empowerment (figure 7.3). The tony town of Copán Ruinas—built on heritage tourism—was surrounded by *aldeas* (small communities), many of which were peopled by descendants of Ch'orti' Mayan speakers.[2] The Ch'orti' population in Honduras is predominantly Spanish-speaking, although efforts are underway to revitalize conversational Ch'orti'. As mentioned in chapter 5, Ch'orti' people (through the political organization of CONIMCHH, Consejo Nacional de Indígenas Maya Ch'orti' Honduras) had occupied the entrance to the World Heritage Site of Copán to press for land reform and for a share of the gate proceeds collected by the state.[3] As in Guatemala, Ch'orti' cultural activists consider archaeological sites to be places of sacred and powerful ancestral forces. The classic Maya dynastic capital of Copán assumed a focal position in the Ch'orti' struggle.[4]

InHerit Partnerships & Grants

Figure 7.2. The Maya region showing places where collaborative heritage programs took place under the umbrella of MACHI, InHerit, and the Alliance for Heritage Conservation. Collaborating organizations are indicated in boldface except when funding was awarded through our two grant competitions: Community Heritage Conservation Grants (CHG) and Bi-Directional Knowledge Exchange Grants (BKE). Name of awardees follow CHG and BKE designations (map by Sarah M. Rowe).

Figure 7.3. A Proyecto Maya workshop in the classroom of a small *aldea* in western Honduras: left to right, Moisés Mancia, one of the workshop facilitators, and Carin Steen, director of Arte Acción Copán Ruinas (photo by author).

We approached schoolteachers about securing time for a cultural enrichment program, and most of the teachers readily freed time during the school day for facilitators to run a class. A few schools in the outlying communities had electricity but many did not, so we needed to design an experience that did not depend on electronics. We discovered that a surprisingly large percentage of schoolchildren had never visited the World Heritage Site of Copán, just a stone's throw from their modest dwellings built of *bajareque* (rammed earth).

Employing young facilitators from the community (figure 7.3), we designed a series of cultural heritage modules that could be implemented in fourth through sixth grades. (Responses to the program are presented in chapter 8.) Carin Steen dubbed the program Proyecto Maya. Each topical module was accompanied by an artistic exercise—such as making a collage—that was loosely linked to the topic of the day (figure 7.4). Textbooks were distributed to each student—for many, the first book they owned (figure 7.5). In the *aldea* schools, students of many ages often are grouped together in the same classroom. For the younger students who were eager to participate, we created a coloring book with drawings by Carin Steen. The contents combined famous monuments and structures of Copán, such as Altar Q (figure 7.6), with images of Ch'orti' cultural practices, such as Tzi'k'in. A short accompanying Spanish text was translated into Ch'orti' by members of CONIMCHH and Teodoro Ramírez de Rosa. The workshop facilitators distributed crayons along with the coloring books.

Figure 7.4. Student in a Proyecto Maya workshop creates a collage of a pyramidal shrine that reaches beyond a canopy of greenery and into the sky (photo by author).

Figure 7.5. Students review their personal copies of the textbook *La Cultura Maya en Copán: Un libro de actividades para niñas/niños* (photo by Shoshaunna Parks).

Figure 7.6. Page 2 of the Ch'orti'-Spanish coloring book showing Altar Q of Copán (illustration by Carin Steen).

Ira twa' e wenib' Q turu tama uparke ojnya'n te k'opan satem.
Yi' ja'xir te wenib' uwira anie e uxmojy inte nuk ajk'amparob' te' k'opan.
Tut tara uwira e inte nuk'ojk'ampar ke uyajk'o e b'aston umen
weptar te penultimo nuk ajkampar.

Este es el Altar Q. Está en el parque arqueológico de Copán Ruinas.
Alrededor del altar se ven los 16 reyes de Copán. Aquí en frente
se ve el primer rey que da el bastón de mando al penúltimo rey.
El penúltimo rey, Yax Pasah mandó hacer este altar para mostrar su poder.

2 ••

Each week the facilitators summoned a small, red moto-taxi for the ride to a different *aldea*. One of our facilitators self-identified as Ch'orti' and lived in a Ch'orti' *aldea*, another lived in Copán Ruinas but also identified as Ch'orti', and other members of our team preferred to think of themselves as Copanecos (residents of the District of Copan). In 2009, at the height of the program, schools in twenty-four communities participated in a program that impacted the lives of over six hundred youths. Beginning in 2007, Carin Steen ran the program. She handed the program over to her facilitators in 2012, after which Asociación Copán administered the program under the guidance of Ricardo Agurcia.

Field trips to the archaeological site of Copán and elsewhere provided a capstone experience for the students, as did periodic *ferias* or festivals and, during one year, the archaeological investigation of a recently abandoned Ch'orti' dwelling (figure 7.7). Although the investigation entailed only mapping and surface collection, student responses indicate that the experience provided them with valuable insights to the methods of archaeology and the conservation concerns that accompany field research. At the close of each year, homeroom teachers and facilitators evaluated the program. We take a close look at those evaluations in chapter 8.

Figure 7.7. Pulling tape to measure a recently abandoned Ch'orti' dwelling, Proyecto Maya, La Pintada, Copán, Honduras (photo by Carin Steen).

B'ELEB'AAL CH'IICH' RE NA'LEB' WITH THE
JULIAN CHO SOCIETY (TOLEDO DISTRICT, BELIZE)

Literally meaning "a traveling vehicle of knowledge" in Q'echi' Mayan, the term *b'eleb'aal ch'iich' re na'leb'* was selected by Cristina Coc, who directed the Julian Cho Society (JCS) of southern Belize (see figure 7.2 for location).[5] As introduced in chapter 5, the society was dedicated to resolving land claims of Indigenous Q'echi' and Mopan peoples who live in the Toledo District of Belize. Lacking secure titles to their traditional-use lands, Toledo Mayan peoples were involved in a protracted legal battle with the government of Belize.[6] Working collaboratively with the JCS, we developed a plan to buy a pickup truck and travel to many of the thirty-two Indigenous communities (ranging in size from 250 to 1,200 persons) of the Toledo District in order to spread the word about cultural heritage and land claims. Throughout Belize, the land-claim issue is highly controversial, as one might imagine; in southern Belize, specifically, the issue of whether land should be privatized or managed communally by elected village authorities evokes impassioned discussion.

After a period of trying out this traveling vehicle of tandem knowledge (land rights and cultural heritage), it became clear that cultural heritage needed a venue separate from the impassioned and high-stakes discussion of land claims. One parent suggested that we take the archaeological discussion into grade-school classrooms, and most parents expressed the desire that their children have an opportunity to learn about Maya archaeology in school. Many believed (and still believe) that their cultural heritage—both tangible and intangible—was slipping away and definitely endangered. We consider these concerns in more detail in chapter 8.

With this advice, we began talking with school principals and teachers and building a curriculum that we hoped would resonate with southern Belizean schoolchildren. Our local facilitator Marvin Coc worked alongside Reiko Ishihara-Brito and then UNC–Chapel Hill graduate student Claire Novotny to design curriculum content. Generating content in written forms of local Mayan languages—in this case, Q'eqchi' and Mopan—was a high priority for us. We produced an eighteen-page illustrated primer to Maya cultural heritage in three languages: English (the official language of Belize), Q'eqchi', and Mopan. Titled *Seeing Our Ancestors* (English), *Qatzolaq Rixeb' Qaxe' Qatoon* (Q'eqchi'), and *U Pektzil Ti Uchb'en Maaya* (Mopan), the booklet proved too text-heavy for third to sixth graders. Children who had been reared speaking Q'eqchi' or Mopan were bewildered by paragraphs of text written in their maternal language. This experience highlighted the distinction between conversational fluency and reading literacy. Marvin Coc, our local workshop facilitator, used PowerPoint images to address topics of cultural heritage, and lectures were enlivened by poster competitions focused on heritage themes (figure 7.8).

Figure 7.8. Winning poster in competition to express themes of heritage conservation, Toledo District, 2009 (photo by Shoshaunna Parks).

At this point, we realized the efficacy of a coloring book in which each of the twenty-four pages contained an image that could be colored followed by two short sentences of explanatory text in one or more languages. The short texts juxtaposed with each other invited translational study rather than posing a difficult-to-comprehend wall of words. We returned to the coloring book that had been created by artist Carin Steen based on Ch'orti' lived experience around Copán. Some of the images translated, but others were out of place in southern Belize. They lacked the localness that is integral to Maya identity, as discussed in chapter 5. For instance, there was no mention of the Deer Dance, which arguably is an extremely important ritual event in southern Belize. So we created a second version of the coloring book that featured Deer Dancers and trilingual text in Q'eqchi', Mopan, and English (figure 7.9). Jimmy Boucher and Thomas Caal translated the text into Mopan, and Roselino Tec Pop handled the Q'echi' translation.

The conflict over land claims continues in southern Belize, but the Julian Cho Society shuttered its doors in early 2010. We were not able to institutionalize the cultural heritage curriculum within the schools, but during the three years in which the workshops were offered, we reached about three hundred children in seven different communities. For her dissertation research, Claire Novotny went on to design a community archaeology project supported by the National Science Foundation with one of the villages that had participated in the

Li xajieb' re ii kej a'an jun re ii ninq'e naqaninq'ehomb'resi' iru. Ça' ii xajok re ii kej ii uuinqeb' nakexjal iix t'ikreb' kama' re ii xujeb' ut aj yo ut nake'xajok ii yoob'k re ii oxloq'ii kej. A'aneb' nakexxaj ii marimb', ii aarp, ut ii tuntun. Li xajok naru uuank chi naab'aj kutan ut chijunii ii ch'ina aieb' nakejulak chi ru riib'aal ut nakexxua' ii poch ii nakexyiib' iix na'eb'.

Le'ek u yok'ot keeh a humb'eel ti ki'oolala. Ichii u yok'oeb'ol a Santo Keeh, walakoo' u heiik u b'ahil ti b'a'aiche'ii i ah ezakii i walakoo' u yok'otik a marimba, aarpa i tamb'or. Ti k'in u pach ti walakoo' u kiolai i walakoo' u b'eel ti cha'an i hanai pooch a tz'ub' a walakoo' u b'etik a na'tzii.

The Deer Dance is one of the festivals we celebrate. In the Deer Dance men dress as animals and hunters and dance the hunting of the holy deer. They dance to the marimba, the harp, and the drum. The dance can last many days and all the children love to watch and to eat the pooch that their mothers prepare.

22

Figure 7.9. Page 22 of the trilingual (Q'eqchi', Mopan, and English) coloring book featuring the Deer Dance; the book was distributed to young schoolchildren in southern Belize (illustration by Carin Steen).

workshops—Aguacate.[7] The community is located very close to an alternative high school called Tumul K'in (new day) with a radio station on which we ran Q'eqchi'-language radio stories about cultural heritage issues. We segue now to our partners in Guatemala and the making of radio *novelas* or soap operas composed around topics of Maya cultural heritage.

ENTRE DOS CAMINOS WITH FUNDACIÓN PROPETÉN (PETÉN, GUATEMALA)

March is the height of the dry season in the Maya region, and heat waves were rippling across the waters of Laguna Petén Itzá as Shoshaunna Parks and I waited to meet with Rosa Chan. We were in a restaurant in Flores—a town founded on an island on top of the fabled stronghold of the Itzaes—the last Maya kingdom to fall in 1697 to the onslaught of Spaniards. In 2006, Rosa Chan directed a local nongovernmental organization (NGO) called Fundación ProPetén (www.prop eten.org) and was involved in community work on environmental and health issues (see figure 7.2 for location). We thought we might find common ground with ProPetén on issues of heritage conservation. As we talked about possibilities, Rosa suggested radio stories (radio *novelas*) about cultural heritage that could address issues of looting and conservation and also present substantive information in a user-friendly fashion. Since Peténeros tend to speak either Spanish or Q'eqchi', radio *novelas* could be broadcast in both languages and, by doing so, also provide support for an Indigenous language. We were captivated by everything but the price tag.

There were many costs involved, Rosa explained. Concepting and writing the script in Spanish, translating the text into Q'eqchi', hiring radio actors to perform the script along with necessary sound effects, recording the performances, and purchasing broadcast time on several radio stations throughout the Petén and Alta Verapaz. The medium of radio was attractive to us because many rural households in the Petén lack electricity and TV, but practically everyone owns a radio and listens to news and programs in the early hours of dawn and at dusk. We vowed to find the resources, and script writing soon began for a series that Rosa called *Entre Dos Caminos* (*Sa' xxaal li b'e* in Q'eqchi' or *Between Two Roads* in English). ProPetén had used the title earlier for a series of environmentally focused radio *novelas*. We liked the active agency suggested by the title, which could be adapted to talk about a critical fork in the road of heritage conservation.

Yadira Vargas, whose grandmother had lived on the north side of the lake, was charged with writing dialogue (figure 7.10). Yadira proved to have a keen understanding of rural issues and an uncanny knack for crafting small-town drama around issues of cultural heritage—a stolen family heirloom, a vulnerable mound in the middle of someone's cornfield, and so forth. She inserted the character of an enlightened schoolteacher who somehow managed to find the resources to take students on field trips to local archaeological sites such as Tikal. The dialogue between teacher and students provided a mechanism for transmitting substantive information about the formidable archaeological sites that cover the Petén. For the Spanish version of the radio *novelas*, local actors from Flores performed and taped the shows in the office of ProPetén (figure 7.11). Roselino Tec Pop translated the text into Q'eqchi', and a group of actors from Sayaxché performed and taped the stories in Q'eqchi' (figure 7.11). You can listen to the radio *novelas* in Spanish and in Q'eqchi' at https://soundcloud.com/inheritp2p/sets/entre-dos-caminos.

After the taping was completed, Edy Romero swung into action. With the smooth and booming bass voice of a Latin American radio announcer, Edy drove through the towns and villages where the radio *novelas* were to be broadcast and announced their imminent airing through a megaphone mounted on the top of his car. During the broadcasts, he introduced each weekly show and then returned to the communities for evaluations of the series. Responses are examined in chapter 9. Edy would convene a focus group under a town *palapa* or pose a series of questions to women in the doorway of their kitchens (figure 7.12). On one occasion when I was able to accompany Edy and Yadira, I heard a range of comments that hovered around the sentiment that it was one of the few radio

Figure 7.10. Yadira Vargas (foreground on right) addresses a group of Petén schoolchildren when the radio *novelas* were adapted to the state-sponsored school curriculum reform in 2010 (photo by Shoshaunna Parks).

Figure 7.11. Performing and taping the radio-*novela* scripts: (top) in Spanish at the office of ProPetén in Flores and (bottom) in Q'eqchi' at a school in Sayaxche, Petén (from the photo archives of MACHI).

shows that had been produced with rural Peténeros and Q'eqchi'-speaking people in mind. The show was for and about rural people of Petén and how they related to the heritage-scape that surrounds them. They were the rock stars of the radio *novelas*; they knew it and appreciated it.

Edy suggested that it would be nice to be able to give something back to the communities in return for asking their opinion of the radio *novelas*. We turned again to Carin Steen to design a Petén-focused version of the coloring book with text in Spanish and Q'eqchi'. The book features famous structures of Tikal, such as Temple 1, and a boy wearing a T-shirt silk-screened with a stylized version of the Tikal emblem glyph. A later page features the Mayejak, a Q'eqchi' celebration dedicated to the earth spirit, Tzuultaq'a. Edy distributed the coloring book as a token of appreciation for feedback on the radio *novelas* (figure 7.13).

When we ran out of funds, we had taped forty episodes in both Spanish and Q'eqchi', which were broadcast over three seasons (2007–2009) on over a dozen

Figure 7.12. Edy Romero collects feedback on the radio *novelas* informally through a kitchen door (from the photo archives of MACHI).

Figure 7.13. Q'eqchi'-Spanish coloring books in use by those who contributed feedback to radio *novelas*: (left) young girl and (right) shopkeepers (photos by Shoshaunna Parks).

radio stations. We never figured out a way to get an exact count of our listening audience, but extrapolating from the responses that Edy received, we reached between two thousand and ten thousand people. In 2010, we decided to archive the shows and rerun them at a later time if we could find less expensive airtime. Then we realized that with only minor adjustments in the dialogue, we could import the Q'eqchi' versions of the radio *novelas* to southern Belize, where a significant Q'eqchi'-speaking population resided. Airtime through the radio station at the Tumul K'in Center of Learning was much more reasonably priced (figure 7.14). As a result, Q'eqchi' speakers of southern Belize listened to the inspired, if melodramatic, stories of Maya cultural heritage from the pen of Yadira Vargas, a descendant of several generations of Peténeros.

One of my colleagues, Miguel Astor-Aguilera, heard about the radio *novelas* and urged us to contact Amadeé Collí at Mayaón—a Yucatec Maya organization located in Felipe Carrillo Puerto (Quintana Roo, México) and dedicated to Maya cultural issues (see figure 7.2 for location). Like Tumul K'in, Mayaón had a close relationship with a radio station (Radio Xenca) and broadcast expenses were negligible, so we produced a Yucatec version of the heritage program. Amadeé wrote twenty-five episodes of a series titled *Raíces, Identidad y Cosmovisión Maya* (Roots, Identity, and Maya Cosmovision). The series was less conversational and more didactic than the ProPetén episodes; however, the local radio audience was

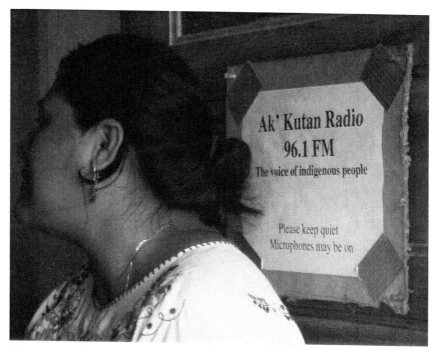

Figure 7.14. Esther N. Sanchez Sho, then director of the Tumul K'in Center of Learning, standing in front of the door to the broadcast booth of Ak' Kutan Radio (photo by Shoshaunna Parks).

enthusiastic about the content and delivery. Amadeé vowed to find funding to reproduce the series in Spanish in order to expand the reach of the program.

Back in the Petén, plans were afoot for a redesign of public grade-school curriculum around concepts of Maya cultural heritage. The Peace Accords of 1996 had promised significant school reform with more emphasis on the revitalization of Mayan languages, but the Escuelas Mayas that had been established were located primarily in the highlands and Alta Verapaz.[8] In 2010, we signed a memorandum of understanding with the Ministry of Education to design a nationally certifiable curriculum that included segments from the radio *novelas*. After securing funding for the staff at ProPetén to design the curriculum collaboratively with teachers, work began on the comprehensive reform. All subjects would be taught—math, science, literature, art, and so forth—by drawing on principles of Maya cultural heritage. It was doable and we did it, although primarily in Spanish.

In 2011, after a workshop in which teachers were introduced to the new curriculum, teachers taught the experimental curriculum to 1,140 students in third and fourth grades (figure 7.15). Surveys administered by ProPetén report that teachers found the new curriculum more satisfying to teach, and some commented that ethnic tensions in the classroom were lowered and more respect was shown to

Figure 7.15. Petén grade-school students hold up new textbooks, *Siguiendo El Camino Maya,* in which curricular topics are approached from the perspective of Maya cultural heritage (photo by Shoshaunna Parks).

Indigenous students. These are positive results that are hard to quantify. Unfortunately, the most quantifiable metric of a curriculum—improvement in test scores—has not yet happened. The children do report excitement about learning traditional school subjects through the lens of cultural heritage. Funding limitations, as always, loom large, and unless the government of Guatemala assumes financial responsibility for the maintenance and expansion of the curriculum, it may not be sustainable. On the upside, this example shows that investing in something that sounds like entertainment—such as radio soap operas—can lead to profound educational reform.

U BE'JIL K-ÚUCHBEN K-CH'I'IBALO'OB WITH KAXIL KIUIC A.C. (YUCATÁN, MÉXICO)

In Yucatán, México, we move to a different project in a different place but nonetheless encounter two recurrent themes of MACHI cultural heritage programs—roads and ancestors. The title of this program is *En el Camino de Nuestros Antepasados*, which translates as *On the Road of Our Ancestors* or *U be'jil k-úuchben k-ch'i'ibalo'ob* in Yucatec Mayan. Our partners for this program were not a local NGO or a society struggling for land rights but a group of archaeologists who had banded together to conserve an archaeological site in the Puuc region of western Yucatán and to create a forest preserve amid the distinctive cone-karst ecology of the Puuc (see figure 7.2 for location). Led by George Bey of Millsaps College and Tomás Gallareta Negrón of INAH (Instituto Nacional de Antropología e Historia) Sureste in Mérida, Kaxil Kiuic A.C. (www.kiuic.org) promotes archaeological research amid the incomparable Late Classic Puuc architecture of the Bolonchén region and also supports the conservation of Yucatec Mayan language and livelihoods.

With a mutual interest in collaboration, discussion turned to the kind of program that might be useful and relevant in the Yucatán. Shoshaunna Parks was excited about the power of puppets to tell stories about cultural heritage and to deal (in a funny and irreverent style) with controversial issues. We originally had in mind puppets along the lines of the Muppets, but that kind of puppet turned out to be way too crude and underdeveloped for Mexican puppet sensibilities, which run along the lines of scaled-down humans or marionettes. In México, marionettes are used in a wider range of media than simply entertainment for children. For public television in Mexico City, Sergio García-Agundis had produced and directed a powerful TV documentary on child sexual abuse (*Es . . . Porque Te Quiero*) using marionettes rather than human actors—an example of the power of puppetry to handle difficult topics.

Although we had originally planned to sponsor live puppet shows at venues throughout Yucatán, Sergio's documentary opened the possibility of filming the puppets live at a series of chosen locations and then distributing the DVD. When Sergio agreed to direct a cultural heritage puppet-mentary in Yucatán, members of the collaboration began to work toward the production of a DVD. Nine marionette figures were produced by puppet-maker Victor Carbajal: two siblings, who would be the stars of the DVD; their mother and grandfather; a mischievous friend of the siblings; their primary-school teacher; an INAH site guard; the rain deity Chaak; and a bunny for comic relief (figure 7.16). We brainstormed scenes and topics, and Shoshaunna Parks and Christa Cesario—then a University of Pennsylvania graduate student conducting ethnographic fieldwork in Yucatán—drew up storyboards. Miguel Gallareta Negrón wrote the Spanish dialogue, which was translated into Yucatec Mayan with adjustments for jokes and dialogue that were "lost in translation." The puppets would speak Yucatec Mayan with optional subtitles in Spanish or English. The soundtrack was produced in Oxkutzcab, Yucatán, with the assistance of a local group of performers.

We filmed on location at the archaeological sites of Kiuic and Chichén Itzá; in a primary school classroom; at the site of road construction, where tangible heritage often is encountered and destroyed; in a cave where a close encounter between the children and the rain deity Chaak occurred; in the interior of a vernacular Yucatec dwelling; and of course along the white-topped roads of Yucatán when the marionettes traveled in the omnipresent yellow tricycles traditionally used for local transportation (figure 7.17).

Figure 7.16. The cast of marionettes (from the photo archives of MACHI).

Figure 7.17. Filming the puppet-mentary on location (counterclockwise from top): on a bus; on a tricycle; in front of the Caracol at Chichén Itzá; and at the Sacred Cenote of Chichén Itzá (from the photo archives of MACHI).

The film presents an idealistic view of the world and how it could be for rural children growing up in Yucatán. In this fictional world, primary-school teachers teach Maya history and students learn to read hieroglyphs; teachers have the resources to take students on field trips to archaeological sites; young people observe and discuss the destruction of archaeological sites, which occurs regularly during road construction; and the old ways—including respect for deities such as Chaak—coexist with modernity without the stark choices that descendant populations are often forced to make. You can see and hear the entire DVD on YouTube at https://www.youtube.com/watch?v=rrb4UCbSPM4.

Even with its idealized and pedagogic content, there is humor, pathos, and plenty of local cultural content in the sixty-minute film. But we didn't have a distribution plan for the DVD until 2009, when we began to talk with the Department of Indigenous Education and the Institute of Culture with the goal of introducing the DVD into primary schools throughout the state of Yucatán. The length of the film precluded its screening in classrooms as a jumping-off point for a discussion of heritage, so we inserted clear breaks between episodes that allowed teachers to show a fifteen-minute clip and then move to discussion and workbook exercises. That worked, but in hindsight dialogue with teachers from the start would have been better than retrofitting the video for classroom use. Shoshaunna Parks and Christa Cesario traveled the length and breadth of Yucatán to distribute the DVD, a teachers' guide, and student workbooks. By the end of a single school year, over fifteen hundred students in more than seventy-five communities had viewed the puppet-mentary. In chapter 9, we examine feedback from teachers and students. Teacher responses to questionnaires suggest that the collaborative net could have been larger and more inclusive—along the lines of the curriculum reform project in the Petén.

Having produced a coloring book for every other partnership, we reasoned that a Yucatec version could be distributed along with the DVDs, thus providing a further opportunity to support language revitalization. This version presents local cultural features of Yucatán such as a reclining *chacmool* figure and the

Figure 7.18. Lourdes Chan Caamal reads the Yucatec text of the coloring book to students, Tahcabo, Yucatán, July 2014 (photo by author).

grand ballcourt of Chichén Itzá, as well as a Ch'a' Chaak ceremony to bring rain. Ana Patricia Martínez Huchim translated the Spanish text into Yucatec Mayan. Recently, we reprinted fifty copies of the coloring book for a heritage-day celebration in the primary school at Tahcabo, Yucatán. A small town on the eastern side of Yucatán (about an hour north of Valladolid), Tahcabo is a place that suffered language loss as a result of national assimilationist policies. At the heritage celebration, children saw written Yucatec and heard spoken Yucatec as Lourdes Chan Caamal read pages of the coloring book aloud, followed by a reading of the Spanish version by Sarah Rowe (figure 7.18).

COMMUNITY MAPPING WITH THE RIECKEN FOUNDATION (HIGHLAND, GUATEMALA)

The initial programs of MACHI—designed to bridge the gap between archaeology and community—had employed pedagogical methods more intensively than I had originally envisioned. The collaborations had succeeded in different ways, and some left a deeper impression than others, but ultimately only time will measure their effectiveness. In the meantime, I wanted to link the methods of archaeology to Indigenous self-representation. In 2009, an opportunity presented itself by way of the Riecken Foundation (www.riecken.org) when Shoshaunna Parks and I spoke with Paul Guggenheim, who was then director of Riecken programs in Guatemala with an office in Antigua (see figure 7.2 for location). Founded by former Peace Corps volunteer Allen Andersson, who was convinced that community libraries were crucial to the survival of rural communities throughout Central America, the Riecken Foundation had built and staffed—in a remarkably collaborative way—twelve community libraries throughout Guatemala and many more in Honduras.

Located primarily in highland regions, the libraries had become community centers par excellence, and each contained a modest collection of books, several computers, and an Internet connection. Participating communities expressed great pride and ownership in their libraries, which formed a hub for community events. All sorts of activities took place in the library: committee meetings, craft and cooking activities, the collection and archiving of oral histories, child care, student research, résumé building, and—via the Internet connection—job searching.

Since the libraries had computers and electricity, our thoughts ran to a community-mapping project. GPS (global positioning system) units could be used to map significant cultural and natural features chosen by the community, and the points and metadata could be downloaded into the library computers and maps produced. By 2009, several communities in the Guatemalan departments of Sololá, Totonicapán, and Quetzaltenango had indicated their interest in a community-mapping program. We contacted a British firm—Helveta LCC—that created icon-driven GPS receivers for community-mapping projects in sub-Saharan Africa. At the time, Helveta was actively applying technology toward the cultural survival of vulnerable populations. After a series of community meetings, the icons (and features to be mapped) were selected, drawn by a local community artist, and sent to Helveta programmers for incorporation into a user interface run on a Motorola GPS receiver. As the technology of the Motorola receivers approached obsolescence, we replaced them with off-the-shelf receivers without icon-driven software with no adverse impact on the mapping program. The process of icon selection (figure 7.19) served to kick-start the project and initiate discussion within communities about which landscape and town features should be mapped. Through mapping outings, additional issues such as how ancillary metadata—oral histories, archival and historical information—might be linked to such features were deliberated.

Community mapping in highland communities with the Riecken Foundation produced dozens of maps—all vetted through community meetings—that range in content from negotiated community boundaries, sacred sites, artisan locations, and environmental hazards. Participating communities quickly adapted the technology to suit local needs and interests. Although field collection of culturally

Figure 7.19. Icon selection for GPS-based community maps (photo by Shoshaunna Parks).

relevant information has ended, community members continue to work with the map data and apply it to different goals, which we have written about elsewhere in significant detail.[9] Within geography, community mapping—especially for the purpose of Indigenous land claims—is approached carefully and critically. Geographers realize that empowerment through Western cartography can be another form of imperial imposition and is not a panacea that will solve all problems wrought by colonization and neoliberal globalization.[10] With these thoughts in mind, we consider the responses of community mapping participants to the value and utility of this initiative in chapter 9.

The collaborative mapping program with the Riecken Foundation took place during several important organizational changes: first, in 2011 MACHI was reinvented (with a less geographically and culturally circumscribed mission) as InHerit: Indigenous Heritage Passed to Present; and second, we started a non-profit legally recognized in 2012 as a 501(c)(3) titled the Alliance for Heritage Conservation. Through the alliance, we could participate in fund-raising using our website (www.in-herit.org) and offer donors a tax-deductible way to participate in the effort (figure 7.20). At the end of 2011, Shoshaunna Parks retired from the business of cultural heritage. In May of 2012, Sarah Rowe, then a graduate student at the University of Illinois, Urbana, became the program director for InHerit. Sarah provided program leadership until 2015, when Claire Novotny became program director.

During 2011, we initiated two new programs that deviated from all previous efforts because they included a request for proposals (RFP) either directly from Indigenous communities or from archaeologists conducting field research in proximity to a community, the ethnic composition of which need not be Indigenous. Titled the Community Heritage Conservation Grant and the Bidirectional Knowledge Exchange Grant, respectively, these competitions provide a window of insight to the cultural heritage interests and priorities of both archaeologists and local communities.

Figure 7.20. Logo for the reinvention of MACHI with a broader geographical scope as InHerit: Indigenous Heritage Passed to Present linked to a 501(c)(3) called the Alliance for Heritage Conservation (from the archives of InHerit).

FUNDING COMMUNITY IDEAS FOR HERITAGE CONSERVATION

Desiring more heritage programs that were entirely grass roots in conception and implementation, we initiated a community-level grant competition (for the location of Community Heritage Grant awardees, see figure 7.2). During the first year, the competition was restricted to Yucatán—an area with a large Yucatec-speaking population and, as discussed in chapter 5, a complex relationship between communities and their deep heritage. We wanted to hear directly from communities about their take on heritage and their plans and desires for heritage conservation. During the first year, we awarded three grants: (1) to a heritage park (Parque A'ak) north of Mérida; (2) to a community endeavor organized by the Motul nonprofit ADIPES to raise children's awareness of the ecological importance of cenotes (large limestone-solution sinkholes) through education and creation of a board game (figure 7.21); and (3) to Manejo Cultural, a Quintana Roo–based heritage conservation organization, which used the funds to create television documentaries about the distinct marine and terrestrial environments as well as the traditional herbal medicines of Quintana Roo (table 7.1).

In the competition of the following year (2012), we emphasized more strongly the importance of local leadership to the creation and execution of the proposals and broadened the competition to the entire Maya region. After in-house review, three proposals were funded (table 7.1): one from Belize and two from Yucatán. In the Belizean proposal, the community of Aguacate (Toledo District)

Figure 7.21. Board game produced by ADIPES with a Community Heritage Conservation Grant. The game highlights the importance and centrality of cenotes to the health and well-being of Yucatec communities (from the archives of InHerit).

Table 7.1. Community Heritage Conservation Grant awards.

Year	Recipient	Project	Place
2011	Ciencia Social Alternativa, A.C.	Parque A'ak (a heritage park)	Yucatán, México
2011	ADIPES, A.C.	Children's Heritage Board Games	Yucatán, México
2011	Manejo Cultural	Heritage TV (stressing environmental heritage)	Quintana Roo, México
2012	Aguacate Conservation Committee & Claire Novotny	"Ancestral Maya Heritage: Supporting Community Patrimony in Southern Belize"	Toledo, Belize
2012	Kaxil Kiuic, Rancho Kiuic descendants & Phillip Boyett	"Restoration of an Historic Cemetery at Rancho Kaxil Kiuic"	Yucatán, México
2012	ADIPES, A.C.	"Proyecto U K'aaxil Maya'ob, Motul, Yucatán, Mexico"	Yucatán, México
2013	Asociación CDRO & ArtCorps	"Strengthening Maya K'iche' Cultural and Environmental Heritage in Totonicapán, Guatemala"	Totonicapán, Guatemala
2013	Seine Bight Village Council & Christian Wells	"Garifuna Community-Based Heritage Conservation in Seine Bight, Belize"	Stann Creek, Belize

partnered with archaeologist Claire Novotny to create a park that would generate ecotourism at Kaq'ru' Ha', a local archaeological site (figure 7.22). In Yucatán, descendant communities whose ancestors had lived and worked at Rancho Kiuic collaborated with the staff of Kaxil Kiuic to restore the historic cemetery (figure 7.23). The Motul-area nonprofit ADIPES won a second award from InHerit to run a series of workshops with children that stressed conservation of *k'aaxil* (fields in varying states of fallow).

The theme of environmental conservation continued to reverberate through the third year of competition. The two funded proposals came from Guatemala and Belize (table 7.1). The Guatemalan proposal was a collaborative effort between ArtCorps and local Totonicapán Asociación CDRO. Together they sought to develop local K'iche' capacity to creatively present information about the environmental and cultural resources located in the San Miguel Forest. Effective conservation and promotion of the forest resources, which provided ingredients for local cuisine and herbal medicines among other benefits, was seen as central to the health and well-being of the district. In a different vein, the proposal from Stann Creek, Belize, concentrated on the heritage and history of a Garifuna (people of Afro-Caribbean and Arawak background) fishing community called Seine Bight. Located on the road to the resort area of Placencia, the community of Seine Bight sought to create a heritage center that might become a must-see stop along the road and lure beachgoers from their cars to visit a community heritage center.

Figure 7.22. Kaq'ru' Ha' eco-park at Aguacate in the Toledo District of Belize developed with a Community Heritage Conservation Grant (photos by Claire Novotny and Matt Stirn).

Figure 7.23. Historical cemetery at Rancho Kiuic restored with a Community Heritage Conservation Grant. Although most families have moved away from the rancho, the cemetery is still in use (photo from the archives of InHerit).

The persistent concern for environmental conservation in the Community Heritage Grant proposals echoes a theme that emerged during a conference on Indigenous Perspectives on Cultural Heritage co-organized in 2008 by MACHI and the Penn Cultural Heritage Center. Thirteen Indigenous leaders from throughout the Western Hemisphere—Alaska to Argentina and Hawai'i—met to discuss cultural heritage issues (figure 7.24). In a final summary statement crafted through consensus, participants made it clear that they do not separate cultural from natural as is common in Western thought. Moreover, participants expressed great concern for the environmental depredations that accompanied colonialism and resource extraction under capitalism. Off the record, a few of the participants stated emphatically that such abuse had not happened "under their watch" (meaning they were not empowered to halt it). There was general agreement that Indigenous peoples likely would suffer more seriously the consequences of climate change. So perhaps it is not surprising that when asked to propose a heritage conservation program to be directed and executed by the community, environmental concerns for the continued health of local landscapes feature prominently. This general concern with conservation is echoed, once more, in the survey responses presented in chapters 8 and 9.

Figure 7.24. Participants in the 2008 conference focused on Indigenous Perspectives on Cultural Heritage cosponsored by the Penn Cultural Heritage Center and MACHI: (standing left to right) Robert Red Hawk Ruth, Richard Leventhal, David Hernández Palmar, J. Ke'eaumoku Kapu, Naxexelhts'i Albert "Sonny" McHalsie, Pedro Cayuqueo Millaqeo, Luis Delgado Hurtado, conference translator, Jorge Antonio Ñancucheo, Christa Cesario, and Kenneth J. Grant; (seated left to right) Mrs. J. Ke'eaumoku Kapu, Shoshaunna Parks, Suzan Shown Harjo, Germán Hernández Brenes, Cristina Coc, Diane Strand, Patricia A. McAnany, Santiago Domínguez Aké, conference translator, and Mrs. Kenneth J. Grant (photo by Louise Krasniewicz).

IMAGINING BIDIRECTIONAL KNOWLEDGE EXCHANGE
BETWEEN ARCHAEOLOGISTS AND COMMUNITIES

A second way in which we sought to effect change in business as usual was to challenge archaeologists to design a program of bidirectional knowledge exchange (BKE; for location of BKE awards, see figure 7.2). Archaeologists have always enjoyed close connections with local communities as employers, friends, and occasional ethnographers, but the lines of hierarchy are clearly established. Seldom is there an exchange of knowledge with communities participating on an equal footing. To work toward mutually beneficial partnerships, we granted funds to archaeologists to initiate an exchange of knowledge with the community that was local to their ongoing archaeological investigation. We also asked archaeologists to record evidence of local looting before and after project implementation in an effort to gauge how effective programs were in changing the way community members relate to archaeological sites in their "backyard."

Between 2011 and 2014, seven proposals received BKE grants (table 7.2). An external board—knowledgeable in collaborative research—evaluated all proposals. The first grants were awarded to ongoing archaeological projects in Yucatán (Scott Hutson and Galvin Can Herrera at Ucí and Kancabal) and Guatemala (Brent Woodfill and Seleste Sanchez at Salinas de los Nueve Cerros). Scott

Table 7.2. Bidirectional Knowledge Exchange Grant awards.

Year	Recipient	Project	Place
2011	Scott R. Hutson & Galvin Masiel Can Herrera	"Strengthening Identification between Ancient Ruins and the Communities of Ucí, Kancabal, and Their Diaspora"	Yucatán, México
2011	Brent Woodfill & Seleste Sanchez	"Community Relations and Development Initiatives in the Salinas de los Nueve Cerros Region, Alta Verapaz, Guatemala"	Alta Verapaz, Guatemala
2012	Kristin Landau & Fredy Rodriguez	"Empowering Youth: Archaeology for Education in Copán, Honduras"	Copán, Honduras
2013	Eric Ponciano, Ruben Larios & Seeds for a Future	"Bi-Directional Knowledge Exchange at Chocolá, Guatemala"	Suchitepequez, Guatemala
2013	Rebecca Zarger & Kristina Baines	"Maya Cultural Heritage Exchange in Southern Belize"	Toledo, Belize
2013	Terry Powis & Jessie Griggs Burnette	"Community Engagement and Collaborative Archaeology in a Contemporary Maya Village"	Cayo, Belize
2013–2014	Jessica Wheeler	"Bi-Directional Knowledge Exchange at Popolá, Mexico"	Yucatán, México

Hutson and Galvin Can Herrera designed a series of activities that improved dialogue between archaeologists and the local community and included participation in *milpa* activities on the part of archaeologists, joint banquet events, and bus rental for a trip to Chichén Itzá, a site that, not surprisingly, few members of the community had visited. At the final community meeting, young project members who had been working with the archaeologists presented the final report—in Yucatec Mayan—of the field season.[11]

Brent Woodfill and Seleste Sanchez faced a challenging field situation at Salinas de los Nueve Cerros. The site is known to have been an important salt-production locale in precolonial times, but little sustained archaeological research has taken place there. Recently, the Q'eqchi' community residing near the site witnessed a series of failed development and ecotourism initiatives.[12] So coming into the situation to investigate this storied salt-production locale required patience, gaining the trust of the community, and figuring out how not to become a pawn of local political forces. Meeting regularly with the community to talk about archaeology, heritage, and to listen to the needs of the community proved crucial to the success of this BKE effort. Woodfill and Sanchez, in collaboration with the community, achieved a wide range of goals from installing new well casings that provided potable water to launching one of the young community members on a path toward a university degree.

Patience, listening, and stretching beyond one's academic comfort zone prove to be important characteristics of successful BKE projects, which tended to extend over longer periods of time than originally planned. In 2012, Kristin Landau and Fredy Rodriguez received a BKE grant to build on the Arte Acción workshops and empower teenage youths of Copán, Honduras, through professional archaeological training. In 2013, four proposals received funding (table 7.2); each conceived project approached heritage conservation from a very different angle. On the Pacific side of Guatemala, at one of the earliest coffee *fincas*, archaeologist Eric Ponciano and architect Ruben Larios planned to collaborate with a local nonprofit called Seeds for a Future and with the community of Chocolá to transform the historical buildings of a coffee *finca* into a heritage center that will provide benefit to the community. Unfortunately, the implementation of this project has been stalled due to the lack of matching funds from the government of Guatemala, but in conception this proposal indicates how sites of painful memories can be usefully deployed toward a frank assessment of heritage. In southern Belize, near the site of Uxbenká, Rebecca Zarger and Kristina Baines are working with the local nonprofit Uxb'enka K'in Ajaw Association (based in the community of Santa Cruz) to establish a network of ethnobotanical trails and train local guides to conduct tours that showcase the botanical wealth of this region and its medicinal applications. To thwart looting (which has been a chronic problem around the archaeological site of Uxbenká), a group of community members have been equipped with GPS to monitor and record evidence of looting.

In the Belizean community of San Antonio (located near the archaeological site of Pacbitun), Terry Powis and Jessie Burnette sought a bidirectional exchange of knowledge through joint participation in sporting events (soccer games) and local festivals, an oral history program, and a formal invitation to the community to visit ongoing excavations. Finally, in Yucatán at the archaeological site and nearby community of Popolà, Jessica Wheeler conducted workshops in Maya hieroglyphs that were open to all community members and coordinated the construction of a *bodega* (storage structure) to conserve the carved stone monuments of Classic-period Popolà.

The BKE proposals have varied widely, but each project entailed a close collaboration between archaeologists and community members, often included some form of training that makes archaeological knowledge more accessible to local communities, and provided benefit to the community that increased the quality of life or improved health. Through these kinds of projects, archaeologists are building bridges to communities and seeking to construct relationships that are less hierarchical than traditional interaction and move the field in the direction of collaborative research partnerships. They are important first steps to creating a balance between archaeological knowledge and local cultural knowledge within the context of fieldwork. In this reconfiguration, there is an emphasis on *process* rather than *product*—the process of collaboration rather than the products of archaeological investigation. For archaeologists, this relational turn is a paradigm shift, as discussed previously. In this context, archaeologists reflect on field methods not narrowly in terms of scientific technique but more broadly in terms of interaction with the local communities that are impacted by field activities.

In chapters 8 and 9, we flip perspective from the archaeologist to the community and focus on responses to the programs implemented directly by MACHI, InHerit, and the Alliance for Heritage Conservation. Through surveys and questionnaires, we critically evaluate the strengths and weaknesses of these programs. Evaluations provide a platform for seldom-heard voices and may provide a path toward a heritage without irony.

NOTES

1. Freire (2002); for other archaeological examples, see Hamilakis (2004) and McGuire (2008).
2. For a comprehensive overview of Ch'orti' Maya history from archaeological times to recent struggles, see Metz, McNeil, and Hull (2009).
3. For further discussion of the Ch'orti' struggle, see McAnany and Parks (2012) and Mortenson (2009) on Ch'orti' identity and tourism at Copán.
4. Euraque (2004).
5. www.jcsbelize.org/pages/aboutJCS.php.

6. For details of the Toledo Maya court cases, see http://amandala.com.bz/news/court-appeal-president-disagrees-toledo-maya-proved-ancestral-rights/.

7. Novotny (2015).

8. For a historical review of Guatemalan educational systems, see Richards and Richards (1996).

9. McAnany et al. (2015).

10. For a critical review of community mapping from the perspective of geographers, see volume 16 of *Cultural Geographies*, which is devoted to Indigenous cartographies, and Bryan (2011), among others.

11. Hutson, Can Herrera, and Chi (2012).

12. Woodfill (2013).

PART III

In Their Own Words

The theory, rationale, and practice of collaborative heritage work examined in parts I and II has set the stage for part III: "In Their Own Words." Chapters 8 and 9 present the responses and opinions of those who participated in the collaborative programs. Although many community archaeology or heritage programs have been initiated globally, few have followed up with questionnaires for participants.[1] Yet this information is critical in order to learn how programming is received and how school workshops, radio programs, or community mapping initiatives are perceived to hold value. The Institutional Review Board, first at Boston University (2007–2008) and thereafter at the University of North Carolina at Chapel Hill vetted the surveys presented here. For longitudinally continuous programs, such as Proyecto Maya in Honduras, change in responses from one year to the next can be examined. For other programs, such as the community mapping initiative in Guatemala, a single questionnaire was made available to participants, who filed their opinions at community libraries at the end of the program.

There are many ways in which this information could be presented. In the interests of hearing community voices, responses have been tabulated and are presented in chapters 8 and 9 outside the confines of a theoretical framing or elaborate conceptual artifice. As themes emerge—such as conservation desires and fixity of identity expression—they are discussed and conclusions drawn, but discussions flow from the responses and not the reverse.

When responses can be condensed into a tabular form, this presentation method is used and integrated into the text, more commonly in chapter 8. Regarding the interpretation of responses, the usual caveats apply. Changes in the structure of the questionnaire, response rate, and a number of other factors intervene when grappling with the diverse response of humans to question prompts. Nonetheless, these responses are unique because they are some of the first to be recorded and presented for heritage programs in the Maya region. As such, they provide a distinctive window into both the opportunities and challenges of future collaborative efforts in reference to conservation and a study of the past.

"In Their Own Words" is divided into three chapters. Chapter 8 provides responses to programs that focus on what George Nicholas calls "education and empowerment."[2] Evaluative words about programs that mix heritage issues with entertainment and performance are presented in chapter 9. Finally, the place to which these efforts are (hopefully) leading—to heritage without irony—is considered in chapter 10.

NOTES

1. On the topic of the effectiveness of communicating with publics through heritage programming, scrutiny tends to be more common with museum exhibits. For pertinent examples of this literature, see Merriman (2004) and Perry and colleagues (2013, 2014), among others.

2. See Nicholas (1997).

8

⌒

Talking Cultural Heritage at School
with Sarah M. Rowe

In contrast with the antidialogical and non-communicative "deposits" of the banking method of education, the program content of the problem-posing method—dialogical par excellence—is constituted and organized by the students' view of the world, where their own generative themes are found.

—Paolo Freire[1]

As Paolo Freire understood, pedagogy—the science and art of teaching—is powerfully instrumental. Within postrevolutionary México, for example, schools were places where Mexican citizenship was inculcated in youth and Indigenous languages actively discouraged.[2] The "generative themes," in the words of Paolo Freire, were set by the state, and the "bank deposit" method of education, so famously critiqued by Freire, was the default method of education in rural schools throughout México and the Maya region.

In Guatemala and elsewhere, cultural activists have called for the reform of public education—not only in content but also in method and language of delivery—to recognize the "generative themes" of Indigenous peoples.[3] In response to this "politics of recognition," bilingual schools emerged in México and Guatemala in the 1980s and more recently, although they remain poorly funded and often lack bilingual teaching materials.[4]

Maya cultural activist Demetrio Cojtí Cuxil has called for schools to be places where students come to "know their ethnic coordinates and not just those of the hegemonic peoples and current nation-state."[5] When students enter into a pedagogic relationship with a teacher, they already embody an ethnic identity that has formed in relation to family and community. That identity is then cast against what is generally a nationalist discourse and identity that—within Latin America and the Caribbean—until recently did not acknowledge or value Indigenous or

African origins. To be left out of the conversation is to be devalued, to be told that your ethnic coordinates are not important or valuable to the larger society in which a child begins to converse via school education. This is the vulnerability discussed in earlier chapters—the dangerous way in which schools and popular culture can perpetuate inequalities and promote something other than pride in one's identity and heritage.

In the Maya region, this vulnerability contains a perverse twist. The "ancient Maya" are valorized for the purpose of heritage tourism, while a popular discourse of discontinuity and nonrelatedness severs links between past peoples and present descendants. This kind of discourse is typical of places in which a relatively recent colonization has created what is often called "settler societies."[6] The political strategy of nullifying claims to place by prior populations through an assertion of nonrelatedness is particularly alienating for children. Integrated into school pedagogy at the point when children (Indigenous or not) are just beginning to relate to a world outside of their immediate surroundings, the negation of deep history and ancestry is disorienting, to say the least.

Referring to the ethnic coordinates of a student is another way of signaling the cultural heritage of a person. As we shall see below, parents and teachers interviewed in the process of evaluating our heritage school programs favored the integration of Maya heritage into curriculum and identified the need for a more balanced curriculum. Initially, the creation of heritage workshops for primary-school students was not on our radar screen as a high priority. We were more interested in reaching adults and creating a dialogue about heritage conservation—in an effort to reduce looting. But as the Maya Area Cultural Heritage Initiative (MACHI) developed, we perceived its importance to children, teachers, and parents. So we worked to continue school programs in the hope that over time they would become sustainable and incorporated into general school curriculum in western Honduras, in the Toledo District of Belize, and in Yucatán. This hope has only been partially fulfilled and in another place altogether—the Petén—where heritage radio *novelas* were transformed into school curriculum.

Partnering organizations proved to be highly influential to the success and sustainability—in both the short and long run—of the programs. Heritage workshops for children were developed collaboratively in the Department of Copán, Honduras, with Arte Acción Copán Ruinas, and in the Toledo District of Belize with the Julian Cho Society. Both workshops ran concurrently, but the Honduran program always seemed to be infused with lots of excitement and innovation. The disparity lay not in the form of the program but in the partnership itself. Neither Arte Acción Copán Ruinas nor the Julian Cho Society counted among their organizational objectives the conservation of heritage places, but both were dedicated to supporting and strengthening local Indigenous communities.

Both organizations accepted the challenge to develop a heritage education program, but it was the nonprofit whose mission was to stimulate creativity in local children (Arte Acción) rather than the organization dedicated to Indigenous land rights (Julian Cho Society) that proved to be more adept at developing content as well as administering, facilitating, and evaluating the program. The different styles of the two organizations also impacted the number of students reached by the two programs. The Copán Department of Honduras contains a much larger population than the Toledo District of Belize—362,226 in Copán and only 30,538 in Toledo (based on 2010 census data). By 2009, twenty-four communities and almost five hundred students were enrolled in Proyecto Maya in Honduras—it had doubled in size. In the Toledo District, on the other hand, the program never scaled up, and at its peak (2008) it reached 250 school students in 8 villages. The Toledo program was half the size of Proyecto Maya, but then again, the population of Toledo is one-tenth that of Copán.

By far, the largest pedagogical impact occurred through the ProPetén radio *novelas*, which were reinvented as the core of a new curriculum based on Maya cultural heritage. In 2012, more than 128 trained teachers taught the curriculum in 38 schools to 3,000 students. The Department of Petén, Guatemala, incidentally hosts the largest population of the three areas—an estimated 450,000 people (2005 census data). In summary, the effectiveness and impact of a program was partially dependent on the partnering organization, but having a critical mass—people-wise—also improved the likelihood that a program would reach more people.

Because questionnaires such as those presented here are not common in archaeologically inspired heritage programs, responses are presented with minimal "varnish." No elaborate interpretive framework is overlaid on the answers to the questionnaires. Students, parents, teachers, and community members simply speak in their own words. The goal of the questionnaires was to evaluate the program rather than extract personal information from the participants. Nonetheless, questions were vetted through the International Review Board (IRB) process. Generally, we worked with our partnering organization to develop and fine-tune questions; the resulting questionnaire was administered by the partnering organization and the responses generally embedded within an annual report. Precautions were taken to ensure that questions were open-ended and not leading, but nonetheless, the power differentials that realistically exist cannot be completely mitigated in heritage programs such as those contained herein.

In the pages to follow, we examine the response of students, teachers, and community members to talking about cultural heritage during schooltime. First, responses to the school program administered by Arte Acción and Asociación Copán (Proyecto Maya) is considered and second, school workshops held in southern Belize. The Petén radio *novelas* and the curriculum derived from the series are reviewed in the following chapter, as is the introduction of a Yucatec puppet-mentary into primary schools. Significantly, themes of conservation, identity, and loss loom large in all of the responses examined.

PROYECTO MAYA IN COPÁN, HONDURAS

After each year of the Proyecto Maya program, our partnering organization, Arte Acción Copán Ruinas, administered a questionnaire to teachers and a sample of students and opportunistically selected community members. After the responses were reviewed, survey questions often were refined for the following year. As a result of this dynamism, straightforward longitudinal information was not generated, but nonetheless, the responses of those involved in Proyecto Maya provide rich food for thought and contain some counterintuitive responses. Carin Steen of Arte Acción administered the 2007–2010 surveys. The 2011 surveys were administered by the Arte Acción facilitators (workshop teachers) supervised by Carin Steen, and for the 2012 surveys, facilitators handled all aspects of the survey. Finally, Asociación Copán—which assumed administration of the program in 2013—distributed the questionnaires and tallied the responses for the 2013 program.

The reach of Proyecto Maya can be seen from table 8.1, which provides a listing of the number of community schools served by the workshops each year, with a peak of 4,980 workshop participants (the sum of students present for each workshop in each community) in 2009. During 2007 and 2008, two trained facilitators (Londin Velásquez and Moisés Mancia) traveled to a school in each of the participating communities once per month to deliver a workshop on Maya cultural heritage during schooltime. When the program was expanded in 2009 and 2010, Elsa Morales became the third facilitator, and the number of communities increased to twenty-four. Personnel losses in 2011–2013 and shifting administration of the program from Arte Acción Copán Ruinas (which shuttered its doors after 2010) directly to a small group of facilitators led by Elsa Morales and Marlen Vásquez and then to Asociación Copán coincided with scaling back the program.

Table 8.1. Impact of Proyecto Maya cultural heritage workshops in Copán, Honduras.

Year	Communities Included	Total Number of Workshops Offered Each Year	Total Number of Workshop Participants (sum of students present for each workshop)
2007	16	150	2,848
2008	18	162	3,181
2009	24	214	4,980
2010	24	219	4,063
2011	11	98	2,070
2012	10	90	2,136
2013	12	84	2,367

Offered to fourth-, fifth-, and sixth-grade students, the workshops were thematic and covered the topics germane to the cultural and natural environment of past and present:

La Antigua Cultural Maya en Copán (The Ancient Maya of Copán);
La Agricultura (Agriculture, offered only in 2007; from 2008 on, this topic was split into La Naturaleza [Nature] and El Maíz [Corn]);
La Naturaleza;
El Maíz;
La Religión (Religion);
Los Gobernantes (Rulers; after 2008, this module was renamed Los Reyes [The Kings]);
Las Ciencias (Sciences, including mathematics);
La Escritura (Writing);
La Arqueología (Archaeology);
La Conservación (Heritage Conservation, combined with other themes after 2007); and
Los Mayas de Hoy (Maya of Today).

Listening to Copán Students

The teachers and administrators of Arte Acción asked a sample of the students what they liked about the workshops. The majority of students responded either that they liked the opportunity to learn about the ancient Maya (with some using the phrase "our ancestors") or that they liked the workshops in general because they were fun and interesting. Carin Steen placed an emphasis on interactivity, physical exercise, and art projects that were incorporated into workshops and created a lively and creative atmosphere.

But which themes really captured the imagination of students? While the ability of the facilitators to teach a theme no doubt factored into student impressions, nonetheless La Naturaleza, complete with a discussion of the role of monkeys and jaguars in Classic Maya cosmology, was the most popular theme every year except the first (when it was combined with Agricultura, which was voted the most popular) and the final year of 2013, when La Antigua Cultura Maya took first place (table 8.2). Other popular themes included El Maíz, in which maize is discussed as part of creation narratives and also in reference to the maize deity. El Maíz ranked second from 2008 through 2010 and tied for third place in 2013. La Arqueología (third in 2007 and second in 2011 and 2012) proved to be a popular theme, and students expressed satisfaction in learning what foreigners did when they disappeared into tunnels under the Copán Acropolis. Los Reyes (which presents the rulers of Copán with attention to the sequence of rulers shown on Copán Altar Q) took third place from 2008 to 2010. During 2007, the theme of La Religión took

Table 8.2. Popularity of different workshop themes.

Workshop Theme	2007	2008[a]	2009	2010	2011	2012[b]	2013
La Antigua Cultura Maya	23%	31	10%	27%	14%		16%
La Agricultura	49%	N/A	N/A	N/A	N/A		N/A
El Maíz	N/A	45	12%	59%	10%		11%
La Naturaleza	N/A	77	28%	63%	19%	1st	13%
La Religión	46%	29	8%	28%	6%		9%
Los Gobernantes (Los Reyes)	33%	40	11%	32%	10%		10%
Las Ciencias (Matematica)	28%	9[c]	4%	13%	7%		9%
La Escritura	33%	33	10%	18%	10%		11%
La Arqueología	37%	34	9%	28%	17%	2nd	11%
La Conservación	11%	N/A	N/A	N/A	N/A		N/A
Los Mayas de Hoy	16%	31	7%	14%	11%		10%

[a]For 2008, themes that were a student's first choice received three points, second choice received two points, and third choice received one point. Thus, scores cannot be converted to percentages as they are weighted.
[b]In 2012, students were only asked to rank their first and second most popular themes.
[c]For this survey, Carin Steen indicated that the children probably did not realize that mathematics was part of the unit, and if they had it would have scored the theme higher because the facilitators perceived that the children really liked the workshop while it was being presented.

second place. The religion theme introduced Maya deities, encouraged students to think about pyramids as once-sacred shrines, and discussed the conversion to Christianity that took place after Spanish political conquest. Finally, La Escritura, which provided a rudimentary understanding of hieroglyphs as a logo-syllabic form of writing, tied for third place in 2013.

Conversely, the least popular themes were La Conservación in 2007 (before being integrated into the other topics), Las Ciencias for three years running (2008–2010), and La Religión in 2011. In 2013, La Religión and Las Ciencias tied for least popular. It's not hard to understand why La Conservación, by itself, was not terribly popular; the theme could hardly compete with jaguars and monkeys for the attention of fourth through sixth graders. From the simple ranking of themes, it's not clear if there was a certain amount of discomfort with the topic of religion and the notion that pyramids could be considered ancient churches and thus the low ranking. Another least favorite—Las Ciencias—covered bar and dot counting, the calendar, and a little astronomy. Perhaps the lack of popularity was due to the complexity of the interlocking calendars, which may have challenged students. Steen did indicate, however, that in 2008 the students particularly liked the counting (mathematical) portion of the workshop. Otherwise, the students seemed to be most interested in the workshops that elaborated upon topics with which they already had a familiarity, such as maize, or which held intrinsic interest, such as wild animals of the forest.

The cultural heritage workshops took place in three kinds of communities: (1) those that self-identified on the community level as Ch'orti'; (2) those that identified as Ladino; and (3) those with a mixture of Ch'orti' and Ladino identities. Starting in 2010, students were asked if they identified as Ch'orti' and if their parents or grandparents identified as Ch'orti' (table 8.3). Despite expectations that fewer students would identify as Ch'orti' than would ascribe Ch'orti' identity to parents or grandparents, there is tremendous intergenerational continuity in ethnic identity. That is, if students identified as Ch'orti', they generally indicated that so did their parents and grandparents. Likewise, when students did not identify as Ch'orti', then most of the time the student indicated that neither parents nor grandparents identified as Ch'orti' either. Ethnic identification is a decision charged with layers of social meaning, and a simple question to youths cannot capture this complexity; however, the stability of the trend does suggest the prevalence of long-term ethnically distinct communities that could push back sixty years or more. Local residents of Copán Ruinas are quick to describe the small surrounding *aldeas* (towns) as Ch'orti' or Ladino but rarely as mixed. Such vernacular distinctions suggest that these differences have been stable through several generations—an example of the vicerality of Indigenous identity discussed by Javier Sanjinés.[7]

The communities that participated in Proyecto Maya fluctuated over the years, and the shifting ratio of Ch'orti' to Ladino *aldeas* is reflected in the survey data. During the two bookend years (2010 and 2013) in which the question of ethnic identity was asked, more Ch'orti' communities participated, and the resultant ratios of Ch'orti' to Ladino self-identity were 54 percent to 46 percent and 55 percent to 45 percent, respectively. In the intervening years of 2011 and 2012, fewer Ch'orti' communities participated, and the ratios fell to 29 percent to 71 percent in 2011 and 35 percent to 59 percent in 2012, with 6 percent of respondents declining to assert an ethnic identity in 2012.

One student (presumably Ladino) was particularly impressed by a statement contained in the Los Mayas de Hoy (Maya of Today) chapter of the student

Table 8.3. Student self-identification as to ethnicity along with ethnic ascription given to parents and grandparents in response to the question, "Are you Maya Ch'orti'?"

	Year																			
	2010						2011						2012		2013					
	Me		My Parents		My Grandparents		Me		My Parents		My Grandparents		Me		Me		My Parents		My Grandparents	
Response	n	%	n	%	n	%	n	%	n	%	n	%	n	%	n	%	n	%	n	%
Yes	97	54%	94	53%	97	54%	29	29%	24	24%	30	30%	42	35%	55	55%	55	55%	55	55%
No	81	46%	84	47%	81	46%	71	71%	74	76%	70	70%	71	59%	45	45%	45	45%	45	45%
No response	0	0%	0	0%	0	0%	0	0%	0	0%	0	0%	7	6%	0	0%	0	0%	0	0%
Total	178	100%	178	100%	178	100%	100	100%	98	100%	100	100%	120	100%	100	100%	100	100%	100	100%

workbook. The chapter states that Maya peoples did not disappear after the Classic period and that there are more than six million people who speak a Mayan language. In responding to the query, "What have you learned about the Maya?" he wrote the following: "*Yo aprendí a no burlarnos de ellos porque no nos gustaría que ellos se burlan de nosotros y también sabemos que existen más de 6 millones de ellos.*" ("I learned that we should not make fun of them because we wouldn't like it if they made fun of us and also we know that there exist more than six million of them."[8]) This student seems impressed and a little intimidated by the sheer size of the Mayan-speaking population, and unfortunately an "us versus them" ethnic polarity comes through quite clearly in this declaration of learning.

Los Mayas de Hoy was the final theme of the workshop series, and by placing it in this capstone position, we had hoped to shore up the fraying edges of Maya cultural heritage and dispel the notion that the Maya peoples who built the massive pyramidal shrines of the classic period had disappeared only to be replaced by pale shadows of the past. After the inaugural year of Proyecto Maya, Londin Velásquez (one of the facilitators) recalled this exchange with workshop students (presumably in a Ch'orti' community) on the subject of the disappearing Maya:

Londin: ¿Piensan que aún hay Mayas hoy? (Do you think that there are still Maya people today?)

Niños: ¡No! Se murieron todos. . . . (No! They all died. . . .)

Londin: Pero yo soy Maya, ¡y ustedes también! (But I am Mayan, and so are you!)

(Unos minutos después) (A few minutes later)

Londin: Entonces, ¿Les da vergüenza ser Maya? (So, are you ashamed to be Maya?)

Niños: ¡¡¡NO!!!

The workshops unapologetically linked the past with the present, but they also addressed the many ways in which life today is much different than during pre-Columbian times. At the end of the year, students were asked what they perceived to be an important difference between Maya peoples of today and those who lived in the past. Here's the question verbatim: "*¿Cuál es la diferencia entre la cultura Maya de antes y la de hoy?*" ("How is Maya culture of today different from the past?") The answers are surprising (table 8.4). The fourth- through sixth-grade students most frequently cited dress as an important distinction between the past and the present. At first glance, this response seems superficial, until one thinks about the fact that our images of Maya life in the past inevitably are drawn from Classic Maya royal iconography. In that medium, men wear lots of jade jewelry and elaborate headdresses (a perennial favorite to re-create during art time), and the women are sheathed in intricately embroidered *huipiles*. They were wealthy, their clothes showed it, and the children perceived that as a major difference.

Table 8.4. Student responses to the question, "How is Maya culture of today different from the past?"

Response	Year									
	2009		2010		2011		2012[a]		2013[b]	
	n	%	n	%	n	%	n	%	n	%
How they dressed	9	15%	24	49%	48	66%	X	—	—	27%
Their religion	6	10%	7	14%	1	1%	X	—	—	3%
Relationship with natural world	8	13%	4	8%	3	4%	X	—	—	0%
Technology	4	7%	5	10%	3	4%	—	—	—	48%
Morality	3	5%	0	0%	2	3%	—	—	—	0%
General differences	15	25%	9	18%	16	22%	—	—	—	22%
No response	16	26%	0	0%	0	0%	—	—	—	0%
Total	**61**	**100%**	**49**	**100%**	**73**	**100%**	**—**	**—**	**—**	**100%**

Note: Totals may not equal 100 percent due to rounding.
[a]In 2012, students were provided with a menu that limited responses.
[b]For 2013, only percentage data were calculated.

The second most important difference to students was religion. The majority of students are nominally Catholic or Evangelical Christians. Few Copán-area students indicated that they have ever participated in a Maya ceremony. For Copán students, Maya religious practices of the past are completely different from the range of Christian religious activities that are present today in their lives. Over the years of the survey, changes in the relationship between people and their natural world ranked almost equal to religion as an important change between then and now. In citing these kinds of changes, some students might have been referring to the general lack of jaguars and monkeys in their immediate landscapes (as opposed to what they imagine to have been the situation in the past), but others may be referencing a visceral angst and critique often voiced by Indigenous adults regarding the dangerous entanglement between the creative destruction of capitalism and the natural world.

Significantly, technology does not rank as a major distinction between now and then except for the final year of the survey. While there is nothing in the survey responses to explain this sudden change, it is possible that new facilitators in the final year emphasized different features of Maya culture. During all previous years, students considered it a minor difference. This intriguing perspective may relate to the fact that students are not living a life that is steeped in technology— some of them don't even have electricity at home or in their school—and so their life technologically doesn't seem so different from the past. Insofar as opportunity can be linked with the accessibility of technology in today's world, this response is very sobering. A final specific difference proposed was a change in morality (table 8.4). Likely linked to the practice of ritual human sacrifice in the past (which was neither emphasized nor denied in the workshops), morality was cited as an important difference by a few students in both the 2009 and 2011 surveys.

Since the theme of heritage conservation wound through the workshops, we wondered how the students thought about objects from the past that they encounter in their daily life. Beginning in 2010, we asked, "*¿En su opinión, qué se debe hacer con un artefacto maya que se encuentra?*" ("In your opinion, what should someone do with Maya artifacts that they find?") During the first two years, responses varied in an intriguing fashion but settled into the standard "Give it to the authorities" response in the last two years (table 8.5). This response dominated in all four years and probably was the response that students thought the program facilitators wanted to hear. Nonetheless, over one-quarter of the 2011 students surveyed preferred to keep the artifact. This response had increased from 3 percent in 2010 but disappeared altogether in 2012 and 2013.

During 2010, one-third of the students responded that the best thing to do would be *to take care of* the artifact. This response dwindled to only 4 percent in 2011 and also disappeared thereafter (table 8.5). The custodial response is intriguing because it doesn't refer to a higher authority and neither does it assume the possessiveness of "keeping it" or the commoditization of "selling it." Rather, it invokes the kind of stewardship toward objects that is written into the Society for American Archaeology Principles of Ethics (discussed in chapter 1). Amazingly, this response comes from third- to fifth-grade students who live an impoverished and increasingly desperate existence and have limited opportunities to attend high school—much less college—or to start a community heritage center at which such objects might be taken care of. This response constitutes an opening for

Table 8.5. Student responses to the question of what should happen to Maya artifacts that are encountered.

	Year							
	2010		2011		2012[a]		2013[a]	
Response	n	%	n	%	n	%	n	%
Give it to the authorities	69	62%	71	62%	—	100%	—	100%
Keep it	3	3%	30	26%	—	0%	—	0%
Take care of it	37	33%	4	4%	—	0%	—	0%
Sell it	2	2%	4	4%	—	0%	—	0%
Paint it	1	1%	5	4%	—	0%	—	0%
Total	**112**	**100%**	**114**	**100%**	**—**	**100%**	**—**	**100%**

Note: Totals may not equal 100 percent due to rounding.
[a]For 2012 and 2013, only percentage data were calculated.

collaboration—a space in which opinions about what should be done with things of the past converge. As has occurred throughout Oaxaca, México,[9] this response signals the interest of local communities in caring for their cultural heritage and their desire to engage locally in such practices.

A small but predictable percentage (2 and 4 percent in 2010 and 2011, respectively) of students would sell the found object, and another small fraction declared that they would paint the object. The artist and program administrator Carin Steen is a painter, and students often painted on paper and other media during workshops. More than one school exterior was adorned with a vibrant polychrome mural painted by Carin Steen and students during the run of the workshops. It's possible that students perceived painting as another way of caring for and conserving a material thing in a traditional manner that is linked to practices of adorning and honoring.

One final student question-and-response to be presented and discussed here touches upon claiming ancient Maya archaeological sites: specifically, "*¿A quién o quiénes pertenecen o deben pertenecer los antiguos sitios mayas?*" ("To whom do ancient Maya sites belong or to whom should they belong?") Admittedly, this question poses a difficulty quandary, even for professional archaeologists and cultural heritage specialists. Nonetheless, we wanted to know what the kids thought about this hot-button issue (table 8.6). As for previous topics, the question was asked in an open-ended fashion in all years, but we only received verbatim student responses in 2010 and 2011. In 2012 and 2013, program

Table 8.6. Student responses to the question, "To whom do ancient Maya sites belong?"

	Year							
	2010		2011		2012[a]		2013[b]	
Response	n	%	n	%	n	%	n	%
To Indigenous Maya people	51	38%	25	22%	—	—	—	10%
To the *pueblo* (town and people)	27	20%	20	17%	X	—	—	—
To the ruins	0	0%	47	41%	X	—	—	—
To archaeologists/experts	19	14%	2	2%	—	—	—	20%
To the Honduran state	26	19%	10	9%	—	—	—	55%
To the world	6	4%	7	6%	X	—	—	—
To elders	5	4%	1	1%	—	—	—	—
To kids	1	1%	2	2%	—	—	—	—
To poor people	1	1%	1	1%	—	—	—	—
To nobody	—	0%	—	0%	—	—	—	15%
Total	**136**	**100%**	**115**	**100%**	**—**	**—**	**—**	**100%**

Note: Totals may not equal 100 percent due to rounding.
[a]In 2012, only a summary of students' responses was provided in the annual report to MACHI.
[b]In 2013, we received percentage data.

facilitators processed student responses and provided us with a summary. An unnumbered list of themes was provided in 2012, while the responses in 2013 were tabulated and converted into percentages without providing raw counts. The themes were consistent across years except for the addition of a new category ("to nobody") in 2013. Despite the differences in data collection over the years, table 8.6 indicates some strong trends; responses are roughly ordered in descending popularity.

The workshop textbooks or sessions offered no programmatic statements about site ownership, yet the idea that the old places belong to Indigenous Maya people was popular. In 2010, over a third of the students voiced this opinion. This fraction decreased to 22 percent in 2011, did not register at all in 2012, and reemerged at 10 percent of the students in 2013. Only slightly less popular was the idea that archaeological sites belong to the *pueblo* (the town and its people) in which the site is located. Gaining 20 percent of the responses in 2010 and 17 percent in 2011, this response made the top-three responses for 2012 but did not make the final list for 2013. A less identity-based response, the attribution of sites to their *pueblos* may reflect the participation of Ladino students, who would see the issue more broadly. Also, the fact that there is a very close linkage between the nearby *pueblo* of Copán Ruinas and the archaeological site no doubt informed student responses.

In the years 2011 and 2012, a significant percentage of students responded enigmatically that sites belonged "to the ruins." A full 41 percent took this position in 2011 and an undocumented fraction in 2012. Apparently, during these years students were thinking about some form of jurisdictional autonomy for archaeological sites. The next three categories of belonging refer to the usual stakeholders: archaeologists/experts, the nation-state, and the world. Over the years, only 2 to 20 percent of students considered archaeological sites to be the possessed domain of archaeologists. From a low of 9 to a high of 55 percent, many students responded that archaeological sites belonged to the nation and all people of Honduras (this response corresponds to Honduran law and the authority vested in the Instituto Hondureño de Antropología e Historia, IHAH). Copán is a World Heritage Site and in this "U.N. sense" is possessed by the world, but most students didn't see it that way. Only 4 to 6 percent (in 2010 and 2011, respectively) cited the world as an important stakeholder of archaeological sites; the world also was present as one of the top-three choices for 2012.

Working down the ranking of responses in table 8.6, the next three entries— elders, kids, and poor people—each received no more than 4 percent of the vote (elders received 4 percent in 2010). This atomic splitting of categories of belonging is reversed in the final entry—"to nobody"—which amazingly received 15 percent of the responses in 2013. It's hard to interpret this category, which could intimate that sites don't belong to any constituency in particular and thus to everyone; or the students could be expressing the thought that a discourse of possession is not appropriate for archaeological sites. It's deep thinking either way.

Although we set out to share archaeological knowledge with students and open a dialogue about heritage conservation, their responses to the questionnaires indicate that something much deeper runs under the surface of poorly funded schools in the outback of Copán Ruinas—a desire to care for things of the past and to keep them close. The student responses proved to be insightful and thoughtful in a philosophical way.

Thoughts of Copán Teachers

Since the workshops interrupted the regular school day and a preestablished lesson plan, we wanted to ask the teachers' opinion about the value of the program to student education. Over the years, between ten and twenty-four teachers participated in the survey (table 8.7; there was no teacher survey in 2012). First, we asked the teachers the following question: *"¿Piensa que es importante que los niños en Copán Ruinas reciban clases sobre la cultura Maya?"* ("Do you think that it is important for the children in Copán to receive classes on Maya cultural heritage?") Possible responses could range from very important to not important at all. The majority felt that the workshops were very important (between 75 percent and 100 percent annually), with the remaining responding that the workshops were important and none responding that the workshops were not very important or not important at all. The teachers who work at rural schools often start their day by ladling out *atole* (maize gruel) to students who may not have had anything to eat that morning. Yet these same teachers felt strongly that talking heritage during schooltime enriched the curriculum in a culturally sensitive manner.

Table 8.7. Responses from teachers when asked if it is important for the children in Copán to receive classes on Maya cultural heritage.

Level of Importance	2007 n/%	2008 n/%	2009 n/%	2010 n/%	2011 n/%	2013 n/%
Very important	14/87.5%	16/84%	17/77%	21/87%	10/100%	9/75%
Important	2/12.5%	3/16%	5/23%	3/13%	0/0%	3/25%
Not so important	0/0%	0/0%	0/0%	0/0%	0/0%	0/0%
Not important	0/0%	0/0%	0/0%	0/0%	0/0%	0/0%
Total	16/100%	19/100%	22/100%	24/100%	10/100%	12/100%

Note: Teacher survey was not administered in 2012.

Next, we asked the teachers to state why they thought the workshops were important. Sometimes teachers listed more than one reason. Each reason was given a tabulation of 1, and the results were converted to percentages in order to compare with years when only percentage tabulations were reported (table 8.8;

note that this question was not asked in 2010; five years of responses are provided in this table). Teachers offered five different reasons why the heritage workshops were important, but one reason was cited more frequently than others. The response "because the Maya are the ancestors of the students" was included in 36 percent to 47 percent of the teachers' answers. From the teachers' perspective—and some of these responses came from teachers working in Ladino communities—students should learn the history of their ancestors. They felt that it should be part of the curriculum. Each year, a significant percentage of teachers (between 10 percent and 33 percent) stated that the heritage workshops would "promote modern culture." It's not clear whether the subtext of this response is the adage "you can't know where you are going until you know where you came from" or if teachers are referring to the need for knowledgeable tour guides in the heritage tourism industry, which was huge in Honduras before the 2009 coup and the uptick in drug-related violence and out-migration.

Table 8.8. Responses from teachers when asked why it is important for students to receive classes on Maya cultural heritage.

Reasons Given	2007	2008	2009	2011	2013
Because the Maya are the ancestors of the students	47%	47%	36%	40%	42%
To promote modern culture	33%	24%	27%	10%	25%
To become capable in tourism and environmental/ local resource management	7%	24%	23%	20%	0%
For general learning	13%	0%	9%	20%	33%
Because the Maya were important	0%	5%	5%	10%	0%

Heritage tourism and related professions of environmental and resource management were directly cited as a reason for the workshops by 7 percent to 24 percent of teachers (table 8.8). It's somewhat surprising that these percentages were not higher since the economy of Copán Ruinas sinks or swims on heritage tourism. From the teachers' perspective, linking classroom content to a potential job was not a strong motivating factor for the workshops. The next reason given, "for general learning," was cited by up to 33 percent of teachers in 2013. This answer provides further support for the notion that teachers did not view the cultural heritage workshop from a vocational-technical vantage point, perhaps because of the young age of the students (in fourth through sixth grade). Rather, the content of the workshops was viewed as providing instruction on a subject that generally was important for students, particularly because of their ancestry, their location near the World Heritage Site of Copán, and because "the Maya were important," a reason cited by 10 percent of teachers in 2011.

We asked the teachers to evaluate whether or not Proyecto Maya contributed to the conservation of Maya cultural heritage, both ancient and contemporary

("*¿Piensa que este proyecto contribuye a la conservación de la cultura Maya, tanto la antigua como la contemporanea? Por qué si, o no?*"). The overwhelming majority of teachers thought that the program did contribute to conservation but for different reasons (table 8.9). A concern with cultural loss was the most prevalent response (between 38 percent and 67 percent), which likely refers to the loss of spoken Ch'orti' and associated cultural practices within the Ch'orti' *aldeas*. The perception of loss stands somewhat at odds with the stability of Ch'orti' communities through time.[10]

A considerable number of teachers (13 percent to 19 percent in 2008, 2009, and 2011) thought that Proyecto Maya workshops resulted in greater conservation of Maya cultural heritage (table 8.9). Linked to this response was the assertion that students become more aware of the need for conservation of archaeological sites after they learn something about the ancient Maya. Up to 31 percent of teacher responses in 2008 made this linkage. Finally, teachers cited the workshop themes as important to heritage conservation.

Each year, the teachers were asked for general ideas and suggestions. All wanted to see the project continue, although one suggested that the workshops be held outside of normal class times. Other teachers suggested offering more workshops (twice rather than once per month) and expanding the cultural enrichment program to all grades. Some teachers requested extra materials and teachers' guides so that they could continue the themes and devote more time to them. One teacher wrote that if the workshops couldn't continue, then the teachers should band together to continue the program.

Teachers also expressed the wish that the Ministry of Education and other government agencies would support the program since the teachers are charged with implementing an intercultural program but resources are scarce to create

Table 8.9. Responses from teachers when asked whether or not Proyecto Maya contributes to the conservation of Maya cultural heritage (both ancient and contemporary).

Contribution to Heritage Conservation	2008	2009	2010	2011[a]	2013[a]
Yes, because people are losing their culture and the program foments interest in it.	44%	38%	N/A	46%	67%
Yes, because the program promotes conservation of sites and artifacts.	13%	19%	N/A	15%	0%
Yes, because the students learn about the ancient Maya.	31%	14%	N/A	8%	0%
Yes, because the themes are important.	6%	19%	N/A	31%	0%
Yes	6%	5%	100%	N/A	N/A
No	0%	5%	0%	N/A	N/A
No response	N/A	N/A	N/A	N/A	33%

Note: In 2012 (not shown here), teachers were given the option of answering either "yes" or "no."
[a] In 2011 and 2013, a "yes" or "no" response was not an option.

new curricula. Printing a textbook for each student constituted one of the major expenses of Proyecto Maya and proved to be an obstacle to garnering support and sustainability for the program with national education ministries in both Honduras and Guatemala. Printed textbooks are very expensive in Latin America—particularly given the modest income of most rural families. Parents routinely cite the price of textbooks as a major reason why their children are not able to attend school after grade 6.

Words of Copán Community Members

During four years of Proyecto Maya (2007, 2008, 2010, and 2013), members of the community of Copán Ruinas and surrounding *aldeas* were asked their opinion of the program. Between nine and thirty-four individuals—generally adults—were queried during each round of opportunistic interviewing. The opening questions were similar to those asked of the teachers, and the responses were also similar. In an effort to gauge how the education program was received within the community, we asked individuals about the specific impacts of Proyecto Maya on the Ch'orti' community ("*¿Piensa que la educación sobre la cultura Maya tiene un impacto [positivo o negative] en la comunidad Maya Ch'orti'?*"). Answers to this question are less generic and more focused (table 8.10).

Learning about past Maya culture ranked high in 2007 and 2008 (37.5 percent and 46 percent, respectively) and was one of the top-three positive impacts cited in 2010 (table 8.10). Connecting people to the past was cited by at least a quarter of those interviewed during three of the four years of community interviews. Many of the interviewed community members self-identified as Ch'orti', so this response can be taken to indicate a desire to feel a greater connection to the past, perhaps to the archaeological site of Copán itself, which increasingly is referred to as a sacred ancestral site by Ch'orti' cultural activists.[11]

In three of the four years, Proyecto Maya was cited as supporting modern cultural identity and language, apparently because of the emphasis on Ch'orti' vocabulary

Table 8.10. Copán community members address the impact of Proyecto Maya on the Ch'orti' community.

Positive Impact for the Following Reasons:	2007	2008	2010[a]	2013[b]
Learning about past Maya culture	37.50%	46%	x	
Connecting people to the past	25%	31%		50%
Supporting modern cultural identity and language	0%	15%	x	50%
Learning about archaeology	0%	0%	x	
Generally positive learning outcomes	12.50%	0%		
Positive, with no additional explanation	25%	8%		

[a]In 2010, only the range of responses was recorded.
[b]In 2013, only percentages were recorded.

during the workshops and the Ch'orti' text in the coloring books that were distributed to the younger schoolchildren. Learning about archaeology in general was cited as one of the top-three positive outcomes in 2010, and during 2007 "generally positive learning outcomes" were mentioned by over 10 percent of interviewees. In short, access to a past that is shaped by archaeologists and also connecting to that past were the top-two positive impacts of the workshops in the opinion of Copán community members. Supporting the survival of the Ch'orti' language was also cited, likely because it is a high-profile issue within the Ch'orti' community.

During 2010 and 2013, interviewees also were asked if they identified ethnically as Ch'orti' Maya and if their parents and grandparents identified as Ch'orti' Maya. The majority responded affirmatively (table 8.11). As with the students, ethnic identity shows stability over three generations, with the fluctuations in table 8.11 likely due to sampling technique. A follow-up question also was asked: "*¿Si usted se considera maya ch'orti', siempre fue así? ¿En el caso que empezó a considerarse maya ch'orti' más tarde, cuando y por qué fue?*" ("If you identify as Ch'orti', has that always been the case? If you have only recently begun to consider yourself as Ch'orti', when and why did the change occur?") The majority of people responded that they either have always considered themselves to be Ch'orti' or "Ch'orti' since childhood." In 2010, one person drew a distinction between being Ch'orti' and belonging to CONIMCHH (Consejo Nacional de Indígenas Maya Ch'orti' Honduras, an Indigenous Ch'orti' organization dedicated to land rights, language revival, and greater involvement in the archaeological site of Copán, among other goals). Also in 2010, two individuals said they realized their Ch'orti' identity when they were undergoing teacher training. In the 2013 survey, a surprising 36 percent of respondents who answered the question affirmatively said that they considered themselves to be Ch'orti' after receiving a parcel of land. (Although the mechanics of land acquisition were not specified in the questionnaire, CONIMCHH has been a strong advocate of land redistribution in the Copán region and probably played a role in what Joy Logan calls the process of "re-ethnification."[12])

Such re-ethnification points to a way in which issues of identity shift through the life cycle of a person. Adults are concerned with having enough land to farm in

Table 8.11. Community member self-identification as to ethnicity along with ethnic ascription given to parents and grandparents in response to the question, "Are you Maya Ch'orti'?"

Response	2010			2013		
	Me	My parents	My grandparents	Me	My parents	My grandparents
Yes	79%	74%	85%	69%	69%	69%
No	18%	26%	—	31%	31%	31%
No response	3%	—	15%	—	—	—

order to feed their families—a concern that youths might only learn as they grow older. Another apparent age-grade distinction between the surveys appeared in the responses to the question, "*¿Ha participado alguna vez en una ceremonia maya?*" ("Have you ever participated in a Maya ceremony?") When students were asked this question, a majority responded that they had not taken part in a Maya ceremony. In contrast, among adult community members 50 percent responded affirmatively in 2010, and in 2013 100 percent of participants declared that they had participated in a Maya ceremony. So either Ch'orti' ceremonies are for adults only or, more likely, schoolchildren did participate but didn't associate the activity with something they would call a ceremony.

Finally, the question of to whom the places of the ancient Maya belong was broached with community members in 2010 and 2013. The wording of the query is repeated here: "*¿A quién o quiénes pertenecen o deben pertenecer los antiguos sitios mayas?*" Similar to student responses, interviewees (between a quarter and a third) expressed the opinion that ancient Maya sites belong to Indigenous people (table 8.12). The idea that sites belong to all Hondurans and thus to the state also was popular among adults and students, as discussed earlier. The sentiment that archaeological sites belong to the places of the past and the people who once inhabited them (ruins among the students and the ancient Maya among community members) was voiced by a small percentage of respondents in 2013. In 2010, over a third of interviewees expressed no opinion about site belonging, and adults definitely did not voice the wide range of opinions and creative options expressed by students (table 8.6).

Table 8.12. Response of community members to the question, "To whom do ancient Maya sites belong?"

Sites Belong To	2010	2013
Indigenous people	35%	23%
The ancient Maya	0%	8%
Hondurans and the state	26%	69%
No opinion	39%	0%

All told, engagement with the past and with current identity in the Copán area is an ongoing concern. Ch'orti' struggles for land and recognition cross-thread with the high-profile World Heritage Site of Copán and combine to create a perfect storm of ethnicity and heritage.[13] Questions about who owns the past and who will benefit from it (via heritage tourism) are front-burner issues. Let's now turn to the Toledo District of Belize, where land rights play a similar and dominant role in ethnic consciousness but have not been linked explicitly to Classic Maya archaeological sites.

HERITAGE WORKSHOPS IN TOLEDO, BELIZE

In collaboration with the Julian Cho Society, heritage workshops in schools were offered from 2007 through 2009 in seven to nine communities of the Toledo District of Belize. Ethnic composition of the students in the workshops was largely Q'eqchi' and Mopan Maya; for many children who attended the workshops, one of these two Indigenous languages was their first and dominant language. As discussed earlier, resolution of conflict over the legal status of traditional-use lands on the so-called Indian reserves in Toledo was a hot-button issue during this time, as were large-scale oil and timber leases awarded by the government to private contractors on lands near or on reserves. Our collaborative partner, the Julian Cho Society, was dedicated to resolving the conflict and securing communal land rights for the several dozen Indigenous communities of the Toledo District. Political discourse was never built into workshop themes or the pedagogical approach, although in the minds of many, our partnership with the Julian Cho Society was proof that we were entangled in the struggle. The workshops did explicitly assert an ancestral connection between the people of Toledo and archaeological features of the Toledo cultural landscape. This patrimonialist discourse placed us in conflict with the government of Belize and the official ideology that everyone living in Belize—including the people of Toledo—is a recent immigrant and thus no one possesses special rights to land.

In 2007, local facilitator Marvin Coc worked with Reiko Ishihara-Brito to develop workshop themes and a series of presentations based on digitized imagery of archaeological sites, iconography, and plants and animals of the Maya region. Topics tracked those of Proyecto Maya but emphasized large, local archaeological sites that have been developed or are under development for tourism: Nim Li Punit, Lubaantun, Uxbenka, and Pusilha. The student textbook, *Seeing Our Ancestors*, was translated into Q'eqchi' and Mopan during this time. In 2008, Claire Novotny completed an internship in Toledo and worked with Marvin Coc to make the workshops more accessible and fun for fourth- to sixth-grade students in the seven participating communities: San Miguel, Silver Creek, Santa Cruz, San Antonio, San Pedro Columbia, Santa Elena, and Indian Creek. The questionnaires and exams completed by 144 students (71 males, 72 females, and 1 nondisclosed) in these communities during the 2008 school year form the basis for reviewing the Toledo workshops. As we shall see, student responses bear certain similarities to those of the Copán schoolchildren—particularly a reticence to engage with the complexities of the old Maya calendar—but also diverge in significant ways that accentuate local tensions surrounding land and government leases for resource extraction. After considering student responses, we turn to teachers' thoughts about the workshops and finally to those of parents and community members.

Students Express Their Thoughts

When Toledo students were asked—in an open-ended fashion—for suggestions about conserving old Maya places and objects, they provided a number of suggestions (table 8.13). The central tendency of their responses hovered around protecting and taking care of sites and objects (this response ranged between 14 percent and 100 percent of suggestions provided within each school). This response is similar to that of Copán schoolchildren and suggests, once again, that an ethic of conservation is not foreign to kids in rural schools in the Maya region. As discussed shortly, some teachers in the Toledo District view archaeologists as active agents of a nonconservation agenda, which strengthens the need for greater dialogue and collaborative effort.

Table 8.13. Student suggestions for conservation of old Maya sites and objects, Toledo, Belize.

	Community						
	San Miguel	Silver Creek	Santa Cruz	San Antonio	San Pedro Columbia	Santa Elena	Indian Creek
Suggestion	n/%	n/%	n/%	n/%	n/%	n/%	n/%
Don't steal or sell objects.	8/40%	6/29%	0	0	2/5%	0	5/16%
Take things from sites.	0	1/5%	0	0	0	0	0
Don't vandalize sites or stelae.	4/20%	4/19%	2/11%	0	12/30%	0	13/41%
Mark stelae/sites.	0	2/9%	0	0	0	0	0
Protect/take care of sites and objects.	8/40%	3/14%	13/72.2%	7/100%	25/62.5%	6/100%	11/34%
Destroy things that don't belong to us.	0	0	0	0	0	0	1/3%
Show visitors and educate people about sites.	0	4/19%	0	0	0	0	0
Keep things in a museum.	0	1/5%	1/5.6%	0	0	0	0
Don't dig for oil.	0	0	0	0	1/2.5%	0	0
Clear land and dig for oil.	0	0	1/5.6%	0	0	0	0
No response	0	0	1/5.6%	0	0	0	2/6%
Total	20	21	18	7	40	6	32

The second most popular suggestion for conservation among schoolchildren was to refrain from stealing or selling objects (from 5 percent to 40 percent of responses within each school; table 8.13). Significantly, no students from Santa Cruz—a town located proximate to the classic Maya site of Uxbenka—offered this suggestion. In the past, "jade hunting" in the mounds of Uxbenka was a pastime that some townspeople freely admitted to. This response did register at other schools proximate to large archaeological sites. Specifically, students who lived near Lubaantun in the towns of San Miguel and San Pedro Columbia (40 percent and 5 percent, respectively) offered this suggestion, as did 16 percent of students living in Indian Creek, which is the community proximate to Nim Li Punit. Third most popular was the suggestion not to vandalize sites or stelae. Again, communities located most proximate to large archaeological sites that have been groomed for tourism were more likely to offer this suggestion (20 percent of San Miguel students, 11 percent of Santa Cruz students, 30 percent of San Pedro Columbia students, and 41 percent of Indian Creek students). In the past, defacement of stelae—as a statement of protest directed toward the policies of the government of Belize or the National Institute of Culture and History (NICH)—has occurred at Uxbenka (adjacent to Santa Cruz) and Nim Li Punit (adjacent to Indian Creek) and students might know of this history.

The shaded rows of table 8.13 indicate counterconservation suggestions that were offered by a very small number of students. It's not clear whether the students misunderstood the question, were joking, or were promoting counterconservation measures. One student from Santa Cruz suggested that digging for oil was one way to conserve Maya cultural heritage. This suggestion relates to the oil exploration underway on and near "Indian reserve" lands. Many Toledo inhabitants view the exploration—for which there is limited local consultation—as destructive and exploitative.

Examining student understanding of past political dynamics, Claire Novotny asked the students to comment on their perceptions of how rulers of the past projected an image of power. There were seven recurrent responses, four of which were particularly popular, and some students offered more than one comment (table 8.14). Warfare placed in the upper tier of student perceptions, indicating recognition of a link between violent conflict and maintaining a large constituency in students' minds. Public worship and sacrifice (sanctioned forms of violence) were also very much on students' minds: 74 percent of Silver Creek students and 43 percent and 33 percent among San Antonio and San Pedro Columbia students, respectively. Projecting power through trading alliances or through the creation of monuments constitute a second tier of popularity. The acquisition of jade—known to be present in both large and small structures in the Toledo District—may have been on students' minds, as well as the delicately carved stelae of Uxbenka and the towering monuments of Nim Li Punit.

Table 8.14. Student perceptions of how past rulers projected an image of power.

Maya Rulers' Projection of Power Through	San Miguel n/%	Silver Creek n/%	Santa Cruz n/%	San Antonio n/%	San Pedro Columbia n/%	Santa Elena n/%	Indian Creek n/%
Powerful marriage alliances	3/11.5%	0	2/11%	0	0	0	2/05%
Warfare	8/31%	0	1/6%	3/43%	18/43%	1/16.7%	9/22.5%
Effective governance	3/11.5%	1/4%	2/11%	0	2/5%	1/16.7%	1/2.5%
Trading alliances	5/19.2%	0		0	0	0	6/15%
Public worship/ sacrifice	3/11.5%	17/74%	7/39%	3/43%	14/33%	1/16.7%	8/20%
Wearing royal costuming	0	2/9%	0	0	1/2%	1/16.7%	2/5%
Creating monuments	0	1/4%	0	0	5/12%	0	4/10%
Other	4/15.3%	2/9%	4/22%	1/14%	0	1/16.7%	5/12.5%
No response	0	0	2/11%	0	2/5%	1/16.7%	3/7.5%
Total responses	26	23	18	7	42	6	40

Note: Percentages may not equal 100 percent due to rounding.

The remaining categories of table 8.14 mentioned by students in more than one school include the following: projection of power through (1) strategic marriage alliances, mentioned in three of seven schools; (2) effective governance, mentioned by a few students in six of seven schools; and (3) wearing royal costuming. Recall that the last response was considered to be a significant difference between Maya of the past and present in Copán also and thus is a recurrent kind of visual analysis in the way that students process workshop content.

Students were asked to identity their most and least favorite themes of the workshops. They chose from the following eight themes: general culture, food and farming, household knowledge, ancient entertainment and writing, calendar and cosmology, architecture and city centers, rulers and kingdoms, and conservation. Responses were all over the chart, indicating a variability of workshop effectiveness from school to school and also pronounced variation among student likes and dislikes. Ancient entertainment and writing was a strong favorite, as were rulers and kingdoms. As happened in Copán, workshops on calendar and cosmology elicited strong reactions—both positive and negative. Among Toledo students who commented on this theme (fifty-four total), 48 percent listed calendar and cosmology as their favorite theme, but for 52 percent of the students, learning about the calendar was their least favorite theme.

In a related query, students were asked to comment on what they had learned from the workshop themes. Several students expressed surprise that there were female rulers during the Classic period. Learning about migration patterns (short and long term) also left a strong impression on the students. Asian origins for Amerind peoples were noted (the timescale may have been compressed in students' minds), and a small group emphasized that they had learned that the First Peoples of Belize were Maya (a reference to the popular allegation that Maya people in Toledo came from Guatemala).

Overall, students responded positively to the workshops. One student registered dislike of the program, 41 percent responded positively but did not qualify their answer, 14 percent liked the workshops because they learned about their ancestors, 39 percent appreciated an opportunity to learn about the ancient Maya, and 3 percent liked the workshops because they were learning how to protect the old places. Granted that conservation was a topic explicitly addressed in the workshops, still it is remarkable that a sample of fourth- through sixth-grade students responded that they liked the program because of the emphasis on conservation—taking care of old places and things.

Teachers Critically Evaluate the Heritage Workshops

For the twelve teachers and school principals interviewed in the seven communities in which the programs were offered, the workshops were seen as beneficial because they allowed students to learn about their deep history (rather than British colonial history) and also, and more generically, about ancient Maya lifeways. When teachers were asked how the heritage workshops added to the school curriculum, many teachers responded that the addition of Classic Maya civilization to the curriculum was most welcome. Others liked the link between farming practices of the past and contemporary agriculture, and still others appreciated the long-term perspective on environmental issues.

When this question was asked in a slightly different way—that is, "Which theme do you think is the most important for students to learn about?"—five teachers indicated that learning about Maya civilization was foremost. Three responded that learning about the traditions and customs of ancestors helped to protect living Maya culture (presumably in shoring up Maya cultural practices and warding off cultural loss—a recurrent theme in the responses of teachers, students, and community members). Two teachers responded that site protection (conservation) was the most important theme for the students, and two thought that all of the themes were of equal importance. The following themes received one vote apiece: learning about migration patterns (how Maya peoples came to the area that is now Belize and where in Central America Maya peoples live); comparing ancient and contemporary Maya cultural practices; delving into the deep tradition of Maya art and aesthetics; and finally, preventing site destruction and exploitation by archaeologists. The final theme conflates the conservation theme with a troublesome conflictive history between archaeological projects and local Toledo communities. We return to this topic shortly.

Next, teachers were asked which of the themes they would like to know more about or wish that their students could learn more about. Respondents offered a wide range of suggestions (table 8.15). Only traditional Maya farming and knowing more about ancient Maya math and numbers were suggested more than once. A teacher from Indian Creek (adjacent to Nim Li Punit) wanted to know more about the specific historical background of temples, while a teacher from Santa Cruz (adjacent to Uxbenka) wanted to know more about the Maya calendar (perhaps because Uxbenka stelae feature long-count dates). Even after lectures in which the long-term resilience of Maya peoples had received great emphasis, one teacher wanted to know "why the Maya disappeared." This question conflates—as happens in popular discourse—the residential abandonment of Classic Maya cities with the disappearance of an ethnic group.

Table 8.15. Themes that Toledo teachers would like to know more about or wish that their students could learn more about.

Want to Know More About . . .	Indian Creek	Silver Creek	San Antonio	Santa Cruz	Santa Elena	San Pedro Columbia	San Miguel
Historical background of temples in Belize	x						
Traditional farming	x					x	
Differences among Maya peoples in Belize today and how different in the past					x		
Calendar				x			
Why the Maya disappeared				x			
Math and numbers						x	x
Religion							x
Writing		x					
Not relevant			x				
Archaeological sites through touring			x				
Caste War			x				
Richness of Maya culture						x	
Conservation						x	

Teachers from San Antonio—which is the largest Mopan community in the Toledo District and not located proximate to a large Classic-period site of heritage tourism—wanted tours of archaeological sites and also more classroom coverage of the so-called Caste War (table 8.15). A major insurrection of the nineteenth century that occurred further north but caused ripple effects through lands that were then claimed as part of the British Empire, the Caste War receives scant coverage in Mexican or Belizean textbooks. Finally, teachers from San Pedro Columbia (located proximate to Lubaantun) asked for more attention to the richness of Maya culture and to conservation issues.

In reference to the activities that accompanied the more didactic material presented in the workshops, five teachers thought that the art projects were the most popular with the students and four teachers responded that students liked the visual information presented via PowerPoint projection. Kids like art projects the world over, but the popularity of this kind of creative expression in both the Toledo program as well as Proyecto Maya in Honduras highlights its novelty. Simple art materials—construction paper, crayons, glue, and scissors—are scarce resources in poorly funded rural schools. Students appreciated both the opportunity for creative expression and the break from drills and rote memorization. Creative projects may also have helped students to cognitively process and remember material presented in the workshops. Seventy-five percent of the teachers commented that students referenced themes of the workshops during regular class time. Another 17 percent noted that students recalled workshop content when prompted.

As in the United States, students take standardized tests (called the PSE or Primary School Examination) in Belize. When teachers were approached about allowing class time for the heritage workshops, some were concerned that the workshops would take time away from drilling students for the exam. In order to gauge whether or not the workshop themes contributed to the preparation of students for the PSE exam, we asked the teachers' opinions after the 2008 cycle of workshops had ended. Teachers responded to this question in paragraph form and often touched upon more than one way in which the workshops and the PSE overlapped (or did not). Table 8.16 presents six of the most frequent responses to this query. In over 50 percent of the replies, teachers found that the heritage themes contributed to student performance on the PSE because the workshops addressed the topic of early civilization (in which students must demonstrate knowledge for the PSE). Other teachers didn't see an application to the PSE because Maya heritage was not specifically part of the exam, and still others thought that Maya heritage and civilization should be part of the PSE. One teacher thought that providing handouts of the material covered in the workshop might help students study the themes and apply them to questions posed in the PSE. Another felt that more content that was specific to Belize would improve overlap, and a final teacher suggested that more content focused on customs, marriage practices, and beliefs would improve overlap.

Table 8.16. Teachers comment on the linkage between the heritage workshops in Toledo and student standardized exam (PSE).

Workshops Helpful (or Not) Because . . .	Indian Creek	Silver Creek	San Antonio	Santa Cruz	Santa Elena	San Pedro Columbia	San Miguel
Not much overlap with PSE	x			x			
Should be more overlap with PSE	x			x			
Helpful because themes address an early civilization	x	x	x		x	x	x
Handouts might improve overlap			x				
More on customs, marriage practices, and beliefs would improve overlap			x				
Discussing more areas of Belize would improve overlap						x	

The final comments from teachers reveal a range of perspectives on the workshops and the troubling, conflictive relationship between archaeologists and communities in this part of the Maya region. One teacher commented that the workshops help to highlight "the importance of conserving our Maya temples and prevention [*sic*] from further destruction and exploitation from the so called conservationist (known as the archeologist)." This comment equates excavation with destruction—which it is in a technical sense, but excavation also creates and disseminates knowledge of the past through analysis and publication. Lacking access to the knowledge produced through excavation and never having been part of the creation of that knowledge, this teacher sees only the destructive part of the process. The bidirectional knowledge exchange (BKE) programs discussed in chapter 7 (as well as many community archaeology projects) were created specifically to address the distance between archaeologists and local communities and to build the rapport and mutual respect that has been shredded by decades of neglect. The charged term *exploitation* is used here and likely refers to excavation for the purpose of grooming a site for tourism, at which point an entrance fee is charged by the government of Belize. From the perspective of this teacher, charging an entrance fee was an exploitation of "our Maya temples." This comment speaks clearly to the work ahead for archaeologists and government ministries alike—to engage in deeper dialogue with local communities in matters of heritage conservation.

Parents and Community Members Give the Final Word

Thirty-one parents (mostly female) were asked about the heritage programs in which their child or children were participating. Four communities participated in the survey: Indian Creek, Silver Creek, San Miguel, and San Pedro Columbia. When asked if their child told them about the program and showed them materials from the workshops, parents revealed varying levels of knowledge. Mothers from Indian Creek were the best informed: 70 percent had heard about the program from their children, and 80 percent had seen program materials. Least informed (by their children) were mothers from San Pedro Columbia: only 20 percent of sampled parents had heard about the program, while 40 percent had seen workshop materials.

Mothers from Indian Creek also were more likely to respond that their entire family displayed interest in the workshops. Parents generally concurred with teachers in feeling that it is important for the children to learn about the "old Maya" (mentioned by 38 percent to 100 percent of respondents within each community). Interestingly, three out of the eight parents consulted in Silver Creek thought that the workshops should include a final exam. Respondents from this community are distinguished by the fact that two of the eight parents surveyed were male—an unusually high ratio.

Although parents generally were supportive of the workshop curriculum, a few reacted negatively because they perceived a conflict between evangelical religious teachings and knowledge of or appreciation for the non-Christian religion of the "old Maya." This conflict between evangelicalism and the old ways is acutely experienced in Guatemala, where active evangelical proselytizing conflicts with efforts by Maya cultural activists to reinterpret the old ways in light of twenty-first-century challenges.[14]

The final constituency consulted in the Toledo District was composed of seventy-three community members from eight communities. In 2008, Claire Novotny asked interviewees a series of open-ended questions to which respondents were free to offer an opinion. In response to why children should learn about the "old Maya," community members offered a range of responses, including that such a curriculum would ensure correct moral upbringing or prevent the old ways from being lost. Some thought that the curriculum would enhance job security by ensuring competency in a tourism-driven heritage economy. Despite overwhelming support for the idea of Maya heritage workshops in schools, less than 10 percent of interviewees had ever visited an archaeological site developed for heritage tourism.

When queried about specific content that should be included in the workshops, community members offered a multitude of ideas, most of which coalesced on a general desire for education about a Maya past. More detailed responses included relearning old technologies and how the "old Maya" interacted with their environment and cared for the land. Several expressed a desire for children to have more access to materials written in a Mayan language. Community members themselves were interested in learning more about Maya origins. This response did not seem to refer to deep-time migrations but rather to the historical movements of Maya peoples in relation to geopolitical boundaries; such knowledge could be deployed in the struggle for land rights. Again, we see how ethnicity and antiquity cross-thread with land struggles.

The desire for the protection and conservation of Maya "ruins" likewise was linked by some interviewees to preserving evidence of Maya landscape inhabitation. Others saw the sites from an archaeological perspective—as repositories of information about the Maya past; still others linked conservation to tourism, citing the importance of well-preserved sites for heritage tourism.

Although community respondents favored site conservation and some looked favorably on heritage tourism, few respondents looked favorably on archaeologists or thought that they had anything to do with the conservation or presentation of Maya cultural heritage to visitors. In fact, those who expressed an opinion about archaeology viewed it as a destructive outside force and commented, "Archaeologists destroy sites" and "It's not fair that archaeologists take artifacts away to places where the local people can't see them." These comments—similar to those of the teacher discussed earlier—are sobering and point to the complicity of archaeologists in heritage alienation. The workshops sought to counter these allegations by linking the results of archaeological research to heritage conservation, but the response of Toledo community members indicates that there is much work still to do.

When community members were asked how they would like to connect with the past, a strong theme of loss emerged from the responses. Some stated that people today are losing the old traditions—that communities don't celebrate ceremonies or perform dances as in the past. Some requested help in working to bring back older cultural practices. The influence of evangelical churches was cited as a culprit in cultural loss. Finally, a few indicated that they would like a museum to be located in their village so that they could see artifacts and learn about Maya history. Heritage centers—so popular in Oaxaca and successful at galvanizing community identity and history—would likely also be enthusiastically endorsed in the Toledo District.

RESPONSES IN GENERAL

Thousands of children and hundreds of adults engaged with MACHI and InHerit programs through school workshops and coloring books, not to mention the radio stories, a puppet-mentary, and the community-mapping program to be discussed in chapter 9. In small, rural communities in both southern Belize and western Honduras, schoolchildren participated in workshops focused on cultural heritage. Particularly in Honduras, students who identified as Ladino were enrolled in the program as well as students who identified as Ch'orti'. Trained instructors stressed the value of Maya identity (traditionally intensely stigmatized), endangered languages, and the fragility of remains of the past.

Responses to the workshops reveal a strong impulse toward conservation (despite the reality of the ease with which rural peoples can become entangled in antiquities trafficking) and, of course, a desire to keep excavated artifacts close to home. Given the strong impulse toward conservation, it's nonetheless a fact that few local inhabitants—student or adult—visit archaeological sites that have been groomed for heritage tourism. Whether the time and expense of a visit or a sense of not being welcome at a site of tourism keeps rural people away is hard to glean from the answers. Regardless of the lack of visitation in western Honduras and southern Belize, a pretty strong sentiment exists that Maya sites "belong" to Indigenous peoples.

For the children, learning about the "old Maya" was appreciated. The creative art projects that accompanied the heritage workshops were generally their favorite part (next to studying the environment, particularly monkeys and jaguars). Although children liked learning about Classic Maya rulers and crafting re-creations of their headdresses, they often cited the opulent clothing worn by Classic Maya rulers as a major difference between today and the past. In a sobering comment on the lack of access to twenty-first-century technology, few Copán students felt that the technology of today was that different from technologies of the past. These responses point to an opportunity to create community archaeology projects that further explore how ordinary peoples of the past lived and how their lives differed (or didn't) from contemporary life away from metropoles.

For children and adults alike, themes of identity and loss loom large and permeate discussions of heritage. In reality, conflict between evangelical ministries and community traditionalists can result in the active repudiation of cultural practices that are linked to the past when evangelical forces work to polarize communities. The loss of ethnic cultural identity also is in line with traditional nationalist desires for an end to ethnic diversity that that has been viewed as an obstacle to the creation of a single national identity. In the Maya region, Indigenous groups can and do place demands on the state for recognition of land rights, bilingual schools, and other resources. But cultural practices are never static. Indigenous peoples of the Americas display a resilience that is truly staggering, and although their dissolution as distinct ethnicities has been foretold many times over the past five hundred years, millions of people still self-identify as Indigenous Americans.

For both western Honduras and southern Belize, the struggle for land informs conversations about cultural heritage, as is apparent in the response of parents and community members. Looking to the past to rebalance the present may be a political use of the past, but it is also reckoning with historical factors that have contributed to the resource inequities that continue to plague Indigenous peoples and to oppressively maintain high poverty levels among rural populations. The heritage workshops did not actively foreground these issues; rather, parents and community members perceived the workshops as "ammunition" in the struggle for land and greater autonomy. Strategically, the workshops made sense. Proximity to hot-button issues such as land reform was not always a comfortable space from which to launch heritage programs, particularly in reference to national bureaucracies and even other archaeologists. But occupying this space did serve the interests and needs of local communities and, over the long run, should enhance the sustainability of archaeology.

The most frequently given reason voiced by teachers and parents in support of the program was that it provided students with an opportunity to know Maya history—even if from an archaeological perspective. For many students, knowledge constitutes their ethnic history. Parents and teachers offered additional reasons for the inclusion of heritage material in schools. There was broad consensus that it is indeed important to talk about cultural heritage during schooltime. That is the takeaway message of the school workshop programs.

NOTES

1. Freire (2002:101).
2. For examples, see Eiss (2004) and Fallow (2004).
3. See Cojtí Cuxil (1996:39–41); also Montejo (2002).
4. Armstrong-Fumero (2013:150–51); Cojtí Cuxil (1996:40); Richards and Richards (1996).
5. Cojtí Cuxil (1996:39).
6. Gosden (2004:25).
7. Sanjinés (2004).
8. All translations are provided by the authors.
9. See the discussion of community heritage museums in Oaxaca in chapter 4.
10. For an expanded discussion of the complexities of Ch'orti' identity, see Metz (2010).
11. Mortensen (2009:246–57).
12. Logan (2009).
13. For more discussion of the Copán situation, see McAnany and Parks (2012).
14. For more on the tension between evangelicals and traditionalists, see McAnany and Brown (2016).

9

⌒

Performing the Past,
Creating a Future

with Sarah M. Rowe

> If the performative must compel collective recognition in order to work, must
> it compel only those kinds of recognition that are already institutionalized, or
> can it also compel a critical perspective on existing institutions?
>
> —Judith Butler[1]

Judith Butler understands well the social magic of performativity and its ability
to compel recognition of existing relations of hierarchy. She also suggests that
through performativity—so integral to subject formation—subjects can reform
and reconstitute themselves. In other words, performativity can play a role in
political contestation of the status quo. In contrast to the hard-wired *habitus* of
Pierre Bourdieu, performativity enables the emergence of new kinds of subjectivity. Butler's words verbatim:

> The performative is not merely an act used by a pregiven subject, but is one of the
> powerful and insidious ways in which subjects are called into social being, inaugu-
> rated into sociality by a variety of diffuse and powerful interpellations. In this sense
> the social performative is a crucial part not only of subject *formation*, but of the
> ongoing political contestation and reformulation of the subject as well.[2]

Here I suggest that the reshaping power of the performative is highly relevant
to the performance of heritage. This kind of performativity can compel recognition of existing modes of subjectivity or it can unsettle them by compelling
imagination of new modes. It is the latter effect—alluded to by Butler in the
opening epigraph—that forms the grist and goal of performing the past. Employing multiple media—including radio, video, and GPS (global positioning system)

mapping—the Maya Area Cultural Heritage Initiative (MACHI) and then In-Herit and the Alliance for Heritage Conservation partnered with nonprofit orga-nizations and communities in an effort to open space for dialogue about heritage and to imagine new forms of interaction with heritage landscapes that might lead to greater self-determination for local communities. These were future-oriented projects, although focused topically on the past. Some performance-based pro-grams employed archaeological methods such as GPS mapping, while others did not. But all are connected to the practice of archaeology in this part of the world by virtue of a focus on engaging local communities in a dialogue about the past.

Setting aside for the moment classroom pedagogy as a vehicle for heritage ed-ucation, we consider the potential of dialogue generated through entertainment and the greater interactivity afforded through GPS mapping to effect change in the status quo. In El Petén, Guatemala, MACHI collaborated with Fundación ProPetén to produce heritage-themed episodes of a radio series called *Between Two Roads (Entre Dos Caminos* in Spanish or *Sa' xxaal li b'e* in Q'eqchi'). A se-ries bearing that name but focused on issues of environment and public health had been created a few years prior to our conservation with Rosa Chan (de-scribed in chapter 5) but were no longer on the air. The program was successful because it used a popular and widely accessible medium (radio broadcasting) to speak to pressing social issues that were embedded within a dramatic story line. The series also proved to be highly adaptable. Later, we were able to incorporate episodes into a specially designed curriculum for third and fourth graders in the Petén region. The curriculum approached traditional school subjects through the lens of Maya culture and emphasized the protection of cultural and natural heritage. The impact of radio in a part of the world where television is not widely available is significant even when content is more didactic, as was the case with the heritage episodes broadcast from Radio Xenca in Felipe Carrillo Puerto, Quintana Roo, México.

In Yucatán, México, MACHI turned toward another form of entertainment—puppets—and the nonprofit Kaxil Kiuic to engage children and to communicate about the Maya past, present, and future. By the program's end in 2010, over fif-teen hundred students and dozens of teachers had watched the puppet-mentary. Their reaction to its content and message are discussed in this chapter.

Finally and most recently, GPS-based community mapping in five communi-ties in highland Guatemala provides a direct mechanism whereby local residents could define their heritage landscape. In the pages to follow, we consider the opinions of the mappers themselves about the performance of mapping.

HEARING ABOUT HERITAGE ON THE RADIO

Depending on content and dialogue, performance over airwaves can provide an effective means of subject formation and reformation. The lack of visual stimuli broadens the imaginative scope of radio performance. The expression "I heard it on the radio" lends authority to the content of a statement (whether well founded or not) while allowing space for a visual imaginary that can take a large range of forms, depending on the background of the listener. With the *Entre Dos Caminos* series, the sound effects of life in a small town—birds singing, machetes chopping, car doors slamming—were as important as the dialogue in lending an air of authenticity to the series. Episodes can be heard at https://soundcloud .com/inheritp2p/sets/entre-dos-caminos.

Unlike the classroom heritage programs, which were divided into distinct themes, the radio broadcasts flowed more organically and attempted to mimic the rhythm and drama of life in a small community. A health-care worker arrives in the fictitious town of San Jerónimo as students gather at school to begin learning about Maya history and archaeology. Later that day, personal dramas take center stage as community members discuss issues of ethnic identity, environmental degradation, and conflict over land inheritance. The strategy of the radio programs was to embed heritage discourse within other issues with which community members were already conversant. We may have succeeded too well in this endeavor, as we shall see shortly.

During two of the three years in which *Entre Dos Caminos* aired—2007 and 2008—Edy Romero and Yadira Vargas surveyed communities to follow up on the impact of the radio programs. During 2007, individuals in nine communities were surveyed; after the 2008 broadcasts, persons in twenty communities were surveyed (table 9.1). Questions were posed individually and to focus groups, the latter in the community of Monte Rico. Although no demographic data were collected during 2007, information about age, sex, religious affiliation, ethnic identity, and years of classroom education was collected during 2008. That information permits deeper insight into the surveys, as we shall see shortly.

In 2008, due to extreme weather and chronic logistical constraints, the communities more proximate to Flores were sampled more heavily than distant towns located in the Department of Alta Verapaz or within the *municipio* of Sayaxche. These more distant communities are the locales where Q'eqchi' is the dominant language and therefore are the places where the Q'eqchi'-language version of the radio *novelas* would have received the largest audience. Unfortunately, we received limited feedback on the episodes broadcast in Q'eqchi'.

The majority of people interviewed following the 2007 broadcasts had listened to the radio *novelas* several times a week (they were broadcast daily within a set time period). Most people said that they liked the series because they learned new things about health issues, cultural heritage, environmental issues, and the importance of conserving archaeological sites. Two questions in particular relate directly to the cultural heritage/conservation content of the radio *novelas*. The questions are restated here, followed by a sample of the answers provided during the surveys. The responses characterize the range of standpoints expressed by the interviewees.

Table 9.1. Communities in which radio-*novela* evaluations were conducted.

Municipio/ Department	Community	Year 2007 Number Interviewed	Year 2008 Number Interviewed
Flores	Monte Rico	Focus group of 6	
	Zocotazal		2
	La Maquina		2
	Yaltutú		5
La Libertad	Tamaris	3	
	Valle Nuevo el Toro		3
	Valle Nuevo San Antonio		2
	Candelaria		5
	La Pista	2	7
San Benito	Belén		3
	San Antonio		5
San José	San Pedro		4
	Jobonpiche		1
San Andrés	Sacpuy	2	
	Cruce	1	
	El Habonero	2	
	Cruce 2 Aguadas		10
	Centro Campesino		3
	Cruce Perdido		1
	El Jobo		1
San Francisco	Acentamiento Nueva Concepción		5
Dolores	Cooperativa Las Flores		4
	Caserio el Fuerzo		1
Alta Verapaz	Chisec	1	
Sayaxche	Kanlech	3	
Unknown		4	11
Total		**24**	**75**

¿Qué entiende por patrimonio cultural y como cuidarlo? (What do you understand about cultural patrimony and how to take care of it?)

Sitios arqueológicos. . . . (Cultural patrimony is archaeological sites.)
Hasta ahora no lo he escuchado. (So far, I have not heard about cultural patrimony.)

Muy poco, no esta claro. (Very little, it's not clear [to me].)

Es importante protegerlo, hacer conciencia de nuestra cultura. (It's important to protect cultural patrimony and to raise awareness of our culture.)

Es de que todo. . . . Se hablada pero hoy en dia nos cuidarlo para saber que es. (Cultural patrimony includes everything—as discussed in the radio *novelas.* Today, we take care of it so as to know it.)

Clearly, there is a continuum of familiarity with the notion of cultural heritage (or cultural patrimony, as the term is generally translated). Some interviewees are comfortable with this kind of dialogue, while others—even after listening to the radio *novelas*—are uncomfortable with the topic and don't want to discuss it. They profess ignorance—which is an indication to us that more dialogue about cultural heritage needs to take place. Others link cultural patrimony with awareness of their culture in a holistic sense, and still others link heritage conservation with the ability to know more about their heritage landscape.

A second question that is pertinent to the issue of cultural heritage goes as follows: *¿Porqué se deberia proteger los sitios arqueológicos y los objetos que hay en ellos?* (Why should one protect archaeological sites and the objects that are found within them?)

Porque tenemos en el pais y hay que cuidarlos. (Because this country contains archaeological sites and we should care for them.)

Por el turismo. . . . (We should protect the sites for the purpose of tourism.)

Ciudad de los mayas, cosas antiguas, que fueron dejados y sirven para conocer. (The ancient Maya cities, artifacts, that were left [i.e., abandoned] provide a basis for knowing about the past.)

Son de nuestros antepasados y hay que cuidarlos. (Archaeological sites are the places of our ancestors and we should take care of them.)

Porque se estan deteriorando y los estan saqueando. (We should take care of the sites because they are deteriorating and being looted.)

Porque es parte de nuestra cultura y su objetivo es la conservacion. (The sites are part of our culture, and conservation is an important objective of cultural heritage.)

Drilling to core rationales and motivations for heritage conservation, this question evoked a wide range of answers. For some, the simple fact that Guatemala is filled with archaeological sites (of considerable size, architectural elaboration, and time depth) is reason enough to practice heritage conservation. In other words, if one lives in Guatemala, one accepts responsibility for conservation of a rich archaeological heritage. Other answers indicate an underlying economic motivation linked to heritage tourism. Another refers specifically to the old places as cities (often a point of animated discussion among archaeologists) that—as a consequence of their abandonment—contain valuable information that will enable us to learn more about the past. This answer is intriguing because of the complexity of the logical linkages among once-vibrant cities, the process of abandonment, and the creation of contexts for knowledge production about the past. One respondent employs a patrimonial discourse by considering archaeological sites to be places of the ancestors, and this provides a sufficient rationale for conservation. Another expresses a more generalized view of sites as simply part of our culture and as such worthy of conservation. A final view cites forces operating against conservation—physical deterioration and looting—as a reason to take care of archaeological sites. These answers indicate the multiple ways in which the radio-*novela* audiences received and digested heritage programming offered in 2007. These responses must be understood in light of existing cultural logics as well as unspecified information gleaned from other sources.

After a new set of radio *novelas* aired in 2008, another round of surveys was conducted with limited overlap by place with 2007 surveys (table 9.1). In 2008, additional demographic information was collected. While seventy-five persons responded to the survey, not everyone responded to every question. The majority of interviewees were female (84 percent), with only 16 percent male respondents. Interviews were conducted during the daylight hours, when males often are engaged either in agricultural work or wage labor. In terms of age, 45 percent of these largely female interviewees were less than or equal to twenty years of age; 25 percent were between twenty-one and thirty; 23 percent were between thirty-one and forty; and only 7 percent were between forty-one and fifty, with fifty years of age being the maximum age of a respondent. The younger female composition of the sample yields a perspective that may not be shared by older females or males (either young or old). But these survey data—skewed as they are—do tap into a demographic that often is difficult to sample, as older males tend to dominate public discourse within rural communities of the Maya region.

In reference to religion, almost half of the young females (47 percent) identified as Catholic, but slightly over a quarter (26.5 percent) were Christian evangelical, and another 26.5 percent professed to practice no religion. When asked about their ethnic affiliation, a full 92 percent self-identified as Ladino (a mixture of Indigenous and Spanish), with only 8 percent identifying as Indigenous Maya. As mentioned previously, this proportion reflects the fact that Q'eqchi' communities that tend to be more distant from Flores (the headquarters of ProPetén) were not well sampled.

Data on level of education are the most sobering demographic to be presented: 29 percent indicated a complete lack of any formal education; 49 percent reported attending some or all of the grades of primary school; 18 percent had received some education in a secondary school; and only 4 percent were fortunate to receive postsecondary education. In a nutshell, the 2008 interviewees were composed primarily of young female Ladino Catholics, most of whom had received less than six years of formal education. Responses to the survey can be considered in light of this demographic.

Most interviewees had listened to most or all of the episodes of the radio *nove-las,* and many were devoted listeners who tuned in every day. Themes relating to health (especially maternal health and herbal medicine) and also care of the environment (including safeguarding potable water) were among the favorite topics. Remember that an earlier version of *Entre Dos Caminos* focused specifically on these topics, and some respondents seem to be referring to these earlier episodes (although the topics of health and clean water also were present in MACHI-produced episodes and woven into heritage dialogue). Of the twenty-three respondents who indicated a specific theme of interest, only two of the responses related to the protection of archaeological sites.

When queried about which of the radio-*novela* themes were completely novel to them, over 50 percent responded that the theme of cultural patrimony (or the ancient Maya) was new to them. For these young women with limited opportunities for education, dialogue about cultural heritage was a new thing. With additional exposure, however, the relevance of these topics would increase. The newness of this dialogue is further emphasized by the fact that many respondents selected "the Maya" or "cultural patrimony" as the theme that they would most like to learn more about.

When interviewees were asked what they understand about the ancient Maya or archaeological sites, the answers tracked responses of the 2007 survey. Thirty-five percent responded that the sites are part of "our history"; 31 percent simply stated that they were aware that the sites were important; 23 percent noted that the ancient Maya were an extraordinary culture; and 11 percent stated that we should protect the sites. When asked if archaeological sites should be protected, an overwhelming majority said yes. When pressed as to why protection was important, answers once again display symmetry with the 2007 survey. Thirty-one percent responded that the sites are part of "our history"; another 31 percent simply asserted that sites "are important"; 16 percent cited tourism as a rationale for site conservation; 9 percent referred to the aesthetic beauty of the sites and their contents; and the remaining 13 percent cited various other reasons.

From these responses, we can conclude that among the young female listening audience, dialogue about cultural heritage is a new and different thing. More distant from their lives than radio-*novela* themes that touched upon family planning, maternal health, and clean water, themes of cultural heritage nonetheless sparked interest and a desire for more information. The inclusion of heritage content with other themes that had immediate relevance to listeners likely expanded the listening audience and promoted a growing awareness of patrimony issues.

The process of adapting radio-*novela* episodes into a primary-school curriculum focused on Maya culture and heritage conservation began in 2010. Area teachers were heavily involved in the process, testing out activities and providing feedback on the organization of the textbooks. A textbook and an activity book were developed for students, accompanied by a guide for third- and fourth-grade teachers. An audio CD of the relevant radio-*novela* episodes accompanied this material (figure 9.1). By the end of 2014, the curriculum had been used in nearly forty schools with six thousand students and had received national approval by the Guatemalan Ministry of Education.

In 2014, surveys were administered to teachers who had implemented the curriculum in the preceding years. Twelve teachers from seven different schools responded to the survey, providing brief but revealing insight into the educational and social impacts of the curriculum on schools in the Petén. All twelve respondents emphasized the "fit" between the heritage curriculum and national educational standards and the ease of teaching the curriculum within the classroom. They identified the clarity of the guides and the simple language in which they were written as factors facilitating adoption of the new curriculum.

Eleven of the teachers said that it was easy to enact the activities included in the curriculum within the classroom, while one disliked the fact that children had to leave the classroom to engage in some of the associated activities. Despite these challenges, all twelve teachers reported that students relate better to the content and activity-focused methods of the new curriculum than they did to previous teaching methods. Of the seven teachers who provided a justification for this assessment, three said it was due to the unique content, which covers subjects

Figure 9.1. Learning materials created in conjunction with radio *novelas* (from the archives of InHerit).

not normally addressed in school. Two teachers simply wrote that the students are more engaged because the content is more interesting. Another two teachers suggested that the students responded well because the new curriculum builds on the students' local knowledge of their landscape and its many archaeological sites.

Because the curriculum builds on local knowledge, the families of students are also engaged with the new curriculum. Students bring their workbooks home to share with parents and siblings, and the message spreads beyond the boundaries of the classroom. Teachers augmented their survey responses with stories of decreased looting of archaeological sites near their schools; however, this theme of conservation was not only applied to archaeological sites but to the natural environment as well. One little girl, the daughter of a poacher who was preparing to go hunting one night, insisted that her father read her textbook. After the girl pointed out that her book said to protect the environment and not to kill endangered species, the father reportedly reconsidered this activity and no longer poaches endangered species.

Only one-quarter of the teachers work at a school with no students who identify as Maya. Conversely, only one teacher reported a student body in which 100 percent self-identify as Maya. The majority of teachers (67 percent) work in a mixed-ethnic teaching environment. While the surveys don't speak directly to the impact of the curriculum on interethnic relations in the schools, Petén teachers reported to Sarah Rowe that there is now greater respect among their students and a deeper appreciation for the cultural background of Maya students in particular.[3] Thus, addressing themes of cultural heritage in the classroom can not only help to protect archaeological sites but also have an impact on the experience of Maya children in the classroom.

ROOTS, IDENTITY, AND MAYA COSMOVISION

Titled *Raices, Identidad y Cosmovisión Maya*, the twenty-five-episode series broadcast in 2010 from Radio Xenca in Felipe Carrillo Puerto, Quintana Roo, México, bore some similarities to *Entre Dos Caminos* but differed in significant ways. Written by Amadeé Collí of Mayaón (a Yucatec Maya organization focused on cultural issues), the series contained far fewer actors than *Entre Dos Caminos* and was less conversational than the ProPetén episodes. Set primarily within a classroom setting, the series used dialogue between teacher and pupils to convey information about Maya culture and Maya archaeology. In the series, the teachers also learn about contemporary Yucatec culture through community visits.

Recorded only in Yucatec Mayan, the series was well received. Amadeé Collí conducted follow-up interviews with forty-seven individuals, and 23 percent of those interviewed commented that they enjoyed the program content especially because it was broadcast in Yucatec. Nonetheless, Amadeé Collí felt that the audience could have been much larger had the series also been broadcast in Spanish, but we were unable to provide funding to translate and tape a Spanish version. The conversation about the language of the broadcasts (Yucatec or Spanish) highlights some of the difficult issues surrounding work on the preservation of Indigenous languages. First, broadcasting only in Yucatec—although great for Yucatec speakers—was exclusionary since the episodes were not accessible to monolingual Spanish speakers. Second, there are more monolingual Spanish speakers who identify ethnically as Maya than had been anticipated. The stigmatized status of Yucatec has led many parents to emphasize Spanish over Yucatec so as to train their children to survive and thrive in a Spanish-speaking world. This constituent was alienated from the broadcasts, as well as those who might not identify as Maya but nevertheless should be part of the conversation. Think back to the young Ladino females who listened to the Spanish version of *Entre Dos Caminos* with such enthusiasm. By way of conclusion, offering radio content in an Indigenous language provides support for language survival, but coupling those broadcasts with episodes translated into the local lingua franca can expand the listening audience in a significantly inclusive fashion.

During the evaluation process, Mayaón unfortunately did not collect the same demographic information as did ProPetén. Nevertheless, insights can be gleaned through the often counterintuitive answers provided to survey questions. About 14 percent of interviewees professed not having heard previously about the importance of archaeological sites or of materials found at sites. An even larger percentage (38 percent) was not familiar with traditional medicine, agriculture, and ceremonies. These responses are surprising given that the radio episodes were aired in and near the municipality of Felipe Carrillo Puerto (population of slightly over seventy-five thousand), which is generally considered to be an area of strong Maya cultural activism and was the epicenter of the nineteenth-century Social War.

When listeners were asked if they had ever visited an archaeological site, about 50 percent responded affirmatively; 19 percent mentioned visiting Chichén Itzá, and 13 percent had toured Tulum. These sites are well known and frequently visited places in Yucatán; coastal Tulum is located somewhat proximate to Felipe Carrillo Puerto, but Chichén Itzá is several hours away by bus or car. In response to a follow-up question asking about interest in visiting an archaeological site in the future, almost 75 percent indicated a desire to do so.

An overwhelming majority expressed the opinion that archaeological sites should be protected (table 9.2). When asked why, answers covered much of the same ground as the respondents interviewed by ProPetén. There was a stronger future orientation to the answers, however, with over 30 percent responding that sites should be protected so that their descendants will know them. Given that the episodes were broadcast in Yucatec, it's not surprising that 20 percent of those interviewed wanted to protect sites because they were viewed as part of their history and identity. Over 10 percent felt that sites must be protected in order to stop looting. Additional answers to the question of why archaeological sites should be protected (each less than 10 percent of the response pool) included the following:

Table 9.2. Reasons given for protecting archaeological sites by radio listeners interviewed by Mayaón.

Archaeological Sites Should Be Protected	Responses[a]
So that future generations (our children) will know them	18
Because they're part of our history/identity	11
So they aren't looted	7
Because they show the Maya exist	5
For tourism	4
Because you can learn a lot from them	2
Because they have lots of value	2
Because of their aesthetic value	1
No Answer	6

[a]Some respondents offered more than one response.

because they exist; for tourism; because you can learn a lot from them; because they have lots of value; and because of their aesthetic value. These answers closely track responses to the ProPetén survey in that answers include similar rationales: acceptance of the existence of archaeological sites as ample justification for their preservation; the economic calculus that well-preserved sites invite tourism; recognition of the knowledge-production potential of archaeological sites; and appreciation of the aesthetic beauty of the old places.

In contrast to the ProPetén interviews, however, respondents were most excited to learn about archaeology and Maya culture, past and present. The other topics that had interested the audience for *Entre Dos Caminos* listeners were not part of the *Raices, Identidad y Cosmovisión Maya* series, and so Maya cultural heritage had taken center stage.

ACTING OUT CULTURAL HERITAGE

As elaborated on in chapter 7, concepts that include roads and pathways recurred throughout the design and implementation of MACHI and InHerit programming. Perhaps this trope presaged the notion of Maya cultural heritage as positioned within a busy intersection. The movement suggested by roads and pathways also provides a metaphor of change, a departure from the status quo. *Be* or road is a basic element of a Yucatec Mayan greeting: *Bix a bel?* means "good day" or "how goes your road?" The title of the puppet-mentary, *U be'jil k-úuchben k-ch'i'ibalo'ob* (*On the Road of Our Ancestors* or in Spanish translation, *En el Camino de Nuestros Antepasados*), seemed a culturally relevant way to approach heritage issues.

In the opening epigraph to this chapter, Judith Butler alluded to the social magic of performativity in its ability to unseat or disrupt the status quo. But for minds that hold to empirical realism, performance is fantasy. Although Butler certainly would argue that empirically observed behaviors are nonetheless social performance, certain actors seem to be able to perform and transgress limits to accepted reality with impunity. Puppets, for instance, are famous for social transgression, and that was part of the allure of using puppets to speak to heritage issues. Technically speaking, the actors are marionettes and almost three feet tall. Throughout the puppet-mentary, a trio composed of an adolescent brother (Eusebio) and sister (Linda) and their friend (Uech) interact with parents, a grandfather, their teacher, an archaeological site guard, the rain deity Chaak, and a quasi-pet rabbit (see figure 7.16 for an image of the marionettes; to view the entire DVD, go to https://www.youtube.com/watch?v=rrb4UCbSPM4).

Although the film originally was conceived as an hour-long documentary, it soon became clear that sixty minutes was a prohibitive length for classroom use. By splicing the film into six- to seven-minute episodes, parts of the puppet-mentary might be shown in a classroom and followed by discussion guided by a teacher as well as workbook exercises. In the ten episodes described below, we follow a few days in the life of these Yucatec speakers as they encounter and discuss their cultural heritage:

1. *Montículos Mayas.* Dawn breaks on a vernacular dwelling in Yucatán as a mother wakes up her children. The brother and sister roll out of their hammocks and get ready for a special class at school while Yucatec-language radio plays in the background. As credits roll for the film, the siblings— along with their mother and grandfather—begin their journey, first to the *maíz* field and then to school. At the field, the family discusses the stone mounds built over thirteen hundred years ago that are ubiquitous on their landscape.

2. *Comida y Agricultura.* As Linda's mom plants corn with a dibble stick, they discuss the cuisine and plants and animals of precolonial times. Their grandfather alludes to the fact that they are descendants of impressive astronomers and mathematicians. Continuing on to school, the brother pedals an orange tricycle (traditional to towns across Yucatán) while his sister rides on the carriage of the tricycle.

3. *Glifos y Números.* At school, the children learn to read Maya hieroglyphs and to count using bar-dot math, a base-twenty system. Their teacher announces that he has a surprise for them after class (field trips to the archaeological sites of Chichén Itzá and Kiuic). The rabbit provides comic relief.

4. *Chichén Itzá.* Impressed by the grandeur of Chichén Itzá and the large number of very pale-skinned tourists, the trio plus their teacher discuss heritage tourism and the benefits (or not) to local residents. The rabbit trails along after the group.

5. *El Juego de Pelota*. Still touring Chichén Itzá, the group stands within the gigantic ballcourt and then moves on to consider the possible astronomical significance of the circular building called El Caracol. After a walk to the sacred cenote, into which the rabbit almost falls, they return to the main pyramid (El Castillo, which is now off-limits to all tourists) and consider the way in which power was materialized in stone. The rabbit displays disapproval that the pyramid cannot be ascended.

6. *La Élite*. Returning from their distant field trip to Chichén Itzá, the group (trio and teacher plus rabbit) tour the Puuc archaeological site of Kiuic—home to Kaxil Kiuic, the nonprofit organization with whom we collaborated to make the film. Uech comments that the buildings are surrounded by forest; the group discusses who lived in the large palaces of Kiuic, as well as issues of heritage conservation and tourism at Kiuic.

7. *El Patrimonio Cultural y la Artesania*. About road building and the destruction of cultural heritage that inevitably accompanies such construction projects, this episode opens with the trio watching bulldozers grade a road surface. (The rabbit comically uses binoculars to see the activity.) Eusebio finds artifacts in the roadbed and plans to show them to his mother and grandfather. When they arrive home, their mother is making tortillas by hand (a highly valued part of Yucatec cuisine). The family discusses the artifacts and decides to contact a local custodian of archaeological sites who assists INAH (Instituto Nacional de Antropología e Historia) archaeologists. While this discussion takes place, the rabbit is trying to steal tortillas.

8. *La Arqueología*. The custodian arrives at their home (on a motorcycle) with a camera, and the family discusses the found artifacts and how fragments of artifacts are still important—even if they can't be displayed in a museum. The importance of archaeological context and heritage destruction also play into the conversation. As the custodian is leaving, Eusebio shows him the complete stone bead that he also found and pocketed but now wants to see displayed in a museum. As the custodian is leaving, the trio poses for photos.

9. *La Cosmovisión*. On their way to school (with a sherd they found in their grandfather's milpa), Eusebio and Linda pause to rest. The rabbit steals the sherd and heads into a cave, which is considered an entrance to the underworld in traditional Maya cosmology. The siblings follow. A voice calls to them. It is none other than Chaak, the deity of rain, who is collecting offerings in the cave. The children converse with Chaak, who is feeling abandoned because he no longer receives much in the way of offerings.

10. *Los Mayas de Hoy y la Conservación*. Linda and Eusebio talk with Chaak about the Ch'a' Chaak ceremony and promise to visit Chaak again and to bring offerings; there is a group hug. The end credits roll. Credits are followed by a short epilogue in which Linda and Eusebio, along with Uech and the rabbit, return to the cave, as promised, to leave an offering to Chaak. As they resurface, they hear thunder—a precursor of rain.

To place the puppet-performed commentary on cultural heritage in schools and relevant institutions throughout Yucatán, we distributed copies of the DVD along with a teacher's guide and the Yucatec coloring book described in chapters 5 and 7. The distribution, spearheaded by Shoshaunna Parks and Christa Cesario, took place in January and February of 2009, during which ninety sets of instructional materials were hand delivered. By September 2009, Shoshaunna and Christa had collected feedback in the form of survey questionnaires from schools (both primary and secondary), libraries, several archaeological sites (the video was used in visitor centers), and a museum in Mérida (Palacio Cantón; see categories listed in table 9.3). In seventy-four different places, the DVD was viewed and evaluated by students, teachers, and program facilitators; the largest audience by far was composed of primary-school students (forty-six primary schools participated)—the intended audience for the DVD. Towns, both large and small, within *municipios* (a township designation) across Yucatán and into Quintana Roo took part in the pilot project (see table 9.4 for a listing of participating *municipios*). We felt that it was particularly important to include small towns such as Kanxoc, small cities such as Valladolid and Felipe Carrillo Puerto, and the largest city on the peninsula, Mérida. Two surveys were designed: one for the teacher (or project facilitator in a nonacademic setting) and one for students (or audiences in a nonschool setting). The response data are extremely unruly, with many partially filled questionnaires and multiple responses provided to popular questions. This translates into a different "n" for each question and poses analytical challenges. In general, though, the response pool for the teachers/facilitators hovered at or below seventy-four and that for students/audience just under two hundred.

Participants in the pilot program responded to the puppet-mentary in varying fashions, which is characteristic of responses to cultural matters in Yucatán, particularly in matters of language. In the circulated DVD, all dialogue took place in Yucatec Mayan with optional Spanish subtitles. Teachers and facilitators at the seventy-four locations viewing the DVD were asked if their audience understood Yucatec; just under half (45 percent) indicated comprehension. At 55 percent of the pilot sites, teachers and facilitators responded that the audience did not

Table 9.3. Institutions participating in viewing and evaluating the experimental puppet-mentary.

Type of Institution	%	n
School, primary	62.1	46
School, secondary	2.7	2
Library	18.9	14
Museum	1.4	1
Private dwelling	2.7	2
Municipal office	1.4	1
Archaeological site	10.8	8
Total	**100**	**74**

Table 9.4. Participating municipalities in Yucatán and Quintana Roo.

Municipality	n
Cuncunul	1
Dzitzas	1
Espita	1
Huhi	1
Kanasin	1
Maní	3
Maxcanú	5
Mérida	9
Motul	1
Muna	3
Oxkutzcab	10
Panaba	1
Peto	5
Santa Elena	2
Sotuta	1
Tekax	2
Tekom	1
Temozon	2
Ticul	3
Tixpehual	1
Tizimin	2
Valladolid	16
Yaxcaba	1
Felipe Carrillo Puerto (QR)	1
Total	**74**

understand spoken Yucatec. At 12.9 percent of the locations, the DVD was shown without Spanish subtitles. When students/audience members were asked about their level of interest and excitement in viewing a Yucatec-language DVD, 44 percent of respondents were excited or pleased, while the remaining 56 percent displayed a range of reactions including unhappiness, confusion, and lack of comprehension. As in the Mayaón radio series, the monolingual presentation—although in an Indigenous language—did engender feelings of exclusion among those not conversant in Yucatec (which included over 50 percent of participants despite our efforts to include rural communities where Yucatec is more likely to be spoken by youngsters).

Given the important visual component of the DVD, however, the episodes could be comprehended—at least partially—without any dialogue. When students were asked about their most and least favorite scenes, a wide range of responses occurred, with 185 indicating their most favorite part(s) and 128 pointing to their least favorite part(s) (figures 9.2 and 9.3). Significantly, the episode in which the marionettes visit Chichén Itzá ranks as the number-one most favorite part of the DVD. This ranking shows that just because many of the program participants had not visited an archaeological site, it doesn't mean that they are not interested in the old places. Rather, this response suggests that students and other audiences are eager to have the opportunity to stroll through Chichén Itzá and discuss the challenges of heritage tourism. Overall, viewers responded that the second most favorite part of the DVD was "*todos*" (everything). We surmise that this indicates a "thumbs up" for the endeavor—gratifying but not terribly informative. Interestingly, the third most popular part was "planting maize"—an activity that occurs at both the beginning and end of the film. The cornfield or milpa has tremendous cultural significance in Yucatán—approaching an iconic moral imperative—and this sentiment is reflected in the popularity of its depiction in the film as central to the life of Yucatec Mayan peoples. As more people gravitate toward urban areas like Mérida or the Maya Riviera to seek employment, the importance of the more distant milpa grows in importance.

Figure 9.2. Responses to the query, "What is your favorite part of the puppet-mentary?"

My least favorite part of the puppet-mentary was . . .

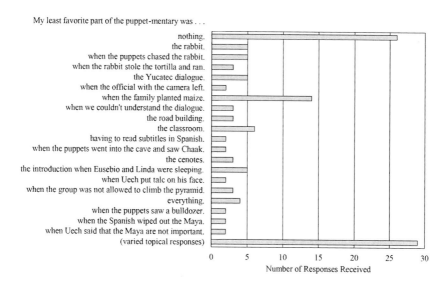

Figure 9.3. Responses to the query, "What is your least favorite part of the puppet-mentary?"

Three scenes tied for the fourth most popular part of the film (figure 9.2): the encounter with Chaak; the antics of the rabbit; and learning about hieroglyphs and bar-dot counting in school. The Chaak scene is a little spooky—it was filmed inside a cave, and the marionette Chaak is much larger than the adolescent marionettes. Students may have enjoyed the slight otherworldliness of this scene, and they may also have been intrigued by the image of a Chaak, the rain deity. This deity managed to survive centuries of religious extirpation campaigns by Spanish friars and is still the focal point of ceremonies calling for rain at the beginning of the planting season. The rabbit was placed in the film explicitly for comic relief, so it's not surprising that rabbit hijinks proved to be entertaining. Finally, students really liked a part of the film that is mostly fantasy—the scene in which young students learn about Maya hieroglyphs and the bar-dot counting system as part of their regular classroom curriculum. This suggests a desire on the part of children to receive this type of instruction.

Students also were asked to comment on their least favorite part of the film (figure 9.3). Many refused to critique any part of the video, while a smaller proportion mentioned many of same scenes that also were ranked as most popular. Planting maize was mentioned as a least favorite part, as was the classroom scene in which the students learn hieroglyphs. A low rumble of displeasure at the antics of the rabbit also came through, as did the encounter with Chaak and even the opening scene in which Eusebio and Linda are sleeping in hammocks. Five students disliked the dialogue altogether—perhaps indicating discomfort with spoken Yucatec. So the most favorite scenes were also the least favorite scenes but among a smaller percentage of the largely student audience.

Over 96 percent of the teachers who showed the DVD in their classes and used lesson plans from the teacher's guide were enthusiastic about the content and of the opinion that the puppet-mentary was useful for teaching about cultural heritage and Maya identity. The same percentage planned to use the DVD in the future. When asked what could be done to increase the effectiveness of the puppet-mentary, one teacher suggested that it be paired with Yucatec-language classes, while another thought that it should be expanded into a series in which the marionettes have different encounters with their cultural heritage. Four teachers (approximately 5 percent) suggested that we continue these types of programs because they help the children and youth of Yucatán remember their culture.

When teachers were asked specifically about the themes of the DVD and which ones worked best in a school setting, about a quarter of the respondents thought that all of the topics worked well (figure 9.4). Other teachers pointed to specific themes that were particularly effective or relevant. In decreasing order, they include rituals and customs of Maya people (a reference to episode 9 and the encounter with Chaak); classic Maya hieroglyphs and the bar-dot counting system; anything to do with Maya culture; archaeological sites; cuisine and agriculture; specifically Chaak, with a vote for inclusion of a Ch'a' Chaak ceremony in another DVD; and anything that provides a "deeper understanding of our culture and patrimony." In short, teachers expressed the sense that including a cultural heritage component in the curriculum was worthwhile and that they wanted to see more rather than fewer curricular materials that facilitated such inclusion.

We asked students what they learned from watching the puppet-mentary—an open-ended question to which students responded in a variety of ways (figure 9.5). The most popular response alluded to learning more about how Maya people lived in the past, followed by increased understanding of the value of archaeological sites and artifacts and of culture and traditions generally. Variations on these responses included learning about the deities, bar-dot numbers, ceremonies and rituals practiced, and Maya cuisine. A few students characterized the DVD as an

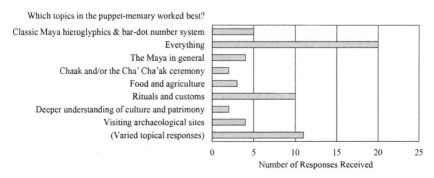

Figure 9.4. Teacher responses to the question, "Which topics of the DVD worked best in a school setting?"

Figure 9.5. Student responses when asked what new things they learned from watching the puppet-mentary.

opportunity to learn about their ancestors or the similarities between their culture and that of the ancient Maya (figure 9.5). These answers suggest that students want to know more about what archaeologists have found and how it has been interpreted. They also appreciate the opportunity to think about the valorization of archaeological sites and artifacts. A close association with the deep history of the Yucatán—as an ancestral history—is also indicated by several of the replies.

In a follow-up question, students were asked if they felt a particular connection to the ancient Maya. Over one-third of the participating students stated that they considered the ancient Maya to be their ancestors, part of their origin and identity, and part of their history. A few students linked the ancient Maya with their parentage and particularly to their grandparents. Although a patrimonialist discourse is not foregrounded in Yucatán in the same manner as in highland Guatemala (more on that soon), it is not very far from the surface—even among primary-school students.

We asked students why they think that the ancient Maya are important. This open-ended question also elicited a wide range of responses that nonetheless do exhibit some modal tendencies (figure 9.6). Topping the chart is the notion that the sheer mass of construction activity—especially temples and important places (likely a veiled reference to Chichén Itzá)—makes the past important. Three different reasons tied for second place. They include "because they [ancient Maya] left us so many things"; because of their culture; and because of their customs and

Ancient Maya are important because they . . .

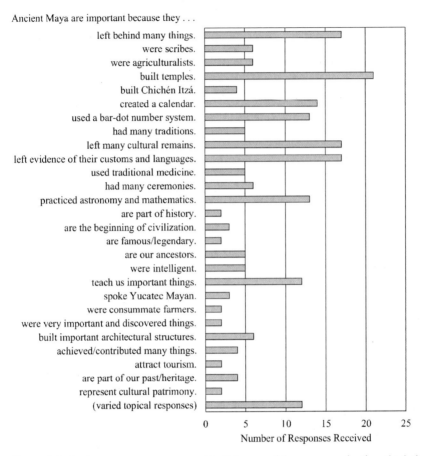

Figure 9.6. Student response to a request to list some of the reasons why they think that the ancient Maya are important.

languages. The third-place rationale for importance was the presence of a complex calendar, while a system of writing numbers and knowledge of astronomy and math tied for fourth place. The fifth-ranked reason that students offered goes like this: that the ancient Maya are important "because they taught us many important things." Browsing the less frequently mentioned reasons for valorizing the ancient Maya, one sees additional links to ancestry, as well as an understanding that the places and things of the old Maya attract tourists and thus provide economic benefits. This answer links back to the most popular one and indicates a keen awareness by these students of the significance of the heritage landscape in which their lives are embedded. The student answers, in fact, display two modal tendencies: the first is to ascribe importance based on the physicality of the footprint of the ancient Maya—their buildings, cities, and artifacts. The second is to nontangible heritage—astronomy or math, for instance—which is perceived as equally significant.

The survey form included a question about ethnicity and whether or not the respondent self-identified as Maya. Interestingly, when the responses discussed above are sorted by ethnic affiliation, the response pattern remains essentially the same, including the responses that addressed the most and least favorite scenes of the DVD. The only discernible difference in response pattern occurred in the more frequent use of "*nosotros*" (us) among those who self-identified as Maya. Both audiences referred to the ancient Maya as "*antepasados*" (ancestors) and "*abuelos*" (grandparents).[4] In fact, a slightly higher percentage of those who did not identify solely as Maya (65.7 percent) used these terms than did self-ascribed Maya respondents (51.1 percent). The fact that heritage terminology and ethnic identification do not run in lockstep will not surprise those who are familiar with the intricacies of Yucatec culture and identity. As discussed earlier, Yucatán is a place where the term *mestiza* is used to refer to a woman who dresses in an embroidered *huipil* (generally considered vernacular Maya clothing); this usage hints at the complexity of ethnic identity in this part of the world and why we need to envision heritage in broad and inclusive ways.

En el Camino de Nuestros Antepasados represents an experiment in dialoguing about cultural heritage using the medium of film with actors that are puppets. Given the response to the DVD, it appears to have achieved the goal of sparking dialogue and reflection about the past and its conservation. However, the longer-term goal of sustaining that spark proved harder to accomplish. Integration into the regular curriculum of third to fifth grades in schools throughout Yucatán is not an impossible goal but would require a sizeable second wave of resources, energy, and close coordination with the secretary of education, the regional branches of INAH, and administrators of bilingual education. Teacher training, as we learned in Guatemala, is a critical part of the equation for which resources and time must be earmarked. Throughout the Maya region, government agencies resist funding the printing and distribution of student textbooks, which means that a new curriculum can never become sustainable until an endowment-like mechanism is established to cover the costs of student learning materials.

The puppets taught us many lessons, not just about heritage but also about sustainability. Dreaming about a different world and imagining it on-screen is a worthwhile endeavor, but it is just as challenging to work against institutional inertia to change the calculus of heritage in a sustainable way. While we contemplated the next chess move in our repartee with the Mexican education system, we also looked to the south, where we had an opportunity to start a different kind of heritage program—one that we hoped would be self-sustaining.

MAPPING HERITAGE IN THE HIGHLANDS OF GUATEMALA

When touring the Riecken-funded community library of Xolsacmaljá, a partnering community in our mapping initiative, one notices that the walls are covered with shapes cut from colorful construction paper. Some shapes mimic patterns found on traditional weavings, while others proclaim "*'Utz Ipetik'*" ("welcome" in K'iche' Maya). A *rincón cultural* (cultural corner) includes pottery, a traditional birthing chair used to seat women in labor, and various handicrafts and symbols of seasonal Guatemalan holidays and Maya rituals (figure 9.7). This culturally rich community building hosts special activities for children and adults alike, as well as offering computers with Internet access to facilitate connections to the world beyond the village. Within dynamic library contexts such as this one, a community-mapping project took place.

The Riecken libraries are woven into the fabric of the communities where they are located. Local towns and municipalities contribute to the initial cost of building the library and the continuing costs of maintaining library personnel. This "buy-in" by the local community increases the perceived value of the library to community members, who in turn generate a rich array of library activities. As a result, each library has a unique set of local programs, and the libraries become an integral part of each community rather than an external imposition. The mapping project was seated within the community libraries and so was incorporated into existing programs. This provided the benefit of existing technological infrastructure and also sent a clear message that the mapping was to be carried out by and for the community.

Figure 9.7. *Rincón cultural* at the community library of Xolsacmaljá, Totonicapan, Guatemala (photo by Sarah Rowe).

Each of the five communities participating in the project hosts a population of between two and three thousand people. While only a small percentage of persons in each community would be engaged directly in recording GPS points or creating the final maps, nearly 100 percent of each community was involved through an approval process whereby each map was discussed in a town meeting. Participation across age and gender was an explicit goal of this project. We particularly encouraged the participation of young persons, who acutely feel the tension between local identity and more cosmopolitan modes of being, and women, who often take a backstage role to any activity that involves public performance. As a result, nearly 70 percent of participants were under the age of eighteen, and 55 percent of all participants were women (table 9.5). Children and adolescents joined the mapping effort with enthusiasm, in part because they have fewer external obligations. Women also participated actively, particularly in reference to maps that feature places of artisan production, such as weaving.

Table 9.5. Age and gender of mapping project participants by community.

Age[a]	Gender	Cabricán	Chiché	Huitán	San Juan la Laguna	Xolsacmaljá	Totals
Children	Female	8	4	9	0	31	52
Children	Male	7	6	6	0	14	33
Teens	Female	6	3	7	10	23	49
Teens	Male	9	7	5	15	17	53
Adults	Female	0	7	0	20	2	29
Adults	Male	4	1	3	12	3	23
Elders	Female	0	0	0	18	0	18
Elders	Male	0	0	0	12	0	12
	TOTAL	34	28	30	87	90	269
						Females	148
						Males	121
						TOTAL	269

Note: These categories were supplied by Riecken coordinators.
[a]Exact age range included within each category is approximated in table 9.6.

Community members designed a protocol for recording locations of important cultural and natural features and for producing maps of these locations.[5] First, a group assembled to map locales belonging to a specific theme, such as locales of artisan production or sacred sites. After data are collected on the relevant features, mappers return to the library to download points and edit the accompanying information for inclusion on a map. Different groups and configurations of mappers would often map the same themes. The repeated experience and expression of community space and community history during group field trips served to highlight the numerous and differing stories that characterize community spaces and encouraged multivocality in the map-making process.

Draft maps are presented at town meetings, during which there is open discussion, and anyone can comment on the features that will appear on a map. Sometimes comments at these meetings result in moving the location of a mapped feature to more accurately reflect specialized knowledge within the community, and at other times the draft maps serve to elicit oral histories, particularly from elders, which can be added to the map archive. Meeting discussion can also result in a location being removed from the map if knowledge of its location and/or existence is deemed too sensitive for open circulation. Only after community meetings have been held and consensus has been reached concerning the content of a map is it printed and distributed within the community.

From the outset, the communities set a goal of recording and mapping natural and cultural resources for community planning. Initial maps created by the communities traced road systems and marked the locations of libraries, schools, municipal buildings, and churches. Community members expanded the scope of the project to include natural and cultural resources in which they are keenly interested, such as bird habitats, tourist routes, water systems, forests, artisan workshops, and the boundary of community-use lands. At a basic level, the purpose of these maps is to facilitate local decision making and self-determination for Indigenous communities.

In order to assess the impact of the project, we developed a survey in conjunction with the Riecken staff in Antigua and community librarians and program coordinators. The survey asked participants what role they had played in the project, what they mapped, their assessments of the impact of the project, and what could be done to improve it. This survey was administered online through Google Forms, which participants accessed in their local library. The survey was also available for participants to fill out on paper within the libraries. Over the course of a month, we collected ninety-eight responses from mapping participants in the five communities (table 9.6). The ratio of male to female respondents and the proportion of respondents under eighteen are commensurate with the demographics of project participants overall.

Demographic information collected in the course of the survey, including gender, age, education, and occupation, also highlighted a recurrent theme found in our work in other regions: many of the respondents were no longer students (even some teenagers) and most people's schooling ended after only a few grades into primary school. This demographic information also highlighted the variety of participants in the project: students, artisans, farmers, tailors, and housewives were all active in the mapping project. Their impressions of the mapping project are provided below with only minor editing, such as subject-verb agreement. Even if a statement is not syntactically elegant, we have not changed it.

The majority of respondents had participated in both mapping workshops and field trips in which GPS points were collected (table 9.7). There seems to have

Table 9.6. Age and gender of survey respondents by community.

Age	Gender	Cabricán	Chiché	Huitán	San Juan la Laguna	Xolsacmaljá	Not Identified	Totals
9–12 (children)	Female	5	0	0	0	5	3	13
	Male	6	0	1	0	0	2	9
13–18 (teens)	Female	2	3	2	2	16	5	30
	Male	9	3	1	2	6	1	22
19–40 (adults)	Female	2	0	3	1	0	1	7
	Male	1	0	1	8	0	0	10
41+ (elders)	Female	0	0	0	4	0	0	4
	Male	1	0	1	0	1	0	3
	Total	26	6	9	17	28	12	98
							Females	54
							Males	44
							TOTAL	98

Table 9.7. Forms of mapping project participation by community.

Form of Participation[a]	Cabricán	Chiché	Huitán	San Juan la Laguna	Xolsacmaljá	Not Identified
Librarian	3[d]	0	1	1[d]		4[b]
Coordinator	2[b,d]	0	1[b]	1[d]	1	4[b]
Participated in a Workshop	23[c](1)	2	8	15[c](8)	28[c](4)	11[c](1)
Collected GPS points	22	5	8	7	24	11
Edited maps	1	1	5	4	5	9
Participated in a community meeting	0	4	6	5	6	7
Archaeological investigation	0	0	0	0	1	0

[a]People often identified more than one form of participation. Thus, the numbers do not equal 98.
[b]There were two official coordinators of the project, one based in Xolsacmaljá and the other in San Juan la Laguna. Other individuals self-identified as coordinators who were not, in an official sense. These people likely were deeply involved in their community or could have been making a bit of a joke (some were quite young).
[c]People sometimes reported that they participated in a workshop but neglected to state that they had collected GPS-point data. However, the same individuals often referred to features that they had mapped in the survey question that followed, suggesting that they had collected GPS points. The number in parentheses indicates the frequency of these individuals.
[d]These individuals only indicated a role as a librarian or coordinator, but from their position in the project and responses to other questions, it is clear that they participated in the full range of activities related to the project.

been some confusion in filling out the survey since some respondents did not state that they used a GPS device but then identified by name features in the community that they had mapped. Relatively fewer had participated in editing maps on the computer or in community meetings at which maps were discussed and approved (or not). This could be due to the relatively young age of the majority of survey respondents, who maybe weren't fully trusted by project staff to manipulate the recorded data or perhaps weren't seen as adult enough to participate in community meetings.

The most common type of features mapped were those pertaining to the natural environment (such as sources of water, animal habitats, or special plants) or infrastructure (streets, community buildings), though cultural sites (such as altars) were also frequently mapped (table 9.8). Only at San Juan la Laguna and Xolsacmaljá were mapped features explicitly labeled as archaeological, although archaeological sites that still carry salience as sacred sites may be folded into the "cultural" category. When asked what communities still need to map, the most frequent responses also dealt with elements of the natural environment and community infrastructure, although archaeological sites and cultural features were also cited (table 9.9). When interpreting these results, it is important to consider that the divisions between various categories are fluid; natural resources are used for cultural purposes (e.g., the location of medicinal plants), and archaeological sites could certainly be lumped with other cultural sites. The frequency of responses to the first question points to the priorities of communities in mapping their landscapes, while the identification of these same categories in responses to the second question emphasizes that a project such as this may have no clear end point—there will always be more information to record.

Participants were asked what they'd learned or discovered through this project (*¿Qué has aprendido/descubierto por medio de este proyecto?*). Approximately half

Table 9.8. Types of features mapped by community.

Type of Feature[a]	Cabricán	Chiché	Huitán	San Juan la Laguna	Xolsacmaljá	Not Identified
Natural	25	0	6	10	25	5
Infrastructure	25	5	8	11	9	10
Cultural	1	1	6	10	10	5
Archaeological sites	0	0	0	6	5	0
Community boundaries	0	0	1	0	1	0
Residences of healers & midwives	0	0	1	0	1	0
None	0	0	1	0	0	0

[a]Respondents generally identified more than one category of points mapped.

Table 9.9. Additional types of features that respondents would like to map by community.

Type of Feature[a]	Cabricán	Chiché	Huitán	San Juan la Laguna	Xolsacmaljá	Not Identified
Natural	2	0	4	7	12	8
Infrastructure	2	0	2	3	11	1
Cultural	14	0	3	3	4	3
Other	1	1	0	1	1	0
Archaeological sites	7	1	1	1	1	4
Community boundaries	0	4	3	1	3	1
Areas for tourism	0	1	0	5	0	0
Businesses	0	0	3	2	0	0

[a]Respondents generally identified more than one category of points to be mapped.

of the responses pertained to technological skills, such as using GPS and taking points, or learning how to make and edit maps (table 9.10). The other half of responses focused more on the intangible qualities of the project, highlighting the discovery of previously unknown, but important, places in their community. Here is a sample of some of the responses to this question:

> *A través de este proyecto he descubierto muchas cosas que son útiles para nuestras comunidades que estaban en abandono.* (Through this project we found many things that are useful for our communities that were abandoned.)
> *He descubierto cosas que no sabia que habían en mi comunidad.* (I found things I did not know were in my community.)
> *Que hay lugares sagrados que muchos de nosotros hemos olvidado.* (There are sacred places that many of us have forgotten.)

Table 9.10. Responses to: *¿Qué has aprendido/descubierto por medio de este proyecto?* (What have you learned or discovered through this project?)

Type of Knowledge[a]	Cabricán	Chiché	Huitán	San Juan la Laguna	Xolsacmaljá	Not Identified
Community knowledge/discovery	16	1	2	7	17	5
Technological knowledge (GPS, computers, etc.)	11	5	8	9	17	7
No response	0	0	0	2	0	1

[a]Respondents generally identified more than one category.

Thus, GPS and mapping familiarity were frequently cited outcomes of the project, but additional responses pointed to the benefits of the project in recovering lost knowledge or enabling a deeper level of familiarity with the local landscape on the part of residents. This concern with knowledge loss, and thus culture loss, is echoed by participants in our programs across the Maya region. While these highland communities generally are identified as "traditional" in that they still retain their language and other outward markers of Indigenous identity such as dress, culture loss remains a persistent concern.

Survey participants were asked two questions that elicited similar responses: *¿Qué tan importantes es para ti el mapeo del sitios comunitarios? ¿Por qué?* (How important is it, for you, to map community sites? Why?) and *¿Qué tan importante es [el proyecto] para la comunidad? ¿Por qué?* (How important is [the project] to the community? Why?) (see table 9.11). The majority of responses in all cases highlighted the importance of the information gathered for the sake of increased knowledge about the community. What follows is a verbatim sample of the responses:

> *Es muy importante porque desconocemos mucho de los sitios. A través del mapeo podemos descubrir nuevas ideas.* (It is very important because we do not know a lot about the sites. Through the mapping we can find new ideas.)
> *Es importante para rescatar cosas perdidas.* (It is important to recover lost things.)
> *Porque a través de estos mapeos transmitimos a nuestras futuras generaciones los recursos que tiene la comunidad.* (Through this mapping project we transmit to future generations knowledge of the resources in the community).

Other respondents highlighted themes that point to the utility of this information in community-development projects. These responses also spoke to one of the driving motivations of the project—to improve the capacity for self-determination:

> *Es muy importante por que a través de los proyectos hay más desarrollo.* (It is very important because through these projects there will be more development.)
> *Para conocer con qué recursos cuenta la comunidad para buscar posibles alternativas para lograr un desarrollo local.* (To know what resources the community has, in order to look for alternatives for local development.)
> *Para conocer los cambios que puedan surgir en el futuro.* (To be aware of the changes that may arise in the future.)
> *Sí es importante porque ayuda a realizar proyectos de desarrollo, porque se puede conocer donde hay necesidades.* (It is important because it helps to carry out development projects, because you can know where the needs are.)

Table 9.11. Responses to: *¿Qué tan importante es el proyecto para la comunidad? ¿Por qué?* **(How important is the project to the community? Why?)**

Type of Response[a]	Total	Cabricán	Chiché	Huitán	San Juan la Laguna	Xolsacmaljá	Not Identified
It's important because of the information we've gathered about the community.	69	21	5	7	11	20	5
It's important for presenting ourselves to visitors.	19	2	0	1	3	9	4
It's important for community development.	12	2	1	1	4	2	2
It's important for the technological knowledge we've gained.	4	1	0	1	0	0	2
No response	4	0	0	1	3	0	0

[a]Respondents occasionally identified more than one category.

These were not distinct motivations, and sometimes various sentiments were bundled together, as in this eloquent response:

Para mí, fue enriquecer mis conocimientos de como es mi comunidad y a su vez poder ser un voluntario para guiar a las personas de otros lugares que desean conocer como es la comunidad de Xolsacmaljá. Porque es necesario saber de lo nuestro primero para fortalecer la protección y mejoramiento de la misma comunidad. (For me [the importance] was to enrich my knowledge of my community, and when I can be a volunteer to guide people from other places, I want to know what my community is like. Because it's necessary to know what we have first, to strengthen the protection and improvement of our community.)

The inverse of these questions—*¿Qué puede pasar si proyectos como este no son implementados en las comunidades?* (What will happen if projects like this are not implemented in communities?)—revealed another dimension of community sentiment toward the value of the project (see table 9.12). Some of the responses were practical—without maps, people would not be able to find their way—but more frequently they pointed to technological illiteracy and lack of community development as likely conditions without the project. The numbers are telling, but a sample of verbatim responses gives finer resolution to the answers:

> *La comunidad no puede saber que es lo que hay dentro de ella y tampoco como puede mejorar.* (The community couldn't know what's inside it and also wouldn't know what to improve.)
>
> *Ignoramos si existen lugares importantes de la comunidad, no hay prosperidad, desconoceríamos muchas cosas de nuestros pueblos.* (If we ignore important places that exist in the community, there is no prosperity, and we would not know a lot of things about our towns.)
>
> *Continuaríamos en el analfabetismo a la par de la tecnología de ahora.* (We would continue to be technologically illiterate.)

The most frequent response to imagined community life without the project emphasized vanishing knowledge and the importance of mapping for articulating the place of their hometown within a wider world.

> *No podríamos transmitir a nuestras futuras generaciones los recursos con los que se cuenta en la comunidad y de esta forma se perderían recursos importantes.* (We could not pass on to future generations the resources of the community, and thus important resources would be lost.)
>
> *Se perdería una gran oportunidad y no se daría ha conocer ante otra gente que quiere conocer nuestra cultura.* (A great opportunity would be lost, and we would not meet other people who want to know our culture.)
>
> *Poco a poco perdemos nuestra identidad ya que por medio de este proyecto con-ocemos más de nuestra identidad.* (Gradually, we [would] lose our identity, but through this [project] we know more of our identity.)
>
> *La comunidad quedaría olvidada y desactualizada.* (The community would be forgotten and outdated.)

These responses mirror statements made on community visits in 2012 and 2014, when participants emphasized the importance of the project for putting their community "on the map." Communities aren't just recording important knowledge within their boundaries, they are also articulating their relationships to other communities, to the Guatemalan state, and to broader forces of globalization that bring people together from far-flung locales.

When asked what aspects of the project could be improved (table 9.13), the most frequent response pertained to recording more places or different kinds of places. This may indicate some internal disagreements about the priority and order of the places that were mapped. Or it may simply be an indication of respondents' desires to continue gathering information. The next most frequent response related to having more time for the project, though this sentiment came mainly from one community, Xolsacmaljá. The integration of school groups into

Table 9.12. Responses to: *¿Qué puede pasar si proyectos como éste no son implementados en las comunidades?* **(What will happen if projects like this are not implemented in communities?)**

Types of Response[a]	Total	Cabricán	Chiché	Huitán	San Juan la Laguna	Xolsacmaljá	Not Identified
We wouldn't know about our community	63	15	2	7	12	20	7
Technological illiteracy	21	1	3	1	6	9	1
Other people wouldn't know about our community	8	4	0	1	2	1	0
There wouldn't be development	5	3	0	1	1	0	0
People would get lost	5	0	0	0	0	3	2
No response or not applicable[b]	5	0	1	0	2	0	2

[a]Respondents occasionally identified more than one category.
[b]Respondents provided no response or repeated their answers to a previous, nonrelated query.

the project at Xolsacmaljá may have resulted in overlarge mapping groups, given the GPS resources available, and reduced time for participation due to other school-scheduling demands.

While some respondents expressed a desire for more financial and technological resources, they more frequently pointed to future steps that would improve the project. These include holding more workshops, getting more people involved in the project (particularly more children), sharing the collected information in more impactful ways, and conducting a more intensive investigation into the places that have already been mapped.

Finally, community members were asked how they think the collected information should be used in the future (*¿Cómo crees que la información recopilada en este proyecto debe ser utilizada en el futuro?*; see table 9.14). The majority of responses from all communities emphasized sharing the recorded information and making it available for posterity. The actual mechanisms to accomplish this information sharing varied from making more maps, storing the data publicly in the library, using it within the schools, or partnering with municipalities. Again, we provide a sample of verbatim responses:

Table 9.13. Responses to: *¿Qué aspectos del proyecto consideras que deberían mejorar?* (What aspects of the project do you think could be improved?)

Type of Response[a]	Total	Cabricán	Chiché	Huitán	San Juan la Laguna	Xolsacmaljá	Not Identified
Record more places	31	16	2	4	4	3	2
Have more time for the project	21	0	0	0	2	15	4
Hold more workshops	14	1	2	3	3	4	1
Get more people participating	13	3	1	1	2	6	0
Share collected information better	11	2	0	1	3	3	2
Do a deeper study of places recorded	7	3	0	0	1	2	1
Have more/better GPS units	6	0	0	0	1	3	2
Provide more money for the project	3	0	0	3	0	0	0
Nothing needs improvement	4	0	1	1	1	0	1
No response	4	1	1	0	2	0	0

[a]Respondents occasionally identified more than one category.

> *Dar a conocer la información a la comunidad, escuelas, colegios; darle seguimiento a la información ya recopilada; involucra a más personas en el proyecto.* (Disseminate information to the community, schools, and colleges; follow up on the information already gathered; involve more people on the project.)
>
> *Tener un archivo de toda la información y mantenerlo visible en la biblioteca para que todos conozcan los recursos con que contamos.* (Have a file with all the information and keep it visible in the library for everyone to know the resources we have.)
>
> *Compartirlo con las demás generaciones para no perder la información recopilada en este taller, y que sepan aprovecharlo de manera eficiente y eficaz.* (Share [the information] with the next generations so as not to lose the information collected in this workshop; know it and use it efficiently and effectively.)
>
> *La información puede estar incluidas en las computadoras y en los telefonos celulares para que se use todos los días.* (The information could be included in computers and cell phones to be used every day.)

Table 9.14. Responses to: *¿Cómo crees que la información recopilada en este proyecto debe ser utilizada en el futuro?* **(How do you think the information gathered in this project should be used in the future?)**

Type of Response[a]	Total	Cabricán	Chiché	Huitán	San Juan la Laguna	Xolsacmaljá	Not Identified
Disseminate information gathered	60	19	4	5	9	15	8
Apply information gathered to development	19	5	0	4	7	2	1
Use the information with visitors	11	0	0	0	1	9	1
Gather more information	11	8	1	0	0	0	2
Include more people in the project	9	2	1	0	2	2	2
No response	1	0	0	0	1	0	0

[a]Respondents occasionally identified more than one category.

Numerous respondents suggested applying the information gathered to different types of development projects.

> *Para buscar que la comunidad se supere en todos los aspectos de la vida, es decir mejorar su nivel de vida.* (To find ways for the community to excel in all aspects of life, that is, to improve the standard of living.)
> *Para generar proyectos de desarrollo sostenible.* (To generate sustainable development projects.)
> *Realizar proyectos como el de rescatar los lugares y especies en peligro de extinción.* (To undertake projects like rescuing sites and endangered species.)
> *Ejecutar proyectos productivos con los datos recopilados para lograr desarrollo de la comunidad, debido a que está en extrema pobreza.* (Run productive projects with the data collected to achieve community development, because it is in extreme poverty.)

Other desired outcomes of the mapping project included increased tourism and visitors to their communities. These responses emphasize that these communities are not inward looking. Respondents are interested in connecting with people beyond their village borders but on their own terms. This desire for connectivity on autonomous terms disrupts the sentiment that "traditional" communities are insular or inward looking, as these verbatim quotes show.

Nos serviría a nosotros mismos y a si darnos cuenta del cambio que a sufrido nuestra comunidad y enseñarle a nuestros visitants. (It would serve us to help realize the changes that our community has undergone and to teach that to our visitors.)

Para promocionar el turismo y colocar mapas en las entradas de las comunidades y ayudar a que los visitantes no se pierdan. (To promote tourism by placing the maps at the entrances to communities to help [visitors] not get lost.)

The responses to the survey as a whole emphasize self-determination. Ultimately, this was the most frequent benefit highlighted by respondents, although in many different ways. The maps provide the information needed in order to care for people and lands and to develop cultural and natural resources according to local cultural beliefs and each community's particular needs. Self-determination takes many forms, but knowing what you have—in terms of both natural and cultural resources—is an essential step in planning for the future.

PERFORMING HERITAGE

The programs and participant feedback examined here highlight that heritage is not a static possession—it is not something that groups have or lack—but rather that heritage as a concept exists only so far as people assign meaning to intangible or tangible elements of their landscape. Heritage resides in the value and valance that such places assume in people's lives. In this sense, Laurajane Smith is correct in asserting that heritage is a relationship. The programs presented here provide opportunities to strengthen that relationship through cultural expression, language, traditional knowledge, or old places, but all programs emphasize living heritage and work to provide space for new dialogues to emerge. Such approaches also provide an opportunity for people to interact with and find meaning in shared heritage. They work to build a bridge between archaeology and local community.

These programs perform heritage in two ways. First, by presenting entertaining performances that engage with heritage themes, a space is opened for audiences to discuss heritage issues. Second, through the performance of heritage documentation—people mapping and making choices about what to map—that heritage is reclaimed and its value enhanced.

Through radio programs broadcast in Guatemala, Belize, and México, listeners were included in debates and conversations about the conservation of archaeological sites and other aspects of local culture and heritage. Whether set in the informal conversational flows of a community or the didactic settings of a classroom, the radio dramas presented themes in a format that allowed people to formulate their own opinions about heritage.

In México, puppets provided unique and transgressive insights into the relationship between local people and archaeology, taking viewers to archaeological sites they had never visited and engaging in debates about the disposition of encountered artifacts. Further, both the radio shows and the puppet-mentary invited viewers to envision a classroom experience where knowledge of the past and value for Indigenous beliefs was presented and supported.

In Guatemala, highland communities developed their ideas of heritage by identifying the resources that they deemed important. Community mappers used this information to design conservation strategies and development plans that empower their determination of heritage within local communities.

The performance of heritage takes many forms, but from the cases presented here it is clear that it can be performed in a manner that disrupts the status quo and encourages a deeper connection between people and a present past. As with all performance, practice helps to develop a voice and to connect with cultural heritage on one's own terms.

NOTES

1. Butler (1999:123).
2. Butler (1999:125).
3. Sarah M. Rowe, personal communication with teachers using the new curriculum, 2014.
4. Federico Navarrete (2011:40) makes a similar point about perceptions of pre-Hispanic heritage throughout México.
5. Additional details about this project can be found in McAnany et al. (2015).

10

⌒⌒

Restoring Balance: Pathways to Heritage without Irony

Roads, pathways, and intersections—the tropes of this book and of the cultural heritage programs detailed herein—signal movement and change. But what is the end game? How do heritage programs relate to archaeological research? How do we move to a more open and collaborative archaeology? In the final analysis, this presentation of collaborative programs, responses from participants, and insights gleaned from successes as well as failures is about a shift in archaeological practice and about sowing the seeds from which a different kind of archaeology can emerge. In this sense, this book joins a host of other books that advocate for a shift in ethical positioning, paradigmatic framework, field practices, and terms of engagement with local and Indigenous communities.[1]

Most approaches to change within the discipline of archaeology note that change does not occur overnight but often is a slow, accretional process—small steps that reverberate into the future. This understanding of change as process structured the heritage programs discussed in chapters 7 through 9, which attempt to narrow the wide chasm that currently separates Maya archaeologists from the local-community context in which research takes place. The programs attempted to bring into dialogue archaeological perspectives on the past with the heritage perspectives of local communities.

This dialogue—also referred to as bridge building in earlier chapters—admittedly is only a first step in a process of moving toward a different and more collaborative research environment. There may be shortcuts or ways of leapfrogging to new kinds of partnerships, but until they come to light, we continue to work toward a rapprochement. Right now, the process of engagement is under reformulation. The product of this new kind of interaction is not yet a freshly minted and codified kind of knowledge that hybridizes archaeological perspectives with

Indigenous Maya perspectives. In fact, that may not be a realistic goal. Collaborative research endeavors—and particularly community archaeology—has a way of thwarting cookbook approaches. When people are added to the research equation, unpredictable but incredibly informative and enriching factors tend to surface.

In the transformed practices imagined here, local communities—many of which self-identify as Indigenous in the Maya region—play important and influential roles in the practice of archaeology from start to finish. Responses to questionnaires indicate that without a doubt there is an interest and willingness to engage. Restoring balance, as signaled in the chapter title, refers to this kind of change: restoring the balance between scientific facts and the value of human lives,[2] between heritage conservation and local livelihood, and between archaeological research and Indigenous self-determination. Issues of incommensurability have a way of dissolving when involved parties are equally empowered and invested in a shared goal. Admittedly, we may never fully arrive at this utopian balance, but we can take steps, even small ones, which over time will create change. If change in this direction can occur, it will move Maya archaeology beyond the trope of the irony generated by the juxtaposition of a past that is greatly valued by archaeologists (and the world in general) with the limited participation and benefit enjoyed by descendant communities.

A very real goal of this journey is to move beyond the paralysis of irony and into a transmodern space in which (descendant) people of value and (archaeological) things of renown are both accorded respect and the former a voice. This world would be one in which tourists and archaeologists alike could not say (or think), "Isn't it ironic that the ancient Maya are such a celebrated culture yet many of their descendants cannot afford more than five years of formal education, live in grinding poverty, and play no role in the study and conservation of the archaeological sites in their backyard?" The previous chapters provide a preview of how this triadic space (in which archaeologists form the third apex of the triangle) might be reshaped by deeper engagement with local communities.[3] Given how such engagements have played out in sociocultural anthropology, archaeological practice—both theory and methods—would be invigorated by such intensified intersectionality. In this final chapter, I focus on pathways into the future by first considering the deeper implications of the phrase "people of value and things of renown." I then apply that discussion to issues of conservation, loss, and sustainability. Finally, I close by returning to the idea of making the extraordinary ordinary.

PEOPLE OF VALUE AND THINGS OF RENOWN

When Annette Weiner published *Women of Value, Men of Renown*,[4] she took a gendered approach to women's crafting and examined the value of that work and its contribution to status rivalry among Trobriand Islands men. Without a woman of value, a man could not become renowned. Synergy between the two produced and reproduced cultural practices that became so seductive to male-focused anthropologists and yet were based, nonetheless, on women's productive labor. The turn of phrase in Weiner's book title resonates with a similar dynamic in the Maya region, where archaeological things and places of renown can be juxtaposed with contemporary people of value. Traditionally, "the people" were valuable to archaeologists, who could not become renowned without the productive labor of Indigenous and local guides, excavators, field cooks, cleaners, and launderers.

Yet *the people* often were undervalued and perceived as pale shadows of the renowned and much celebrated archaeological culture. Their position as descendants of a storied past is frequently questioned and in a persistent manner that can only be understood in terms of postcolonial dynamics. Archaeologists have been slow to acknowledge this dynamic and to confront the haunting questions that linger in the aftermath of colonial disenfranchisement from a homeland. The vignette of chapter 1—an event that occurred over twenty-five years ago—provides a good example of how slow the rate of gestation can be. The wide prevalence of what can be called the *myth of extinction* demands a more honest and precise presentation by archaeologists of the Late Classic political crisis in the lowlands in order to dispel the idea that everyone simply died. But there is a deeper, rotten core to the myth that is more difficult to reconcile with archaeological research. The myth of vacant terrain (supported by the extinction narrative) is one of the most prevalent tropes of colonialism and nation building.

How does this relates to collaborative research and heritage programs? Are archaeologists now expected to fight the battles of postcolonialism in addition to raising funds to excavate sites, analyze findings, and construct narratives about the past? No, but most archaeological projects—particularly in the Maya lowlands—could be more inclusive of local populations without sacrificing the goals of archaeological research. Moving toward such inclusion is not only forward thinking, it is strategic planning. Recall the survey results presented in chapters 8 and 9. Despite the heavy toll of postcolonial nation building on rural populations, there was strong consensus among children, adults, and teachers that sites "belong" to Indigenous peoples rather than to the state or the world. This sentiment is all the more remarkable in light of the fact that—as we learned from the questionnaires—only a small percentage of those living in rural communities have visited an archaeological site that has been groomed for tourism. As the land rights of Indigenous peoples are recognized by court after court, it becomes increasingly clear that the days of archaeologists as exclusive stewards of the past are drawing to a close. Responses to questionnaires clearly indicate that local communities would welcome a dialogue about site conservation and desire to play a role in the management of their heritage landscape.

In this sense, archaeology is not exempted from the crisis of representation that reshaped sociocultural anthropology, it is simply coming to archaeology on a delayed timetable. The lag is fortuitous and provides time to put in place collaborative practices that build horizontal (rather than hierarchical) networks in the rhizomatic sense as proposed by Gilles Deleuze and Félix Guattari.[5] Such networks would accord nodal positions to both people of value and things of renown. Through such a collaborative nodal network, archaeological research can become sustainable.

In light of responses reported upon here, the value ascribed to women and children deserves special attention. Women particularly exhibited high levels of interaction with the Petén radio shows and community mapping, which enhanced the multivocality of these programs in terms of important but often difficult-to-achieve gender representation. Many of the heritage programs reported upon here touched the lives of fourth to sixth graders, and their responses highlight the vulnerability of children living in rural districts throughout the Maya region. With a school curriculum that traditionally has been disconnected from local heritage, their "ethnic coordinates," in the words of Demetrio Cojtí Cuxil,[6] can become understandably confused. This need not be the case. The convergence of ethnic identity with school curriculum—taking place in Petén rural schools as discussed in chapter 9—has the potential to strengthen identity by valuing Maya cultural heritage without excluding those who may not self-identify as a member of a Mayan ethnolinguistic group. The heritage programs presented here also highlight the complex and delicate balance between supporting Indigenous languages without alienating those with no Indigenous-language skills. Giving more voice to traditional languages through radio shows and in the puppet-mentary distanced and frustrated those who lacked the linguistic background to follow the dialogue.

CONSERVATION, LOSS, AND SUSTAINABILITY

Themes of conservation as well as loss of cultural identity and of cultural knowledge loomed large in the survey responses discussed in chapters 8 and 9. In reference to the tangible heritage of archaeological sites, a strong ethic of caring for place was present in responses regardless of whether the heritage program took place in the *aldeas* around Copán, in southern Belize, the Petén, the Guatemalan highlands, or Yucatán. Questions about what should be done with archaeological sites and artifacts consistently yielded the response that we should take care of these things of the past. A number of reasons were offered—some quite archaeological in referring to the information value of artifacts and sites—while other rationales emphasized a respect for the alterity of the past, revealing an understanding that Bjørnar Olsen would characterize as materiality.[7] Still others stressed the importance of assuming responsibility for conserving the old places that are proximate to where one lives, and some cited the importance of well-preserved sites for heritage tourism. These responses strengthen the call for comanagement of archaeological sites—whether the site is a tourist magnet or a special place prized by a local community. On a global scale, states have demonstrated only limited ability to monitor and protect old places from the ravages of neglect, development, and looting. Collaboration and site-stewardship programs initiated with local communities provide the best odds for conserving old and distinctive places.

All of the heritage programs presented here discussed conservation within a larger topical menu that included topics such as the Classic Maya dynastic calendar, deities of old, and agricultural practices of past and present. Yet the topic of caring for old places elicited the widest range of comments. Even if respondents were not conversant in the discourse of cultural patrimony—recall the young Ladino women living in rural towns of the Petén—they still felt comfortable voicing an opinion about the importance of conserving archaeological sites. And often these same respondents had never had an opportunity to visit one of the large nearby sites—hubs of a lucrative international heritage tourism industry.

E. N. Anderson has pondered the reasons why those who engage in what he terms *traditional landscape management* often express a refined philosophy of caring for place.[8] In reference to Yucatán specifically, he describes a system of environmental ethics and the "extreme knowledge, efficiency, and care in which the morals are embedded."[9] Anderson also stresses that in Yucatán, there is no strict division between cultural and natural resources.[10] Caring for archaeological places then may be an extension of a more general approach to landscape in which an astute eye and ear detects the ubiquity of the human imprint, which is only obvious to nontraditionalists when played out on a monumental scale.

A persistent and deep concern with environmental conservation—as part of cultural heritage—was particularly apparent in the Community Heritage Conservation Grant applications, as well as the community-mapping program in the Guatemalan highlands (both discussed in chapter 7). At first, there was a sense of disappointment that communities were prioritizing nature over culture in their proposals until it became apparent that communities were acting upon what Anderson had come to understand many years earlier in Yucatán: nature and culture are inseparable, and elements of each are indispensable to heritage conservation and cultural identity. Such nonpolarity also was evident in responses to the Yucatec puppet-mentary. When asked to identify their favorite scenes, respondents most often turned their thoughts to the marionettes filmed on location at Chichén Itzá, secondly to the impact of the film in total, but thirdly to the *milpa* scenes that bracket the beginning and end of the film. There was positive approval for the important role accorded to *milpa*, which has been described elsewhere as emblematic of cultural identity and increasingly of cultural loss as wage labor on the Maya Riviera leaves scant time for farming. *Milpa* as an icon of self-sustainability has assumed a position of moral authority in Yucatán that few Maya people would question. In reference to environmental stewardship, the irony lies not in the valorization of the past when juxtaposed with the disenfranchisement of present peoples but rather in allegations of poor environmental stewardship in the past juxtaposed against repeated contemporary demonstrations of careful environmental stewardship.[11]

A more diffuse kind of knowledge loss was cited as an issue of concern among community mappers in the highlands of Guatemala. Armed with GPS (global positioning systems) and mapping landscape themes, such as sacred sites or locales central to oral histories, mappers were alarmed when they contemplated how easily such places could be erased from community memory and cease to be part of the social fabric of the community. Mappers considered the ability to curb cultural loss in a self-determinative manner as a major benefit of the mapping project.

Plans of action to curb cultural loss and improve livelihoods reside close to the collaborative heritage programs reported upon here. More than one survey respondent wrote that sites should be conserved because well-preserved sites can lead to heritage tourism, which provides local economic benefit. Most every archaeologist who works in the region has been approached by a nearby community that is pinning hopes of economic development on a small archaeological site that realistically few tourists could be persuaded to visit. This does not mean that the site is worthless or not important to local identity, but it does mean that we have to move beyond and decouple a celebration of local heritage from a heritage-tourism-as-economic-development strategy.

Alternative and creative models of visitation are badly needed, and the highland mapping project may provide some answers. Mappers articulated a desire for greater connectivity with the world on terms that enhance rather than diminish self-determination, which suggests that local communities are not looking for a contract with an international cruise line that would seek to dictate the financial terms of such connectivity. Respondents also indicated an openness to visitors who can appreciate local culture, of which tangible heritage is only one part, which indicates that these communities are not closed but rather seek to play a larger role in a global community in which they and their heritage are valued.

Although pursuing Maya archaeology as business as usual is not sustainable, neither is converting the lowlands into one large archaeological theme park groomed for tourism. Honduras provides an excellent example of the dangers and unpredictability of heritage tourism as a central strut of economic development. Undergoing what Darío Euraque calls the Mayanization of Honduras,[12] the Honduran state invested in a huge advertising campaign to rebrand itself as a nation of Maya descendants and in the process devalued the ethnic diversity that is central to Honduran identity.[13] A political coup erupted in 2009, which destabilized the transportation infrastructure as well as national security. Honduras subsequently was unable to control drug- and gang-related violence, and the U.S.

State Department responded by placing a travel warning on Honduras, which further curbed tourism—particularly high-end tour packages. Even Copán, which is a World Heritage Site and one of the most spectacular dynastic capitals of the late classic period, suffered a drastic downturn in visitors.

From a global UNESCO perspective, Diane Barthel-Bouchier questions whether the network of World Heritage Sites can be sustained for an elite class of cultural heritage tourists.[14] Many World Heritage Sites are directly impacted by climate change due to their location, and still more have a checkered history in terms of bringing economic benefit to local people. Can heritage tourism deliver local benefit while conserving world heritage? And can heritage tourism be sustained? These questions drive to the heart of local/global tensions that characterize the heritage industry. UNESCO proclamations turn the eyes of the world to a specific place but with many not-so-flexible rules and strings attached to that penetrating gaze. The concern for old places voiced by participants in heritage programs provides hope that local solutions can emerge if seldom-heard voices are heeded.

Global forces often override local needs and desires and in the process diminish the probability of sustainability. Worse yet, World Heritage status can involve the transformation of a heritage place into a "no-go" zone for local people, who can no longer step foot upon what were perceived as traditional-use lands. Are traditional strategies of landscape management so diametrically opposed to conservation? From the discussion above, it seems not to be the case, and more attention needs to be given to restoring a balance between heritage conservation and local livelihood. Unfortunately, heritage specialists seem more inclined to study the global forces of heritage rather than local needs. Also badly needed are studies that tack back and forth between the local and the global in the fashion employed by Sally Engle Merry in her study of human rights and gender violence.[15] Only by examining how UNESCO site designation is vernacularized can transparency be improved and the designation ultimately made more beneficial locally.[16]

In contrast to the global heritage industry, local heritage endeavors focused on attracting visitors are more flexible, can be customized to fit the needs and interests of local communities, and thus have a better shot at sustainability. Although such grassroots initiatives rarely yield the big payback that can occur when the industry gets involved, benefit can be more equably distributed and the long-term impact in improvement of livelihood more significant, especially if changes in education are included. Archaeologists are uniquely suited to engage with and understand the localness of community-based approaches to heritage. Recall that only 4 to 6 percent of Copán-area schoolchildren recognized "the world" as a significant stakeholder in local archaeological sites.

A final issue raised in the responses that touches upon sustainability involves the transport of artifacts away from the location of excavation. A respondent in Toledo, Belize, expressed the anger of many local communities with the following words: "Archaeologists take artifacts away to places where the local people can't see them." Archaeologists transport artifacts in order to safeguard and study them and often to comply with permit regulations. Nonetheless, locals perceive this action as secretive and as denying them access to objects found in their sphere of inhabitation. While the popularity of local heritage centers (discussed in chapter 4) needs to be balanced with concerns for the security and long-term curation of objects, archaeologists are obliged to think more creatively about postcolonial approaches to artifact storage, curation, and exhibition.

MAKING THE EXTRAORDINARY ORDINARY

As Sarah Rowe and I were compiling responses to the multiyear heritage programs, I realized that I had not seen another study in which in-depth responses to grassroots efforts had been collected and published. While this realization gave me hope that archaeologists would be attracted to this book because it is different, at the same time I felt a bit apprehensive that—except for a small group of ethnographers studying the ethnography of archaeology[17]—there had not been a steady stream of publications about community reactions to archaeology in the Maya region or elsewhere. No one would read this book and say, "Not another one!"

In the Petén, where archaeologists invented the trope of the Mysterious Maya and spend countless hours and millions of dollars excavating Late Classic political capitals located in less accessible places, how can it be that there has been so little local dialogue about cultural patrimony? How is it possible that (as discussed in chapter 9) over 50 percent of the young females who listened to the radio *novelas*, self-identify as Ladino, and live in the rural communities of the Petén had no prior exposure to the topic of cultural heritage? They were literally in the dark, they knew it and expressed a desire to learn more—to become conversant with the archaeology of their backyards. This is the reality of archaeological fieldwork in the lowlands. This situation will only change when young women such as the radio-*novela* listeners have an opportunity to learn about and visit archaeological sites—such as Tikal—that have been groomed for heritage tourism. Efforts to start a dialogue about heritage issues are neither extraordinary nor expensive when viewed in the larger scheme of things as a contribution toward restoring balance.

By rendering the extraordinary ordinary, we actively carve out a path toward heritage without irony. Admittedly, this space of dialogue is uncertain and contains the challenge of incommensurability. Charles Hale refers to this space as *compromised*[18] because it is the place where research meets reality, and things get bent. The trope of a shaky bridge has been used here to convey the notion that dialogue and collaboration are components of a purposeful construction that if successful, will lead the field of archaeology to a more sustainable future with amazing community partners.

NOTES

1. Most notably but not exclusively, see Atalay (2012), Atalay et al. (2014), Meskell (2009), and Phillips and Allen (2010).

2. Dietz (2014).

3. For more discussion of the triadic relationship, see McAnany and Rowe (2015).

4. Weiner (1987).

5. Deleuze and Guattari (1987); for specific examples of participatory research methods, see Strand et al. (2003) and Wilmsen et al. (2008).

6. Cojtí Cuxil (1996:39).

7. Olsen (2012).

8. Anderson (2014).

9. Anderson (2014:122).

10. Anderson (2014:118).

11. For a recent example of forest stewardship, see Ford and Nigh (2015).

12. Euraque (2004).

13. For a case study of the Mayanization process on the Honduran island of Roatan, see Figueroa, Goodwin, and Wells (2012).

14. Barthel-Bouchier (2013).

15. Merry (2006).

16. Helen Human (2015) provides a sobering analysis of vernacularization of the UNESCO process at Çatalhöyük.

17. See particularly Castañeda and Matthews (2008).

18. Hale (2006).

References

Achugar, Hugo
2009   Foundational Images of the Nation in Latin America. In *Building Nineteenth-Century Latin America: Re-rooted Cultures, Identities, and Nations*, edited by W. G. Acree and J. C. González Espitia, pp. 11–31. Vanderbilt University Press, Nashville, TN.

Acree, William G., Jr., and Juan Carlos González Espitia (editors)
2009   *Building Nineteenth-Century Latin America: Re-rooted Cultures, Identities, and Nations.* Vanderbilt University Press, Nashville, TN.

Alexander, Rani T.
2004   *Yaxcabá and the Caste War of Yucatán: An Archaeological Perspective.* University of New Mexico Press, Albuquerque.

Anderson, Benedict
1991   *Imagined Communities: Reflections on the Origin and Spread of Nationalism.* Verso, London and New York.

Anderson, E. N.
2014   *Caring for Place: Ecology, Ideology, and Emotion in Traditional Landscape Management.* Left Coast Press, Walnut Creek, CA.

Ardren, Traci
2002   Conversations about the Production of Archaeological Knowledge and Community Museums at Chunchucmil and Kochol, Yucatán, México. *World Archaeology* 34(2):379–400.

2004   Where Are the Maya in Ancient Maya Archaeological Tourism? Advertising and the Appropriation of Culture. In *Marketing Heritage*, edited by Y. Rowan and U. Baram, pp. 103–13. AltaMira Press, Walnut Creek, CA.

Armstrong-Fumero, Fernando
2011   Words and Things in Yucatán: Poststructuralism and the Everyday Life of Mayan Multiculturalism. *Journal of the Royal Anthropological Institute* (N.S.) 17:63–81.

2013   *Elusive Unity: Factionalism and the Limits of Identity Politics in Yucatán, Mexico.* University Press of Colorado, Boulder.

213

Armstrong-Fumero, Fernando, and Julio Hoil Gutierrez
  2010   Community Heritage and Partnership in Xcalakdzonot, Yucatán. In *Handbook of Postcolonial Archaeology*, edited by J. Lydon and U. Z. Rizvi, pp. 405–11. Left Coast Press, Walnut Creek, CA.
Atalay, Sonya
  2006   No Sense of the Struggle: Creating a Context for Survivance at the NMAI. *American Indian Quarterly* 30(3):597–618.
  2008   Multivocality and Indigenous Archaeologies. In *Evaluating Multiple Narratives: Beyond Nationalist, Colonialist, Imperialist Archaeologies*, edited by J. Habu, C. Fawcett, and J. M. Matsunaga, pp. 29–44. Springer Science and Business Media, New York.
  2012   *Community-Based Archaeology: Research With, By, and For Indigenous and Local Communities.* University of California Press, Berkeley.
Atalay, Sonya, Lee Rains Clauss, Randall H. McGuire, and John R. Welch (editors)
  2014   *Transforming Archaeology: Activist Practices and Prospects.* Left Coast Press, Walnut Creek, CA.
Barth, Fredrik
  1969   Introduction. In *Ethnic Groups and Boundaries: The Social Organization of Culture Difference*, edited by F. Barth, pp. 3–38. Little, Brown, Boston.
Barthel-Bouchier, Diane
  2013   *Cultural Heritage and the Challenge of Sustainability.* Left Coast Press, Walnut Creek, CA.
Bartu Candan, Ayfer
  2007   Remembering a Nine-Thousand-Year-Old Site: Presenting Çatalhöyük. In *The Politics of Public Memory in Turkey*, edited by E. Özyürek, pp. 70–94. Syracuse University Press, Syracuse, NY.
Bastos, Santiago, and Manuela Camus
  2004   Multiculturalismo y Pueblos Indígenas: Reflexiones a Partir del Caso de Guatemala. *Revista Centroamericana de Ciencias Sociales* 1:87–112.
Beck, Wendy, Dee Murphy, Cheryl Perkins, Tony Perkins, Anita Smith, and Margaret Somerville
  2005   Aboriginal Ecotourism and Archaeology in Coastal NSW, Australia: Yarrawarra Place Stories Project. In *Indigenous Archaeologies: Decolonizing Theory and Practice*, edited by C. Smith and H. M. Wobst, pp. 226–41. Routledge, London.
Benavides, O. Hugo
  2001   Returning to the Source: Social Archaeology as Latin American Philosophy. *Latin American Antiquity* 12(4):355–70.
Bernal, Ignacio
  1980   *A History of Mexican Archaeology: The Vanished Civilizations of Middle America.* Thames & Hudson, London and New York.
Bhabha, Homi
  1994   *The Location of Culture.* Routledge, London.
Blum, William
  2004   *Killing Hope: U.S. Military and CIA Interventions since World War II*, updated edition. Common Courage Press, Monroe, ME.

Bonfil Batalla, Guillermo
1996   *México Profundo: Reclaiming a Civilization*, translated by P. A. Dennis. University of Texas Press, Austin.
Borgstede, Greg
2010   Social Memory and Sacred Sites in the Western Maya Highland: Examples from Jacaltenango, Guatemala. *Ancient Mesoamerica* 21:385–92.
Borgstede, Greg, and Jason Yaeger
2008   Notions of Cultural Continuity and Disjunction in Maya Social Movements and Maya Archaeology. In *Archaeology and the Postcolonial Critique*, edited by M. Liebmann and U. Z. Rizvi, pp. 91–107. AltaMira Press, Lanham, MD.
Bourdieu, Pierre
1977   *Outline of a Theory of Practice*. Cambridge University Press, Cambridge.
Bray, Tamara L., and Thomas W. Killion (editors)
1994   *Reckoning with the Dead: The Larsen Bay Repatriation and the Smithsonian Institution*. Smithsonian Institution Press, Washington, DC.
Breglia, Lisa C.
2006   *Monumental Ambivalence: The Politics of Heritage*. University of Texas Press, Austin.
2005   Keeping World Heritage in the Family: A Genealogy of Maya Labour at Chichén Itzá. *International Journal of Heritage Studies* 11(5):385–98.
Brown, Bill
2001   Thing Theory. *Critical Inquiry* 28(1):1–22.
Brumfiel, Elizabeth M.
2000   Making History in Xaltocan. In *Working Together: Native Americans and Archaeologists*, edited by K. E. Dongoske, M. Aldenderfer, and K. Doehner, pp. 181–90. Society for American Archaeology, Washington, DC.
Bryan, Joe
2011   Walking the Line: Participatory Mapping, Indigenous Rights, and Neoliberalism. *Geoforum* 42:40–50.
Butler, Judith
1999   Performativity's Social Magic. In *Bourdieu: A Critical Reader*, edited by R. Shushterman, pp. 113–28. Blackwell Publisher, Oxford, UK, and Malden, MA.
Callahan, Robey
2007   Apocalypto in Cobá. *Anthropological News* 48(6):28–29.
Castañeda, Quetzil
1996   *In the Museum of Maya Culture: Touring Chichén Itzá*. University of Minnesota Press, Minneapolis.
2004   "We Are *Not* Indigenous!" An Introduction to the Maya Identity of Yucatan. *Journal of Latin American Anthropology* 9(1):36–63.
Castañeda, Quetzil, and Christopher N. Matthews (editors)
2008   *Ethnographic Archaeologies: Reflections on Stakeholders and Archaeological Practices*. AltaMira Press, Lanham, MD.
Castro-Klarén, Sara
2003   The Nation in Ruins: Archaeology and the Rise of the Nation. In *Beyond Imagined Communities: Reading and Writing the Nation in Nineteenth-Century Latin America*, edited by S. Castro-Klarén and J. C. Chasteen, pp. 161–95. Johns Hopkins Press, Baltimore, MD.

Catherwood, Frederick
1844   *Views of Ancient Monuments in Central America, Chiapas, and Yucatan.* Bartlett and Welford, NY.

Caton-Thompson, Gertrude
1931   *The Zimbabwe Culture: Ruins and Reactions.* Clarendon Press, Oxford, UK.

Chasteen, John C.
2003   Introduction: Beyond Imagined Communities. In *Beyond Imagined Communities: Reading and Writing the Nation in Nineteenth-Century Latin America*, edited by S. Castro-Klarén and J. C. Chasteen, pp. ix–xxv. Johns Hopkins University Press, Baltimore, MD.

Clarence-Smith, William G., and Steven Topik
2003   *The Global Coffee Economy in Africa, Asia and Latin America, 1500–1989.* Cambridge University Press, Cambridge.

Clark, Geoffrey A.
2000   NAGPRA, the Conflict between Science and Religion, and the Political Consequences. In *Working Together: Native Americans and Archaeologists*, edited by K. E. Dongoske, M. Aldenderfer, and K. Doehner, pp. 85–90. Society for American Archaeology, Washington, DC.

Coe, Michael D.
1993   From *Huaquero* to Connoisseur: The Early Market in Pre-Columbian Art. In *Collecting the Pre-Columbian Past*, edited by E. H. Boone, pp. 271–90. Dumbarton Oaks, Washington, DC.

1999   *Breaking the Maya Code*, revised ed. Thames & Hudson, New York.

Cogolludo, Diego López de
1688   *Historia de Yucathan.* Juan Garcia Infanzon, Madrid.

Cojtí Cuxil, Demetrio
1996   The Politics of Maya Revindication. In *Maya Cultural Activism in Guatemala*, edited by E. F. Fischer and R. M. Brown, pp. 19–50. University of Texas Press, Austin.

Cojti Ren, Avexnim
2006   Maya Archaeology and the Political and Cultural Identity of Contemporary Maya in Guatemala. *Archaeologies* 2(1):8–19.

Collier, George Allen, and Elizabeth Lowery Quaratiello
2009   *Basta! Land and the Zapatista Rebellion in Chiapas*, 3rd ed. Food First Books, Oakland, CA.

Colwell-Chanthaphonh, Chip
2005   The Incorporation of the Native American Past: Cultural Extermination, Archaeological Protection, and the Antiquities Act of 1906. *International Journal of Cultural Property* 12:375–91.

2012   Archaeology and Indigenous Collaboration. In *Archaeological Theory Today*, 2nd ed., edited by I. Hodder, pp. 267–91. Polity Press, Cambridge, UK.

Colwell-Chanthaphonh, Chip, and T. J. Ferguson
2008   Introduction: The Collaborative Continuum. In *Collaboration in Archaeological Practice: Engaging Descendant Communities*, edited by C. Colwell-Chanthaphonh and T. J. Ferguson, pp. 1–32. AltaMira Press, Lanham, MD.

Colwell-Chanthaphonh, Chip, T. J. Ferguson, Dorothy Lippert, R. H. McGuire, George P. Nicholas, Joe E. Watkins, and L. J. Zimmerman

2010   The Premise and Promise of Indigenous Archaeology. *American Antiquity* 75(2):228–38.

Cooke, Bill, and Uma Kothari (editors)

2001   *Participation: The New Tyranny?* Zed Books, New York.

Corntassel, Jeff, and Richard C. Witmer

2008   *Forced Federalism: Contemporary Challenges to Indigenous Nationhood.* American Indian Law and Policy Series. University of Oklahoma Press, Norman.

Daes, Erica-Irene A.

1996   Working Paper on the Concept of "Indigenous People." UN Doc. E/CN.4/SUB.2/AC.4/1996/2. Accessed May 18, 2000. www.documents.un.org/results .asp.

Davis-Salazar, Karla L., E. Christian Wells, and José E. Moreno-Cortés

2007   Balancing Archaeological Responsibilities and Community Commitments: A Case from Honduras. *Journal of Field Archaeology* 32:196–205.

Dawdy, Shannon Lee

2009   Millennial Archaeology: Locating the Discipline in the Age of Insecurity. *Archaeological Dialogues* 16(2):131–42.

Dearborn, Lynne, and John C. Stallmeyer

2010   *Inconvenient Heritage: Erasure and Global Tourism in Luang Prabang.* Left Coast Press, Walnut Creek, CA.

del Cid, Mario, and Arthur A. Demarest

2004   Desarrollo eco-turístico del sitio arqueológico Cancuen: Un modelo para la conservación del patrimonio y desarrollo participativo. In *XVII Simposio de Investigaciones Arqueológicas en Guatemala, 2003*, edited by J. P. Laporte, B. Arroyo, H. Escobedo, and H. Mejia, pp. 117–27. Ministerio de Cultura y Deportes, Guatemala City.

del Cid, Mario, and Davíd García

2005   Cuevas Candelaria, Alta Verapaz: Demitificando la participación comunitaria en la conservación del patrimonio cultural. In *Simposio XVIII de Investigaciones Arquelógicas en Guatemala*, edited by J. P. Laporte, B. Arroyo, and H. Mejía, pp. 375–82. Museo Nacional de Arquelogía y Etnología, Guatemala City.

Deleuze, Gilles, and Félix Guattari

1987   *A Thousand Plateaus: Capitalism and Schizophrenia*, translated by B. Massumi. University of Minnesota Press, Minneapolis.

Deloria, Vine, Jr.

1969   *Custer Died for Your Sins: An Indian Manifesto.* Macmillan, New York.

Demarest, Arthur A., and Tomás Barrientos

2004   Los proyectos de arqueología y de desarrollo comunitario en Cancuen: Metas, resultados y desafíos en 2003. In *XVII Simposio de Investigaciones Arqueológicas en Guatemala, 2003*, edited by J. P. Laporte, B. Arroyo, H. Escobedo, and H. Mejia, pp. 450–64. Ministerio de Cultura y Deportes, Guatemala City.

Diamond, Jared

2005   *Collapse: How Societies Choose to Fail or Succeed.* Viking, New York.

218   *References*

Dietz, Thomas
2014   "Science, Values, and Decision-Making for Sustainability." Lecture delivered at the University of North Carolina, Chapel Hill, April 17, 2014.
Di Giovine, Michael A.
2009   *The Heritage-scape: UNESCO, World Heritage, and Tourism.* Lexington Books, Lanham, MD.
Dongoske, Kurt E., M. Aldenderfer, and Karen Doehner (editors)
2000   *Working Together: Native Americans and Archaeologists.* Society for American Archaeology, Washington, DC.
Edgeworth, Matt (editor)
2006   *Ethnographies of Archaeological Practice: Cultural Encounters, Material Transformations.* AltaMira Press, Lanham, MD.
Eiss, Paul K.
2004   Deconstructing Indians, Reconstructing Patria: Indigenous Education in Yucatán from the Porfiriato to the Mexican Revolution. *Journal of Latin American Anthropology* 9(1):119–50.
England, Nora C.
1996   The Role of Language Standardization in Revitalization. In *Maya Cultural Activism in Guatemala*, edited by E. F. Fischer and R. M. Brown, pp. 178–94. University of Texas Press, Austin.
Euraque, Darío
2004   *Conversaciones Historicas con el Mestizaje y su Identidad Nacional en Honduras.* Centro Editorial, San Pedro Sula, Honduras.
Fairclough, Graham (editor)
2008   *The Heritage Reader.* Routledge, London.
Fallow, Ben
2004   Rethinking Mayan Resistance: Changing Relations between Federal Teachers and Mayan Communities in Eastern Yucatan, 1929–1935. *Journal of Latin American Anthropology* 9(9):151–78.
Falzon, Mark-Anthony (editor)
2009   *Multi-sited Ethnography: Theory, Practice and Locality in Contemporary Research.* Ashgate, Surrey, UK.
Farriss, Nancy M.
1984   *Maya Society under Colonial Rule: The Collective Enterprise of Survival.* Princeton University Press, Princeton, NJ.
Figueroa, Alejandro J., Whitney A. Goodwin, and E. Christian Wells
2012   Mayanizing Tourism on Roatán Island, Honduras: Archaeological Perspectives on Heritage, Development, and Indigeneity. In *Global Tourism: Cultural Heritage and Economic Encounters*, edited by S. Lyon and E. C. Wells, pp. 43–60. AltaMira Press, Lanham, MD.
Finamore, Daniel
2008   Furnishing the Craftsmen: Slaves and Sailors in the Atlantic Mahogany Trade. In *American Furniture*, edited by L. Beckerdite, pp. 61–87. Chipstone Foundation, Milwaukee, WI.
Fischer, Edward F.
1996   Induced Culture Change as a Strategy for Socioeconomic Development: The Pan-Maya Movement in Guatemala. In *Maya Cultural Activism in Guatemala*,

edited by E. F. Fischer and R. M. Brown, pp. 51–73. University of Texas Press, Austin.

2001   *Cultural Logics and Global Economies: Maya Identity in Thought and Practice.* University of Texas Press, Austin.

Fischer, Michael J.

2003   *Emergent Forms of Life and the Anthropological Voice.* Duke University Press, Durham, NC.

Ford, Anabel

2006   Adaptive Management and the Community of El Pilar: A Philosophy of Resilience for the Maya Forest. In *Of the Past, for the Future: Integrating Archaeology and Conservation*, edited by N. Agnew and J. Bridgland, pp. 105–12. Getty Conservation Institute, Los Angeles.

2011   Afterword: El Pilar and Maya Cultural Heritage: Reflections of a Cheerful Pessimist. In *Contested Cultural Heritage: Religion, Nationalism, Erasure, and Exclusion in a Global World*, edited by H. Silverman, pp. 261–66. Springer Science and Business Media, New York.

Ford, Anabel, and Ronald Nigh

2015   *The Maya Forest Garden: Eight Millennia of Sustainable Cultivation of the Tropical Woodlands.* Left Coast Press, Walnut Creek, CA.

Foucault, Michel

1979   *Discipline and Punish: The Birth of the Prison.* Vintage Books, New York.

Fournier, Patricia

1999   La Arqueología Social Latinamericana: Caracterización de Una Posición Teórica Marxista. In *Sed Non Saciata: Teoría Social en la Arqueología Latinamericana Contemporánea*, edited by A. Zarankin and F. Acuto, pp. 17–32. Tridente, Buenos Aires.

Fraser, Nancy

1996   *Justice Interruptus.* Routledge, New York.

Freire, Paulo

2002 [1970]   *Pedagogy of the Oppressed*, 30th anniversary ed. Continuum, New York.

Fruhsorge, Lars

2007   Archaeological Heritage in Guatemala: Indigenous Perspectives on the Ruins of Iximché. *Archaeologies* 3(1):39–58.

Gabbert, Wolfgang

2004   Of Friends and Foes: The Caste War and Ethnicity in Yucatan. *Journal of Latin American Anthropology* 9(1):90–118.

Geertz, Clifford

1973   *The Interpretation of Cultures.* Basic Books, New York.

Gero, Joan, and Dolores Root

1990   Public Presentations and Private Concerns: Archaeology in the Pages of *National Geographic*. In *The Politics of the Past*, edited by P. Gathercole and D. Lowenthal, pp. 19–37. Unwin Hyman, London.

Gnecco, Cristóbal, and Patricia Ayala

2011   What Is to Be Done? Elements for a Discussion. In *Indigenous Peoples and Archaeology in Latin America*, edited by C. Gnecco and P. Ayala, pp. 11–27. Left Coast Press, Walnut Creek, CA.

Gomez, Felipe
    2010   The Struggle for a Law on Sacred Sites in Guatemala. *Compas: Endogenous Development Magazine* 6:26–29.
González, Roberto
    2004   From Indigenismo to Zapatismo: Theory and Practice in Mexican Anthropology. *Human Organization* 63(2):141–50.
González-Stephan, Beatriz
    2009   Forms of Historic Imagination: Visual Culture, Historiography, and the Tropes of War in Nineteenth-Century Venezuela. In *Building Nineteenth-Century Latin America*, edited by W. G. Acree Jr. and J. C. González Espitia, pp. 101–32. Vanderbilt University Press, Nashville.
Gosden, Chris
    2004   *Archaeology and Colonialism: Cultural Contact from 5000 BC to the Present.* Cambridge University Press, Cambridge.
    2012   Post-colonial Archaeology. In *Archaeological Theory Today*, 2nd ed., edited by I. Hodder, pp. 251–66. Polity Press, Cambridge, UK.
Gossen, Gary H.
    1996   Maya Zapatistas Move to the Ancient Future. *American Anthropologist* 98(3):528–38.
Graeber, David
    2011   *Debt: The First 5,000 Years.* Melville House, Brooklyn, NY.
Graham, Ian
    2002   *Alfred Maudslay and the Maya.* University of Oklahoma Press, Norman.
Grandia, Liza
    2012   *Enclosed: Conservation, Cattle, and Commerce among the Q'eqchi' Maya Lowlanders.* University of Washington Press, Seattle.
Groarke, Leo, and Gary Warrick
    2006   Stewardship Gone Astray? Ethics and the SAA. In *The Ethics of Archaeology: Philosophical Perspectives on Archaeological Practice*, edited by C. Scarre and G. Scarre, pp. 163–77. Cambridge University Press, Cambridge.
Haber, Alejandro F.
    2007   This Is Not an Answer to the Question "Who Is Indigenous?" *Archaeologies* 3(3):213–29.
Habu, Junko, Clare Fawcett, and John M. Matsunaga
    2008   *Evaluating Multiple Narratives: Beyond Nationalist, Colonialist, Imperialist Archaeologies.* Springer Science and Business Media, New York.
Hale, Charles R.
    2006   Activist Research v. Cultural Critique: Indigenous Land Rights and the Contradictions of Politically Engaged Anthropology. *Cultural Anthropology* 21(1):96–120.
    2011   Resistencia Para Que? Territory, Autonomy and Neoliberal Entanglements in the "Empty Spaces" of Central America. *Economy and Society* 40(2):184–210.
Hall, Gillette, and Harry A. Patrinos
    2006   *Indigenous Peoples, Poverty, and Human Development in Latin America.* Palgrave Macmillan, New York.
Hamilakis, Yannis
    2004   Archaeology and the Politics of Pedagogy. *World Archaeology* 36(2):287–309.

Hanks, William F.
  2010   *Converting Words: Maya in the Age of the Cross.* University of California Press, Berkeley.
Harris, Charles H., III, and Louis R. Sadler
  2003   *The Archaeologist Was a Spy: Sylvanus G. Morley and the Office of Naval Intelligence.* University of New Mexico Press, Albuquerque.
Hervik, Peter
  2003   *Maya People Within and Beyond Boundaries: Social Categories and Lived Identity in Yucatan.* Routledge, New York.
  1998   The Mysterious Maya of *National Geographic. Journal of Latin American Anthropology* 4:166–97.
Hickey, Samuel, and Giles Mohan (editors)
  2004   *Participation: From Tyranny to Transformation? Exploring New Approaches to Participation in Development.* Zed Books, London.
Hill, Robert M., and John Monaghan
  1987   *Continuities in Highland Maya Social Organization: Ethnohistory in Sacapulas, Guatemala.* University of Pennsylvania Press, Philadelphia.
Hinton, Alexander Laban
  2002   The Dark Side of Modernity: Towards an Anthropology of Genocide. In *Annihilating Difference: The Anthropology of Genocide,* edited by A. L. Hinton, pp. 1–41. University of California Press, Berkeley.
Historial de las Insignias de Guatemala
  1971   Sociedad de Geografía e Historia de Guatemala Publicacion Especial No. 16. Tipografía Nacional, Guatemala.
Hodder, Ian
  2008   Multivocality and Social Archaeology. In *Evaluating Multiple Narratives: Beyond Nationalist, Colonialist, Imperial Archaeology,* edited by J. Habu, C. Fawcett, and J. M. Matsunaga, pp. 196–200. Springer, New York.
Hodder, Ian, and Scott Hutson
  2003   *Reading the Past: Current Approaches to Interpretation in Archaeology,* 3rd ed. Cambridge University Press, Cambridge.
Hollowell, Julie, and George Nicholas
  2009   Using Ethnographic Methods to Articulate Community-Based Conceptions of Cultural Heritage Management. *Public Archaeology: Archaeological Ethnographies* 8(2/3):141–60.
Hoobler, Ellen
  2006   To Take Their Heritage in Their Hands: Indigenous Self-Representation and Decolonization in the Community Museums of Oaxaca, Mexico. *American Indian Quarterly* 30(3/4):441–60.
Hoopes, John W.
  1997   Ordeal in Chiapas: Archaeologists Survive Attack during Attempt to Rescue Maya Altar from Looters. *Society for American Archaeology Bulletin* 15(4). Accessed August 12, 2014. www.saa.org/Portals/0/SAA/publications/saabulletin/15-14/SAA12.html.
Houston, Stephen D., and Takeshi Inomata
  2009   *The Classic Maya.* Cambridge University Press, New York.

Human, Helen
  2015   Democratizing World Heritage: The Policies and Practice of Community In-
          volvement in Turkey. *Journal of Social Archaeology* 15(2):160–83.
Huner, Michael Kenneth
  2009   Toikove Ñane Retã! Republican Nationalism at the Battlefield Crossings of Print
          and Speech in Wartime Paraguay, 1867–1868. In *Building Nineteenth-Century
          Latin America*, edited by W. G. Acree Jr. and J. C. González Espitia, pp. 79–97.
          Vanderbilt University Press, Nashville.
Hutson, Scott R., G. Can Herrera, and G. A. Chi
  2012   Maya Heritage Entangled and Transformed. *International Journal of Heritage
          Studies* 19:1–17.
Ivic de Monterroso, Matilde
  2004   The Sacred Place in the Development of Archaeology in Guatemala: An Analy-
          sis. In *Continuities and Change in Maya Archaeology: Perspectives at the Millen-
          nium*, edited by C. W. Golden and G. Borgstede, pp. 295–307. Routledge, New
          York.
Jameson, Fredric
  1991   *Postmodernism; or, the Cultural Logic of Late Capitalism.* Duke University Press,
          Durham, NC.
Jones, Grant D.
  1989   *Maya Resistance to Spanish Rule: Time and Resistance on a Colonial Frontier.*
          University of New Mexico Press, Albuquerque.
Joseph, Gilbert M.
  1982   *Revolution from Without: Yucatán, Mexico, and the United States, 1880–1924.*
          Cambridge University Press, Cambridge.
Joyce, Rosemary A.
  2003   Archaeology and Nation Building: A View from Central America. In *The Politics
          of Archaeology and Identity in a Global Context*, edited by S. Kane, pp. 79–100.
          Archaeological Institute of America Colloquia and Conference Papers 7, Boston.
Kaeding, Adam
  2013   Negotiated Survival: An Archaeological and Documentary Investigation of Co-
          lonialism in Beneficios Altos, Yucatan, Mexico. Unpublished PhD dissertation,
          Department of Archaeology, Boston University, Boston.
Killion, Thomas W. (editor)
  2008   *Opening Archaeology: Repatriation's Impact on Contemporary Research and
          Practice.* School for Advanced Research, Santa Fe, NM.
Kintigh, Keith, Jeffrey H. Altschul, Mary C. Beaudry, Robert D. Drennan, Ann P. Kinzig,
          Timothy A. Kohler, W. Frederick Limp, Herbert D. G. Maschner, William K.
          Michener, Timothy R. Pauketat, Peter Peregrine, Jeremy A. Sabloff, Tony J.
          Wilkinson, Henry T. Wright, and Melinda A. Zeder
  2014   Grand Challenges for Archaeology. *Proceedings of the National Academy of Sci-
          ences (PNAS)* 111(3):879–80.
Kohl, Philip, and Clare Fawcett (editors)
  1995   *Nationalism, Politics, and the Practice of Archaeology.* Cambridge University
          Press, Cambridge.
Labadi, Sophia, and Colin Long (editors)
  2010   *Heritage and Globalisation.* Routledge, New York.

Langfield, Michele, William Logan, and Máiréad Nic Craith (editors)
    2010   *Cultural Diversity, Heritage and Human Rights.* Routledge, New York.
Lapolla Swier, Patricia
    2009   Unveiling the Mask of Modernity: A Critical Gendered Perspective of *Amistad
            funesta* and the Early Chronicles of José Martí. In *Building Nineteenth-Century
            Latin America: Re-rooted Cultures, Identities, and Nations,* edited by W. G.
            Acree and J. C. González Espitia, pp. 227–45. Vanderbilt University Press, Nash-
            ville, TN.
La Salle, Marina J.
    2010   Community Collaboration and Other Good Intentions. *Archaeologies: Journal of
            the World Archaeological Congress* 6(3):401–22.
Law, Danny, John Robertson, Stephen Houston, and Robbie Haertel
    2009   Most Maya Glyphs Are Written in Ch'olti'an. In *The Ch'orti' Maya Area: Past
            and Present,* edited by B. E. Metz, C. L. McNeil, and K. M. Hull, pp. 29–42. Uni-
            versity Press of Florida, Gainesville.
Levy, Janet
    2006   Prehistory, Identity, and Archaeological Representation in Nordic Museums.
            American Anthropologist 108(1):135–47.
Liebmann, Matthew
    2008   Introduction: The Intersection of Archaeology and Postcolonial Studies. In *Ar-
            chaeology and the Postcolonial Critique,* edited by M. Liebmann and U. Z. Rizvi,
            pp. 1–20. AltaMira Press, Lanham, MD.
Lilley, Ian
    2008   Archaeology, the World Bank, and Postcolonial Politics. In *Archaeology and
            the Postcolonial Critique,* edited by M. Liebmann and U. Z. Rizvi, pp. 141–64.
            AltaMira Press, Lanham, MD.
Lippert, Dorothy
    2005   Building a Bridge to Cross a Thousand Years. *American Indian Quarterly*
            30(3/4):431–40.
    2008   Not the End, Not the Middle, but the Beginning: Repatriation as a Transfor-
            mative Mechanism for Archaeologists and Indigenous Peoples. In *Collabora-
            tion in Archaeological Practice: Engaging Descendant Communities,* edited by
            C. Colwell-Chanthaphonh and T. J. Ferguson, pp. 119–30. AltaMira Press,
            Lanham, MD.
Little, Barbara J., and Paul Shackel
    2014   *Archaeology, Heritage, and Civic Engagement: Working toward the Public Good.*
            Left Coast Press, Walnut Creek, CA.
Little, Walter E.
    2004   *Mayas in the Marketplace: Tourism, Globalization, and Cultural Identity.* Uni-
            versity of Texas Press, Austin.
    2008   Living within the Mundo Maya Project: Strategies of Maya Handicrafts Vendors.
            Latin American Perspectives 35(3):87–102.
Logan, Joy
    2009   Constructing Indigeneity in Argentina: At the Crossroads of Mountaineering,
            Tourism, and Re-ethnification. *Journal of Latin American and Caribbean An-
            thropology* 14(2):405–31.

Low, Setha
  2011   Claiming Space for an Engaged Anthropology: Spatial Inequality and Social Exclusion. *American Anthropologist* 113(3):389–407.
Low, Setha M., and Sally Engle Merry
  2010   Engaged Anthropology: Diversity and Dilemmas (an Introduction to Supplement 2). *Current Anthropology* 21, Supplement 2:S203–S226.
Lowenthal, David
  1985   *The Past Is a Foreign Country.* Cambridge University Press, Cambridge.
Luke, Christina
  2006   Diplomats, Banana Cowboys, and Archaeologists in Western Honduras: A History of the Trade in Pre-Columbian Materials. *International Journal of Cultural Property* 13:25–57.
Lutz, Catherine, and Jane Collins
  1993   *Reading National Geographic.* University of Chicago Press, Chicago.
Lydon, Jane, and Uzma Z. Rizvi (editors)
  2010   *Handbook of Postcolonial Archaeology.* Left Coast Press, Walnut Creek, CA.
Maca, Allan L.
  2009   Ethnographic Analogy and the Archaeological Construction of Maya Identity at Copan, Honduras. In *The Ch'orti' Maya Area: Past and Present*, edited by C. L. McNeil and K. M. Hull, pp. 90–107. University Press of Florida, Gainesville.
Magnoni, Aline, Traci Ardren, and Scott Hutson
  2007   Tourism in the Mundo Maya: Inventions and (Mis)Representations of Maya Identities and Heritage. *Archaeologies* 3(3):353–83.
Maldonado, Doris Julissa
  2011   Reconfiguring Archaeological Practice: Lessons from Currusté, Honduras. Unpublished PhD dissertation, Department of Anthropology, University of California, Berkeley.
Manz, Beatriz
  2004   *Paradise in Ashes: A Guatemalan Journey of Courage, Terror, and Hope.* University of California Press, Berkeley.
Marcus, George E.
  1995   Ethnography in/of the World System: The Emergence of Multi-sited Ethnography. *Annual Review of Anthropology* 24:95–117.
Marcus, George E., and Michael M. J. Fischer
  1999   *Anthropology as Cultural Critique*, 2nd ed. University of Chicago Press, Chicago.
Marshall, Yvonne
  2002   What Is Community Archaeology? *World Archaeology* 34(2):211–19.
Martin, Simon, and Nikolai Grube
  2008   *Chronicle of the Maya Kings and Queens: Deciphering the Dynasties of the Ancient Maya*, 2nd ed. Thames & Hudson, London.
Martínez Cobo, José R.
  1986   Study of the Problem of Discrimination against Indigenous Populations. Vol. 5, Conclusions, Proposals and Recommendations. UN Doc E/CN.4/Sub.2/1986/7/Add.4. Accessed May 1, 2010. www.un.org/en/documents/.
Maxwell, Judith M.
  1996   Prescriptive Grammar and Kaqchikel Revitalization. In *Maya Cultural Activism in Guatemala*, edited by E. F. Fischer and R. M. Brown, pp. 195–207. University of Texas Press, Austin.

McAnany, Patricia A.
   2010   *Ancestral Maya Economies in Archaeological Perspective.* Cambridge University Press, New York.
   2014   Transforming the Terms of Engagement between Archaeologists and Communities: A View from the Maya Region. In *Transforming Archaeology: Activist Practices and Prospects*, edited by S. Atalay, L. R. Clauss, R. H. McGuire, and J. R. Welch, pp. 159–78. Left Coast Press, Walnut Creek, CA.
McAnany, Patricia A., and Linda Brown
   2016   Perceptions of the Past within Tz'utujil Ontologies and Yucatec Hybridities. *Antiquity* 90(350):487–503.
McAnany, Patricia A., and Tomas Gallareta Negrón
   2010   Bellicose Rulers and Climatological Peril? Retrofitting 21st Century Woes on 8th Century Maya Society. In *Questioning Collapse: Human Resilience, Ecological Vulnerability, and the Aftermath of Empire*, edited by P. A. McAnany and N. Yoffee, pp. 142–75. Cambridge University Press, New York.
McAnany, Patricia A., and Shoshaunna Parks
   2012   Casualties of Heritage Distancing: Children, Ch'orti' Indigeneity, and the Copan Archaeoscape. *Current Anthropology* 53(1):80–107.
McAnany, Patricia A., and Sarah M. Rowe
   2015   Re-visiting the Field: Collaborative Archaeology as Paradigm Shift. *Journal of Field Archaeology* 40(5): 499–507.
McAnany, Patricia, Sarah Rowe, Yisrael Quic Cholotio, Evelyn Caniz Menchú, and Jose Mendoza Quic
   2015   Mapping Indigenous Self-Determination in Highland Guatemala. *International Journal of Applied Geospatial Research* 6(1):1–23.
McGhee, Robert
   2008   Aboriginalism and the Problems of Indigenous Archaeology. *American Antiquity* 73(4):579–97.
McGuire, Randall H.
   2008   *Archaeology as Political Action.* University of California Press, Berkeley.
   2013   Steel Walls and Picket Fences: Rematerializing the U.S.-Mexican Border in Ambos Nogales. *American Anthropologist* 115(3):466–79.
McGuire, Randall H., and Rodrigo Navarrete
   2005   Between Motorcycles and Rifles: Anglo-American and Latin American Radical Archaeologies. In *Global Archaeological Theory: Contextual Voices and Contemporary Thoughts*, edited by P. P. Funari, A. Zarankin, and E. Stovel, pp. 309–36. Kluwer Academic/Plenum Publishers, New York.
McNiven, Ian J., and Lynette Russell
   2005   *Appropriated Pasts: Indigenous Peoples and the Colonial Culture of Archaeology.* AltaMira Press, Lanham, MD.
Menchú, Rigoberta
   1984   *I, Rigoberta Menchú: An Indian Woman in Guatemala*, edited and introduced by Elisabeth Burgos-Debray, translated by Ann Wright. Verso, London.
Merlan, Francesca
   2009   Indigeneity: Global and Local. *Current Anthropology* 50(3):303–33.
Merriman, Nick (editor)
   2004   *Public Archaeology.* Routledge, London.

Merry, Sally Engle
2006   *Human Rights and Gender Violence: Translating International Law into Local Justice*. University of Chicago Press, Chicago.
Meskell, Lynn (editor)
2009   *Cosmopolitan Archaeologies*. Duke University Press, Durham, NC.
Meskell, Lynn
2012   The Social Life of Heritage. In *Archaeological Theory Today*, 2nd ed., edited by I. Hodder, pp. 229–50. Polity Press, Cambridge, UK.
Metz, Brent
2010   Questions of Indigeneity and the (Re-)Emergent Ch'orti' Maya of Honduras. *Journal of Latin American and Caribbean Anthropology* 15(2):289–316.
Metz, Brent E., Cameron L. McNeil, and Kerry M. Hull (editors)
2009   *The Ch'orti' Maya Area: Past and Present*. University of Florida Press, Gainesville.
Mignolo, Walter
2000   *Local Histories/Global Designs: Coloniality, Subaltern Knowledges, and Border Thinking*. Princeton University Press, Princeton, NJ.
Mintz, Sidney W.
1985   *Sweetness and Power: The Place of Sugar in Modern History*. Penguin, New York.
Montejo, Victor D.
2002   The Multiplicity of Mayan Voices: Mayan Leadership and the Politics of Self-Representation. In *Indigenous Movements, Self-Representation, and the State in Latin America*, edited by K. B. Warren and J. E. Jackson, pp. 123–48. University of Texas Press, Austin.
Morandi, Steven
2010   Xibun Maya: The Archaeology of an Early Spanish Colonial Frontier in Southeastern Yucatan. Unpublished PhD dissertation, Department of Archaeology, Boston University, Boston.
Morgan-Smith, Mary Margaret
2014   Creating Ties, Incurring Debts: Exploring the Role of Life Events through Archival Documents and Oral History from Rancho Kiuic, Yucatán, México. Paper presented at the 78th Annual Meeting of the Society for American Archaeology, Austin, Texas.
Mörner, Magnus
1967   *Race Mixture in the History of Latin America*. Little, Brown, Boston.
Mortensen, Lena Michaela
2009   Copan Past and Present: Maya Archaeological Tourism and the Ch'orti' in Honduras. In *The Ch'orti' Maya Area: Past and Present*, edited by B. E. Metz, C. L. McNeil, and K. M. Hull, pp. 246–57. University of Florida Press, Gainesville.
Mortensen, Lena Michaela, and Julie Hollowell (editors)
2009   *Ethnographies and Archaeologies: Iterations of the Past*. University of Florida Press, Gainesville.
Nadasdy, Paul
2005   The Anti-politics of TEK: The Institutionalization of Co-management Discourse and Practice. *Anthropologica* 47:215–32.
Navarrete, Federico
2011   Ruins and the State: Archaeology of a Mexican Symbiosis. In *Indigenous Peoples and Archaeology in Latin America*, edited by C. Gnecco and P. Ayala, pp. 39–52. Left Coast Press, Walnut Creek, CA.

Nicholas, George P.
  1997 Education and Empowerment: Archaeology With, For, and By the Shuswap Nation. In *At a Crossroads: Archaeology and First Peoples in Canada*, edited by G. P. Nicholas and T. D. Andrews, pp. 85–104. Archaeology Press, Burnaby, BC, Canada.
  2008 Melding Science and Community Values: Indigenous Archaeology Programs and the Negotiation of Cultural Difference. In *Collaborating at the Trowel's Edge: Teaching and Learning Indigenous Archaeology*, edited by S. W. Silliman, pp. 228–49. University of Arizona Press, Tucson.
  2010 Seeking the End of Indigenous Archaeology. In *Bridging the Divide: Indigenous Communities and Archaeology into the 21st Century*, edited by C. Phillips and H. Allen, pp. 233–52. Left Coast Press, Walnut Creek, CA.
Nicholas, George P. (editor)
  2011 *Being and Becoming Indigenous Archaeologists*. Left Coast Press, Walnut Creek, CA.
Nicholas, George P., and Thomas D. Andrews
  1997a Indigenous Archaeology in the Postmodern World. In *At a Crossroads: Archaeology and First Peoples in Canada*, edited by G. P. Nicholas and T. D. Andrews, pp. 1–18. Archaeology Press, Burnaby, BC, Canada.
  1997b On the Edge. In *At a Crossroads: Archaeology and First Peoples in Canada*, edited by G. P. Nicholas and T. D. Andrews, pp. 276–79. Archaeology Press, Burnaby, BC, Canada.
Niezen, Ronald
  2003 *The Origins of Indigenism: Human Rights and the Politics of Identity*. University of California Press, Berkeley.
Nigh, Ronald
  1994 Zapata Rose in 1994: The Indian Rebellion in Chiapas. *Cultural Survival Quarterly* 18(1):9–13.
Novotny, Claire
  2015 Social Identity across Landscapes: Ancient Lives and Modern Heritage in a Q'eqchi' Maya Village. Unpublished PhD dissertation. Department of Anthropology, University of North Carolina, Chapel Hill.
Olsen, Bjørnar
  2012 Symmetrical Archaeology. In *Archaeological Theory Today*, 2nd ed., edited by I. Hodder, pp. 208–28. Polity Press, Cambridge, UK.
Overholtzer, Lisa
  2015 A Model for Initial Implementation of a Collaborative Archaeology Project. *Advances in Archaeological Practice* 3(1):50–62.
Pagán Jiménez, Jaime, and Reniel Rodríquez Ramos
  2008 Toward the Liberation of Archaeological Praxis in a "Postcolonial Colony": The Case of Puerto Rico. In *Archaeology and the Postcolonial Critique*, edited by M. Liebmann and U. Z. Rizvi, pp. 53–71. AltaMira Press, Lanham, MD.
Palka, Joel W.
  2005 *Unconquered Lacandon Maya: Ethnohistory and Archaeology of Indigenous Culture Change*. University Press of Florida, Gainesville.
Parks, Shoshaunna, and Patricia A. McAnany
  2007 Reclaiming Maya Ancestry. In *Look Close, See Far: A Cultural Portrait of the Maya*, edited by B. T. Martin, pp. 17–26. George Braziller, New York.

2011   Heritage Rights and Global Sustainability via Maya Archaeology. *Anthropology News* 52(5):27.

Parks, Shoshaunna, Patricia A. McAnany, and Satoru Murata
2006   The Conservation of Maya Cultural Heritage: Searching for Solutions in a Troubled Region. *Journal of Field Archaeology* 31(4):425–32.

Patch, Robert W.
1985   Agrarian Change in Eighteenth-Century Yucatan. *Hispanic American Historical Review* 65(1):21–49.

Patterson, Thomas C.
1994   Social Archaeology in Latin America: An Appreciation. *American Antiquity* 59:531–37.
1995   Archaeology, History, Indigenismo, and the State in Peru and Mexico. In *Making Alternative Histories: The Practice of Archaeology and History in Non-Western Settings*, edited by P. R. Schmidt and T. C. Patterson, pp. 69–85. School of American Research Press, Santa Fe, NM.
2008   A Brief History of Postcolonial Theory and Implications for Archaeology. In *Archaeology and the Post-colonial Critique*, edited by M. Liebmann and U. Z. Rizvi, pp. 21–34. AltaMira Press, Lanham, MD.

Pendergast, David M.
1967   *Palenque: The Walker-Caddy Expedition to the Ancient Maya City, 1839–1840.* University of Oklahoma Press, Norman.

Perry, S., and A. Chrysanthi
2014   Site Visualisation and Presentation 2014. In *Çatalhöyük 2014 Archive Report*, edited by B. Tung, pp. 173–85. Çatalhöyük Research Project, Stanford University, CA. www.catalhoyuk.com/archive_reports/.

Perry, S., A. Chrysanthi, and T. Frankland
2013   Site Visualisation and Presentation 2013. In *Çatalhöyük 2013 Archive Report*, edited by B. Tung, pp. 289–310. Çatalhöyük Research Project, Stanford University, CA. www.catalhoyuk.com/archive_reports/.

Phillips, C., and H. Allen (editors)
2010   *Bridging the Divide: Indigenous Communities and Archaeology into the 21st Century.* Left Coast Press, Walnut Creek, CA.

Pikirayi, Innocent
2001   *The Zimbabwe Culture: Origins and Decline of Southern Zambian States.* AltaMira Press, Walnut Creek, CA.

Politis, Gustavo G., and José Antonio Pérez Gollán
2004   Latin American Archaeology: From Colonialism to Globalization. In *A Companion to Social Archaeology*, edited by L. Meskell and R. W. Preucel, pp. 353–73. Blackwell Publishing, Malden, MA.

Preucel, Robert W., and Craig N. Cipolla
2008   Indigenous and Postcolonial Archaeologies. In *Archaeology and the Postcolonial Critique*, edited by M. Liebmann and U. Z. Rizvi, pp. 129–40. AltaMira Press, Lanham, MD.

Pyburn, K. Anne
2003   Archaeology for a New Millennium: The Rules of Engagement. In *Archaeologists and Local Communities: Partners in Exploring the Past*, edited by L. Derry and M. Malloy, pp. 167–84. Society for American Archaeology, Washington, DC.

2004   We Have Never Been Postmodern: Maya Archaeology in the Ethnographic Present. In *Continuities and Change in Maya Archaeology: Perspectives at the Millennium*, edited by C. W. Golden and G. Borgstede, pp. 287–93. Routledge, New York.

2011   Engaged Archaeology: Whose Community? Which Public? In *New Perspectives in Global Public Archaeology*, edited by K. Okamura and A. Matsuda, pp. 29–42. Springer, New York.

Pyburn, K. Anne, and Richard R. Wilk

2000   Responsible Archaeology Is Applied Archaeology. In *Ethics in American Archaeology*, 2nd ed., edited by M. J. Lynott and A. Wylie, pp. 78–86. Society for American Archaeology, Washington, DC.

Quezada, Sergio

2014   *Maya Lords and Lordship: The Formation of Colonial Society in Yucatán, 1350–1600*, translated by T. Rugeley. University of Oklahoma, Norman.

Rama, Angel

1996   *The Lettered City*, translated by John C. Chasteen. Duke University Press, Durham, NC.

Raxche' [Demetrio Rodríguez Guaján]

1996   Maya Culture and the Politics of Development. In *Maya Cultural Activism in Guatemala*, edited by E. F. Fischer and R. M. Brown, pp. 74–88. University of Texas Press, Austin.

Renan, Ernest

1990   What Is Nation? In *Nation and Narration*, edited by H. Bhabha, translated by M. Thom, pp. 8–22. Routledge, New York.

Restall, Matthew

2004   Maya Ethnogenesis. *Journal of Latin American Anthropology* 9(1):64–89.

2009   *The Black Middle: Africans, Maya, and Spaniards in Colonial Yucatan*. Stanford University Press, Stanford, CA.

Restall, Matthew, and Solari Amara

2011   *2012 and the End of the World: The Western Roots of the Maya Apocalypse*. Rowman & Littlefield, Lanham, MD.

Restall, Matthew, and John F. Chuchiak IV

2002   A Reevaluation of the Authenticity of Fray Diego de Landa's Relación de las cosas de Yucatán. *Ethnohistory* 49(3):651–69.

Restrepo, Eduardo, and Arturo Escobar

2005   Other Anthropologies and Anthropology Otherwise: Steps to a World Anthropologies Framework. *Critique of Anthropology* 25(2):99–129.

Richards, Julia Becker, and Michael Richards

1996   Maya Education: A Historical and Contemporary Analysis of Mayan Language Education Policy. In *Maya Cultural Activism in Guatemala*, edited by E. F. Fischer and R. M. Brown, pp. 208–21. University of Texas Press, Austin.

Río, Don Antonio del

1822   *Description of the Ruins of an Ancient City Discovered near Palenque, in the Kingdom of Guatemala, in Spanish America*, translated by P. F. Cabrera. Henry Berthoud, London.

Rizvi, Uzma Z.

2008   Decolonizing Methodologies as Strategies of Practice: Operationalizing the Post-colonial Critique in the Archaeology of Rajasthan. In *Archaeology and the Post-colonial Critique*, edited by M. Liebmann and U. Z. Rizvi, pp. 109–27. AltaMira Press, Lanham, MD.

Robles, Nelly M.

2010   Indigenous Archaeology in Mexico: Recognizing Distinctive Histories. In *Being and Becoming Indigenous Archaeologists*, edited by G. P. Nicholas, pp. 277–85. Left Coast Press, Walnut Creek, CA.

Rodriguez, Timoteo

2006   Conjunctures in the Making of an Ancient Maya Archaeological Site. In *Ethnographies of Archaeological Practice: Cultural Encounters, Material Transformations*, edited by M. Edgeworth, pp. 161–72. AltaMira Press, Lanham, MD.

Ross, Anne, Kathleen Pickering Sherman, Jeffrey G. Snodgrass, Henry D. Delcore, and Richard Sherman

2011   *Indigenous Peoples and the Collaborative Stewardship of Nature: Knowledge Binds and Institutional Conflicts*. Left Coast Press, Walnut Creek, CA.

Rowan, Yorke M., and Uzi Baram (editors)

2004   *Marketing Heritage: Archaeology and the Consumption of the Past*. AltaMira Press, Walnut Creek, CA.

Rugeley, Terry

1996   *Yucatan's Maya Peasantry and the Origins of the Caste War*. University of Texas Press, Austin.

2009   The Imponderable and the Permissible: Caste Wars, Culture Wars, and Porfirian Piety in the Yucatan Peninsula. In *Building Nineteenth-Century Latin America*, edited by W. G. Acree Jr. and J. C. Gonzalez Espitia, pp. 177–201. Vanderbilt University Press, Nashville.

Rus, Jan

2003   Coffee and the Recolonization of Highland Chiapas, Mexico: Indian Communities and Plantation Labor, 1892–1912. In *The Global Coffee Economy in Africa, Asia and Latin America, 1500–1989*, edited by W. G. Clarence-Smith and S. Topik, pp. 257–85. Cambridge University Press, Cambridge.

Sabloff, Jeremy A.

2008   *Archaeology Matters: Action Archaeology in the Modern World*. Left Coast Press, Walnut Creek, CA.

2011   Where Have You Gone, Margaret Mead? Anthropology and Public Intellectuals. *American Anthropologist* 113(3):408–16.

2015   On the History of Archaeological Research in Mesoamerica, with Particular Reference to Pre-Columbian Maya Civilization. In *Globalized Antiquity: Uses and Perceptions of the Past in South Asia, Mesoamerica, and Europe*, edited by U. Schüren, D. M. Segesser, and T. Späth, pp. 219–29. Dietrich Reimer Verlag GmbH, Berlin.

Said, Edward

1978   *Orientalism*. Pantheon Books, New York.

1996 [1993]   *Peace and Its Discontents: Essays on Palestine in the Middle East Peace Process*. Vintage, New York.

Sánchez de Aguilar, Pedro

    1639   *Informe contra idolorum cultores del obispado de Yucatán.* Iuan Gonçalez, Madrid.

Sanford, Victoria

    2003   *Buried Secrets: Truth and Human Rights in Guatemala.* Palgrave Macmillan, New York.

Sanjinés, Javier C.

    2004   *Mestizaje Upside-Down: Aesthetic Politics in Modern Bolivia.* University of Pittsburgh Press, Pittsburgh, PA.

Scarre, Chris, and Geoffrey Scarre (editors)

    2006   *The Ethics of Archaeology: Philosophical Perspectives on Archaeological Practice.* Cambridge University Press, Cambridge.

Schackt, Jon

    2001   The Emerging Maya: A Case of Ethnogenesis. In *Maya Survivalism*, edited by U. Hostettler and M. Restall, pp. 3–14. Verlag Anton Saurwein, Markt Schwaben, Germany.

Schele, Linda, and Nikolai Grube

    1996   The Workshops for Maya on Hieroglyphic Writing. In *Maya Cultural Activism in Guatemala*, edited by E. F. Fischer and R. McKenna Brown, pp. 131–40. University of Texas, Austin.

Schensul, J.

    2010   Engaged Universities, Community Based Research Organizations and Third Sector Science in a Global System. *Human Organization* 69(4):307–20.

Schlesinger, Stephen, and Stephen Kinzer

    1990   *Bitter Fruit: The Untold Story of the American Coup in Guatemala.* Anchor Books, New York.

Scott, James C.

    1990   *Domination and the Arts of Resistance: Hidden Transcripts.* Yale University Press, New Haven, CT.

Seneviratne, Sudharshan

    2008   Situating World Heritage Sites in a Multicultural Society: The Ideology of Presentation at the Sacred City of Anuradhapura. In *Archaeology and the Postcolonial Critique*, edited by M. Liebmann and U. Z. Rizvi, pp. 177–95. AltaMira Press, Lanham, MD.

Sharer, Robert J., and Loa P. Traxler

    2006   *The Ancient Maya*, 6th ed., revised from earlier editions by Sylvanus G. Morley (1946) and George W. Brainerd (1956). Stanford University Press, Stanford, CA.

Silliman, Stephen W. (editor)

    2008   Collaborative Indigenous Archaeology: Troweling at the Edges, Eyeing the Center. In *Collaborating at the Trowel's Edge: Teaching and Learning in Indigenous Archaeology*, edited by S. W. Silliman, pp. 1–21. University of Arizona Press, Tucson, AZ.

Silverberg, Robert

    1968   *Mound Builders of Ancient America: The Archaeology of a Myth.* New York Graphic Society, Greenwich, CT.

Silverman, Helaine

    2002   Touring Ancient Times: The Past and Presented Past in Contemporary Peru. *American Anthropologist* 104(3):881–902.

Silverman, Helaine (editor)

  2006   *Archaeological Site Museums in Latin America.* University Press of Florida, Gainesville.

Silverman, Helaine, and D. Fairchild Ruggles (editors)

  2007   *Cultural Heritage and Human Rights.* Spring Science and Media, New York.

Smith, Claire, and H. Martin Wobst (editors)

  2005   *Indigenous Archaeologies: Decolonizing Theory and Practice.* Routledge, Taylor and Francis, London.

Smith, Laura

  2008   Indigenous Geography, GIS, and Land-Use Planning on the Bois Forte Reservation. *American Indian Culture and Research Journal* 32(3):139–51.

Smith, Laurajane, and Emma Waterton

  2009   *Heritage, Communities, and Archaeology.* Duckworth, London.

Smith, Linda Tuhiwai

  2012   *Decolonizing Methodologies: Research and Indigenous Peoples,* 2nd ed. Palgrave Macmillan, New York.

Smith, Monica

  2005   Networks, Territories, and the Cartography of Ancient States. *Annals of the Association of American Geographers* 95(4):832–49.

Spivak, Gayatri Chakravorty

  1988   Can the Subaltern Speak? In *Marxism and the Interpretation of Cultures,* edited by C. Nelson and L. Grossberg, pp. 271–316. University of Illinois Press, Urbana.

Stephen, Lynn

  2002   *Zapata Lives! History and Cultural Politics in Southern Mexico.* University of California Press, Berkeley.

Stephens, John Lloyd

  1993   *Incidents of Travel in Central America, Chiapas, and Yucatan,* edited by Karl Ackerman. Smithsonian Institution Press, Washington, DC.

Stoler, Ann L. (editor)

  2006   *Haunted by Empire: Geographies of Intimacy in North American History.* Duke University Press, Durham, NC.

Stottman, M. Jay (editor)

  2010   *Archaeologists as Activists: Can Archaeologists Change the World?* University of Alabama Press, Tuscaloosa.

Strand, Kerry, Sam Marullo, Nick Cutforth, Randy Stoecker, and Patrick Donohue

  2003   *Community-Based Research and Higher Education.* Jossey-Bass, San Francisco.

Sturm, Circe

  1996   Old Writing and New Messages: The Role of Hieroglyphic Literacy in Maya Cultural Activism. In *Maya Cultural Activism in Guatemala,* edited by E. F. Fischer and R. McKenna Brown, pp. 114–30. University of Texas, Austin.

Sullivan, Paul

  1989   *Unfinished Conversations: Maya and Foreigners between Two Wars.* University of California Press, Berkeley and Los Angeles.

Taylor, Sarah R.

  2014   Maya Cosmopolitans: Engaging Tactics and Strategies in the Performance of Tourism. *Identities: Global Studies in Culture and Power* 21(1):219–32.

Tedlock, Dennis

1993   Torture in the Archives: Mayans Meet Europeans. *American Anthropologist* 95(1):139–52.

1996   *Popol Vuh: The Definitive Edition of the Mayan Book of the Dawn of Life and the Glories of Gods and Kings.* Simon and Schuster, New York.

Thomas, David Hurst

2000   *Skull Wars: Kennewick Man, Archaeology, and the Battle for Native American Identity.* Basic Books, New York.

2008   Foreword. In *Collaboration in Archaeological Practice: Engaging Descendant Communities*, edited by C. Colwell-Chanthaphonh and T. J. Ferguson, pp. vii–xii. AltaMira Press, Lanham, MD.

Thompson, J. Eric S.

1966   *The Rise and Fall of Maya Civilization*, 2nd ed. University of Oklahoma Press, Norman.

Toledo Maya Cultural Council

1997   *Maya Atlas: The Struggle to Preserve Maya Land in Southern Belize.* North Atlantic Books, Berkeley, CA.

Tozzer, Alfred M. (translator)

1941   *Landa's Relación de las Cosas de Yucatán.* Papers of the Peabody Museum of American Archaeology and Ethnology, Vol. 18. Harvard University, Cambridge, MA.

Trigger, Bruce G.

2003   All People Are [Not] Good. *Anthropologica* 45:39–44.

2006   *A History of Archaeological Thought.* Cambridge University Press, Cambridge.

Valle Escalante, Emilio del

2009   *Maya Nationalisms and Postcolonial Challenges in Guatemala: Coloniality, Modernity, and Identity Politics.* School for Advanced Research, Santa Fe, NM.

Vance, Erik

2014   Losing Maya Heritage to Looters. *National Geographic*, August 10. http://news .nationalgeographic.com/news/2014/08/140808-maya-guatemala-looter-antiq uities-archaeology-science/.

Vázquez, Luis

2003   *El leviantán arqueólogo: Antropología de una tradición científica en México.* CIESAS-Porrúa, Mexico.

Vitelli, Karen D., and Chip Colwell-Chanthaphonh

2006   *Archaeological Ethics*, 2nd ed. Altamira Press, Lanham, MD.

Vogt, Evon Z.

1964   The Genetic Model and Maya Cultural Development. In *Desarrollo Cultural de los Mayas*, edited by E. Z. Vogt and A. Ruz Lhuiller, pp. 9–48. Universidad Autónoma de México, México.

1976   *Tortillas for the Gods: A Symbolic Analysis of Zinacanteco Rituals.* Harvard University Press, Cambridge, MA, and London.

Wagner, Henry R., and Helen Rand

1967   *The Life and Writings of Bartolomé de las Casas.* University of New Mexico Press, Albuquerque.

Wainwright, Joel
  2008   *Decolonizing Development: Colonial Power and the Maya.* Blackwell Publishing,
          Malden, MA.
Warren, Kay B.
  1996   Reading History as Resistance: Maya Public Intellectuals in Guatemala. In *Maya
          Cultural Activism in Guatemala*, edited by E. F. Fischer and R. McKenna Brown,
          pp. 89–106. University of Texas, Austin.
  1998   *Indigenous Movements and Their Critics: Pan-Maya Activism in Guatemala.*
          Princeton University Press, Princeton, NJ.
  2002   Voting against Indigenous Rights in Guatemala: Lessons from the 1999 Refer-
          endum. In *Indigenous Movements, Self-Representation, and the State in Latin
          America*, edited by K. B. Warren and J. E. Jackson, pp. 149–180. University of
          Texas Press, Austin.
Watkins, Joe
  2000   *Indigenous Archaeology: American Indian Values and Scientific Practice.* AltaMira
          Press, Walnut Creek, CA.
  2005   Through Wary Eyes: Indigenous Perspectives on Archaeology. *Annual Review of
          Anthropology* 34:429–49.
Webster, David
  2002   *The Fall of the Ancient Maya: Solving the Mystery of the Maya Collapse.* Thames
          & Hudson, London.
Weiner, Annette B.
  1987   *Women of Value, Men of Renown.* University of Texas Press, Austin.
Wilcox, Michael
  2009   *The Pueblo Revolt and the Mythology of Conquest: An Indigenous Archaeology of
          Contact.* University of California Press, Berkeley.
  2010a   Marketing Conquest and the Vanishing Indian: An Indigenous Response to
          Jared Diamond's Archaeology of the American Southwest. In *Questioning Col-
          lapse: Human Resilience, Ecological Vulnerability, and the Aftermath of Empire*,
          edited by P. A. McAnany and N. Yoffee, pp. 113–41. Cambridge University
          Press, New York.
  2010b   Saving Indigenous Peoples from Ourselves: Separate but Equal Archaeology Is
          Not Scientific Archaeology. *American Antiquity* 75(2):221–27.
Willey, Gordon R., and Jeremy A. Sabloff
  1993   *A History of American Archaeology*, 3rd ed. W. H. Freeman, New York.
Wilmsen, Carl, William Elmendorf, Larry Fisher, Jacquelyn Ross, Brinda Sarathy, and Gail
          Wells (editors)
  2008   *Partnerships for Empowerment: Participatory Research for Community-Based
          Natural Resource Management.* Earthscan Publishing, London.
Wolf, Eric
  1957   Closed Corporate Peasant Communities in Mesoamerican and Central Java.
          Southwestern Journal of Anthropology 13(1):1–18.
  1982   *Europe and the People Without History.* University of California Press, Berkeley.
Woodfill, Brent K.
  2013   Community Development and Collaboration at Salinas de Los Nueve Cerros,
          Guatemala. *Advances in Archaeological Practice* 1(2):105–20.

Woons, Marc (editor)

2014   *Restoring Indigenous Self-Determination: Theoretical and Practical Approaches.* E-International Relations, Bristol, UK.

Wright, Amy E.

2009   Novels, Newspapers, and Nation: The Beginnings of Serial Fiction in Nineteenth-Century Mexico. In *Building Nineteenth-Century Latin America*, edited by W. G. Acree and J. C. González Espitia, pp. 59–78. Vanderbilt University Press, Nashville, TN.

Wylie, Alison

1995   Alternative Histories: Epistemic Disunity and Political Integrity. In *Making Alternative Histories: The Practice of Archaeology and History in Non-Western Settings*, edited by P. R. Schmidt and T. C. Patterson, pp. 255–72. School of American Research Press, Santa Fe, NM.

2008   The Integrity of Narratives: Deliberative Practice, Pluralism, and Multivocality. In *Evaluating Multiple Narratives: Beyond Nationalist, Colonialist, Imperial Archaeology*, edited by J. Habu, C. Fawcett, and J. M. Matsunaga, pp. 201–12. Springer, New York.

2015   A Plurality of Pluralisms: Collaborative Practice in Archaeology. In *Objectivity in Science: New Perspectives from Science and Technology Studies*, edited by F. Padovani, A. Richardson, and J. Y. Tsou, pp. 189–210. Springer International Publishing, Switzerland.

Yaeger, Jason, and Greg Borgstede

2004   Professional Archaeology and the Modern Maya: A Historical Sketch. In *Continuities and Changes in Maya Archaeology: Perspectives at the Millennium*, edited by C. Golden and G. Borgstede, pp. 259–85. Routledge, New York.

Yaeger, Jason, and David Hodell

2008   The Collapse of Maya Civilization: Assessing the Interaction of Culture, Climate, and Environment. In *El Niño, Catastrophism, and Culture Change in Ancient America*, edited by D. H. Sandweiss and J. Quilter, pp. 187–242. Dumbarton Oaks Research Library and Collection, Washington, DC.

Index

DATE DUE

6/4/18 OLV

PRINTED IN U.S.A.